THE
ANIMATION
PIMP

By Chris Robinson
Drawn by Andreas Hykade

AWN
PRESS

President and Co-Publisher, AWN Press: Ron Diamond
COO and Co-Publisher, AWN Press: Dan Sarto
Senior Book Editor, AWN Press: Jon Hofferman

Publisher and General Manager, Thomson Course Technology PTR: Stacy L. Hiquet
Associate Director of Marketing: Sarah O'Donnell
Manager of Editorial Services: Heather Talbot
Marketing Manager: Heather Hurley
Executive Editor: Kevin Harreld
Marketing Assistant: Adena Flitt
PTR Editorial Services Coordinator: Erin Johnson

ISBN-10: 1-59863-403-8
ISBN-13: 978-1-59863-403-7

Library of Congress Catalog Card Number: 2007923309
Printed in the United States of America
07 08 09 10 11 TW 10 9 8 7 6 5 4 3 2 1

Cover Illustration by Andreas Hykade

AWN Press
A division of AWN, Inc.
6525 Sunset Blvd., GS 10
Los Angeles, CA 90028
http://www.awn.com

Thomson Course Technology PTR,
a division of Thomson Learning Inc.
25 Thomson Place
Boston, MA 02210
http://www.courseptr.com

For Richard Meltzer,
a good friend and mentor.

Contents

Acknowledgments   11
Foreword by Nick Tosches   15

PIMPOLOGY   **17**
The Beginning of the End of the Beginning. . .   19
The Beginning of the End of the Beginning, Part 2: Revolver   25
The Beginning of the End of the Beginning, Part 3: The Tent   33
Frolicking in the Tent   40

FESTIVALS AND THEIR DISCONTENTS   **49**
The Animation Pimp   51
Annecy, Audiences, Art and Sandwiches   54
Proposal Modest A   59
Greetings from St. Helena   63
Via Slug's Saloon   69
Rant   76
How To Avoid Pissing Me Off or...Ottawa Festival Entry Tips   84
From Quays to Krays?   91
ASIFA-East Festival. May 16, 2004. Manhattan.   95

THE AESTHETICS OF ANIMATION   **101**
In Search of STUFF, Part 1: (F)art   103
In Search of STUFF, Part 2: Yummy and Yucky   111
In Search of STUFF, Part 3: Fear of a Non-Narrative Planet   117
Aural Allochezia*   121

SEX & DEATH   **125**
"Long Live Tits"   127

Shrekxxx 130

Animation to Get Off To? 135

"And Never Die... And Never Die..." 140

Father Who Takes the Darkness Away 147

STYLES OF RADICAL ANIMATION 153

Pierre Hébert and the Work of Animation in the Age of Digital Reproduction 155

Why is it Not Done? 161

Clinging to a small piece of nothing in the middle of nowhere 165

Chillax 173

Andreas Hykade's Great Balls of Fire 176

Scratch Fever 180

IDENTITY POLITICS 185

Just Like Us? 187

ανΦρωπος μορΦη 192

Like Everyone, I'm Not Like Everybody Else 199

Is There a Gay in the House? 205

TUBULAR DISTRACTIONS 211

A Modest Request 213

Pleasure and Pain: Ren & Stimpy's Adult Cartoon Party 217

Justice League—What's with These People? 223

Harvey Birdman: A Tale Told by an Idiot 228

HUMAN FRAILTY 233

Can't Escape You 235

You Never Know 243

Donald Duck is an Asshole 247

Carnivale 253

Ryan 259

Just Kept Walkin' 267

SEASONAL DYSPHORIA 271

Speaking of Bloated Asses... 273

Ho Ho Ho 277

Elbows and Cakeholes 284

Chaos x Order + Fragments x Whole + Process x End(s) = The 2003 Year in Review! 290

FRINGE BENEFITS 309

The Old Man and The Sea: A Plagiarism (not the film) 311

You Don't Kick a Zombie When It's Down, You Shoot It in the Head 313

The Stars 323

WHO'S WHO 333

Acknowledgments

First and foremost, I want to thank everyone at Animation World Network especially Ron Diamond, Dan Sarto, Heather Kenyon and Annick Tenninge. They not only allowed me the opportunity to write this column, but came to my defense whenever the Pimp was attacked —and that was often, early on. With maybe two exceptions they let me write whatever I wanted. That's as close to paradise as any writer can get.

I want to thank Jon Hofferman for coming on board to edit this book. I was really worried at first that an editor might radically alter my often-chaotic rants. My worries evaporated during my first phone call with Jon when he said that the Pimp reminded him a bit of this guy named Richard Meltzer. I knew we'd get along from that point on.

I cannot say enough about the support, encouragement, generosity and passion that Andreas Hykade brought to this project. Over the course of about a month he sent me something like 80-90 drawings for the book. Each of them was something special. I first approached Andreas in November 2000 about doing the Pimp 'logo'. I seemed to recall that he quickly grabbed a piece of paper and did it on the spot. And, as usual, it was a perfect fit.

I wanna thank the many Pimp lovers and haters. These columns got people talking. Aint nothing bad about that.

Finally, I want to thank my wife Kelly, mother-in-law, Betty, and my sons, Jarvis and Harrison (born as I put the finishing touches on this book). They have put up with a LOT over the years and have always stood by me. Kelly IS an angel. I have no doubt about that.

And one more thanks to Ron Diamond and Dan Sarto. It's one thing to publish the column, quite another to take a chance on them as a book. We've had our hassles here and there, but at the end of the day, there's a lot of respect on both sides. I thank them for their faith in this project.

Chris Robinson
April 2007
Ottawa

Foreword

Writers who don't, so to speak, pull off their britches when they write don't write anything worth reading. It is good, in a pathetic sort of way, that so few writers do, so to speak, pull off their britches when they write. Otherwise, there would be far too much to read, and life is far too short.

But Chris Robinson has made a book that should be read. His honesty, what he has to say, and how he says it are enthralling. That is what makes this collection of columns more than just a bunch of writings strewn through the years and gathered together with binder's glue. This is the real thing, a real book by a real writer.

That Robinson here speaks ill of one of my own books is as representative of his willingness to reveal his humanity in all its imperfection as it is of my grace and understanding, which allow me to write the words that I have here written. May we both be praised, not necessarily in alphabetical order.

It's uncanny, very uncanny, that if you're looking for a book about animation, you'll find it here, and if, like me, you're not, you won't. I don't quite know how this can be, but it is.

Nick Tosches

PIMPOLOGY

The Beginning of the End of the Beginning. . .

Jesus said, "Have you discovered the beginning,
that you search for the end? In the place where that
beginning is, there the end will be."
– The Gospel of Thomas

And you may ask yourself—Well... How did I get here?
– Talking Heads, "Once in a Lifetime"

Summer '91. Just came back from—get this—Sheridan College. Media Arts. Dropped out. Too commercial. Wasn't all worthless. Phil Hoffman was a great teacher. D.D. remains one of my bestest friends. And that twin from the animation dept. She was so sexed up she scared me. Just a little boy. Wrote some absurd stories for an Ottawa weekly. One was about a guy who wore pylons on his arms and thought they gave them superpowers. They weren't so good. Had fire-colored hair. Only job I could get was working at a parking lot. They actually griped about my hair color but let it go. Best job I ever had. I can back up a car better than most can drive forward. Took coins from cars as tips. Left there and worked at Greenpeace for two weeks. Went door-to-door trying to convince people that saving whales was a good thing. They only paid you if you got a minimal amount of cash. Scam. I got chased from lawns. Fuck the whale. Best thing about the summer was going to a clothing store to buy a hat and meeting K.N.

Fall '91. Before Sheridan, I had taken a year or two of film studies at university—yes, film studies is like political science; you take it when you've no clue what you want to do with your life. Animation is NOWHERE near the map... or at least I

19

didn't see it on the map just yet. It never was near me. A sort of friend at school (Nathalie) helps get me a job ripping tickets at a cinema for the Canadian Film Institute (CFI). Working as a class projectionist and skipping film class at university. Living in a claustrophobic downtown shithole on a fold-up cot, writing bad songs, skipping rent, drinking nightly (most memorably, a 48-hour bender with this gal from school) and getting stoned to the point where I thought someone was shooting at me. Taking bus rides to Toronto just to get laid. Doing the dishes in the tub. No idea where things are going.

Spring '92. CFI organizes some animation festival. This short-bearded guy appears in the office one day. His name was Not or something. He gives me work typing names and dates and places into the computer. I loved this place. There were maybe five to six people working there. The CFI was near the end of a tailspin that saw it drop from as many as 30 employees to a handful. They had a cinema dept (where I was working under McSorley), non-theatrical division (where this big guy named Brian spent the day getting his furniture fixed), and animation. There was a dir. of development (John)—really funny and smart guy… and, I still can't believe this, a full-time accountant. There's a funny story there. It happened before my time.

During Ottawa '90, they needed someone to run over to the National Arts Centre to deliver some invitations. The only person available was the accountant's sister. John asked her to go and she said, "Will there be big dogs?" A startled John said, "Big dogs?" "Yes, big dogs. Big dogs bite. Big dogs bite," she replied with her French accent. John assured the woman that there would unlikely be any big dogs on her route since most of it was through the shopping mall. But she kept mumbling, "Big dogs bite. Big dogs, they bite." John quietly turned, walked away and delivered the invites himself. He didn't meet any big dogs. In fact, I don't think any of us ever encountered a big dog along that route. She's dead now. It's sad really. So I worked part-time taking cinema tickets and once the school year finished, did the festival by day.

During the parking lot job, I watched this cute gal go to work every day. She was stylish. Wore red rubber boots. She was a waitress at the restaurant next to the lot. I never had the courage to ask her out. Out drinking with some classmates one night. We're getting flooded. Vaguely remember seeing red rubber woman at a nearby table. Next thing I remember is waking up next to her. She asked me if I knew her name. That was awkward. We did nothing but fuck for about a month. Then she dumped me. I got angry. Smashed a guitar and left the pieces on her doorstep. Tried to kill myself. Police busted in that night to make sure I didn't. How embarrassing. I never took rejection well.

Late March. I'm a projectionist for a film class. K.N. is taking that class. I ask her out. She gives me her number. I call. It's the wrong number. Finally get it right the next week. Our first date is at this dive. We drink quarts; I talk about how much I hate people. Real charmer. She dumped me a few weeks later too. I was heartbroken again. Couldn't do nothing right. Alone in this shithole pad, feeling sorry for myself.

My big job was entering the submissions into a database. There were hundreds of packages in the middle of the floor… they flooded in each day. I struggled to keep up. It was mind-numbing work but I liked reading all the synopses. Usually got a laugh out of how serious they were. Had no idea who any of these people were. Didn't care.

That summer I took over some gal's downtown apartment. It was paradise compared to where I was living. One night I was passed out on the couch. I got up to piss and, as I passed by the kitchen, I noticed a glow from the fire escape. I ignored it and pissed. I came back and moved closer to the glow… and there was someone attached to it. K.N. was sitting there. She said she missed me. She had climbed the apartment's fire escape stairs to see me. We never really parted from that moment on. I forgot about how secure and happy that moment made me feel.

All the entries were in. Now there were five animation people coming to town to watch them. Karen Aqua, Ellen Meske, Chris Cassady, Mark Langer and Joyce Borenstein. The festival had a small budget. Apparently the previous director had crippled the place financially. This left this Not guy with little room to work. So these five would also be the jury. Some animators' association didn't like that. Turned out that my job would be to take these people from their hotels to the viewing area every day and sit with them while they watched all the submissions. I had to get them breakfast, lunch and dinner. Some of them thought I was their houseboy. Fuck them. Wonder if it's a coincidence that they never got a film in Ottawa after 1996? Heh, heh. Just kidding.

Anyhow… I had to put the tapes in and take them out of the machine and cue the projectionist. There wasn't much video so most days were spent in the cinema. We watched submissions from about 9:00 am till sometimes as late as 9:00 pm. I seem to remember that they pretty much watched everything right the way through. But there were maybe 600-700 entries. They had time. I really didn't know anything about animation films. Like most, I'd seen Disney films. On Saturdays, I'd watched "The Bugs Bunny/Road Runner Hour." But beyond that I didn't know nuttin' about cartoons. I vaguely remember anything from that selection period. There was *Stimpy's Invention*. I remember that being an early favourite. A bunch of shorts from something called Liquid Television. Really crazy, different-looking stuff.

But the film I remember most of all was this German piece called *Crossroads*. It was black-and-white and basically had stick figures. The drawing was really simple. It looked like anyone could do it. I remember a character approached a crossroad. There are three other guys—all reflections of the same person. And somehow no matter what road the guy traveled down he would end up back at the same place. The way this animator used the space was incredible. I'd never seen anything like it. How did he get so much depth out of these black line drawings? It was like a 3D film. It was magic really. But more than that there were these themes. The film was maybe six or seven minutes, but in that time it dealt with this existential crisis in a very smart and funny way. I was big into Bergman and Buster Keaton at the time and this film seemed to have it all. It was one-stop shopping. It fused Bergman, Keaton and Beckett into this short cartoon. I got

23

such a buzz from this film. I just had no idea that cartoons could do this. It was the right film at the right moment.

I didn't like the committee all that much and I don't remember much about the '92 festival except arguing with a French woman who ranted and raved about my lack of French. Most days I sat at a table and went home at 5:00 pm. Maybe I went to a party or two. Can't remember. Only thought about K.N. Just wanted to be with her. I wasn't there yet, but that big small German film by some guy named Raimund Krumme had put me on a road that headed toward the door of the tent.

(January, 2005)

The Beginning of the End of the Beginning, Part 2: Revolver

I wanna be either old or young
Don't like where I've ended up or where I begun
I always feel I must get things in the can
I just can't handle it the way I am
              – Pete Townshend, "Misunderstood"

Idiot wind, blowing through the buttons of our coats,
Blowing through the letters that we wrote.
Idiot wind, blowing through the dust upon our shelves,
We're idiots, babe.
It's a wonder we can even feed ourselves.
              – Bob Dylan, "Idiot Wind"

So...after *Crossroads* and Ottawa 92...well...kept ripping tickets at the Canadian Film Institute, projecting films, was a teaching assistant at Carleton U. and slowly getting my degree. Winter '93 I moved in with Kelly and her merry band of roommates. It wasn't so bad. We became a little dysfunctional family. Kelly got work at Carleton U. That was great 'cause they had a massive collection of films on VHS. When it became clear that some union wank was gonna push Kelly out of the job, we brought home as many tapes as possible each night so I could dub everything. For a while we amassed a pretty decent library of rare stuff (days before dvd). There were good days and lots of bad. Getting thrown out of clubs. Screaming matches with strangers. Drinking increasing. Vomiting in cabs. Before or after 1994? Can't even remember. Around that time. 1994 came. Finally graduated—at least I think I did. Did an indie study on the early films of Ingmar Bergman. That prof of mine, Peter Harcourt. Guy was a real legend in Canadian film studies. I admired the fuck out of him because he was a guy who wrote and taught from the heart. He was a passionate, sensitive, self-centred guy who, for me, injected some humanity back into film studies, which was increasingly being dominated by scientists with all their theories. I like the theories a bit more now, but in the day I just couldn't grasp the idea that 'taste' or 'judgement' shouldn't exist, that we couldn't simply say we liked or disliked a film. Sure, I get it. I know what they're saying about examining films in a larger, more complex context, but fuggit, I got a brain, a heart, a soul. I ain't no robot. If I don't like a film, I don't like a film. So be it. Harcourt was in this vein. He was more interested in the psychology of the filmmakers, of their characters... what it all said about life. Just writing that sentence I realize how much influence Peter Harcourt still has on me. Strangely, he didn't like me. I mean...yeah...I'm difficult at times... what were Brenda's last words to Nate in "Six Feet Under" (man...am I glad that show is over. Loved it, but enough already)? "You're a narcissist, you can't commit to anyone, not even yourself." I'm still brushing off the dust of thinking I know everything. Still...I was Harcourt's #1 fan. I wrote articles (hmm...another root...I started writing reviews and small shit for the Carleton U newspaper...and oh... did I tell you I had some stories published in an Ottawa weekly, circa 1991? One was called "Pylon Man." Was about an idiot who figured that if he put a pylon on his arm, he'd have superpowers. Wrote another about a man who turned into a fruit. State of mind circa '91... Did an interview with Harcourt proclaiming him as the department's great guy. No thanks, nothing. What was my sin? I didn't pretend to be sophisticated. I was a slug. Harcourt, for all his talk, wanted to be an aesthete... he loved the role of prof...was like a Philip Roth scholar... just looking to get laid and applauded. See, that was the biggest issue: I was a guy. I didn't have titties. So...finished my indie study. Harcourt said the paper itself was an A, but the effort was a B... so he gave me a B+. That still irks me a bit (not much). If the paper was that good despite the lousy effort... shouldn't I get an A+? Well...bygones be. He's retired. Just got some Order of Canada. I ain't doin so bad myself. Graduated. Immediately planned to go to grad. school for Canadian studies...but backed out. Wasn't up to it. Couldn't handle structure.

Back at the festival. 1994. This was another real turning point. Had the same job. Sorting out entries and babysitting the selection committee. Difference was that this committee was great. Among the four members were Marc Glassman, Otto Alder and Linda Simensky. Three pretty decent friendships grew out of that. They were funny, smart and patient. That year we had problems with the projectionist. We were saddled with a knob who didn't know anything about 35mm film. He burned a print one day, came in late another because he was having problems with his girlfriend. Ha…I remember…when we were showing Derek Jarman's *Blue*. It's just a blue screen with a voice-over for 70 minutes. Somehow the projectionist managed to get some white in there. There were a lot of delays…and yet these guys were patient. Well…okay…Otto wasn't, but it was funny. He'd seen many of the films, so he'd vote to move on pretty quickly. Marc and Linda were often more patient…and wanted to see more of a film. Otto would start doing handstands in the back of the room or saying "COME ON!! How can you watch this shit!!??" The 'come on' line remains today. He did it in a friendly way and often just left to go for a smoke. Linda was quiet most of the time, but was easy going. It wasn't until we saw her doodles after the selection that we realized what a nifty sense of humour she had. Marc was Mr. Fast Forward. He wanted to be sure about everything and always asked to fast forward through the film to make sure we weren't missing anything. We had time for dinners… I got a chance to hang out with Otto a lot…and really liked how down to earth and honest he was. He didn't hide his feelings. It was really refreshing. By the end of the week, I really loved these three. I was excited to go to work every day and hang out with them. All the while I thought Linda was gonna be some stuck-up TV executive (she was at Nick)… but she was anything but. She never complained (even if she wanted to!)… and was funny, modest and human. If more TV execs were like Linda… oh man… things would be oh-so-good.

Ottawa '94 was a much different experience. I was there day

and night. My job was to be the stage manager and make sure the projection went well. It was a stressful job. I knew many of the films, but I was dealing with union people. They were okay, but a couple of them hated to work… and like most projectionists, the idea of checking for sound and focus was a foreign concept to them. We had a few problems which the directors remember to this day. Steve Dovas' 10-sec ID for MTV was shown without sound. John Hays's hillbilly series for MTV was shown without sound (twice) and that prompted the audience to make their own dialogue and sound effects. I think we fugged up a JJ Sedelmaier shortie too. Oh god…I remember the looks on their faces when they were introduced following their film. Through the glare of the spotlight they stared up at the projection window, anger dripping from their nostrils. All three guys remember the fug-up to this day.

Also the site of my first worst hangover ever. After a red wine night with Marc Glassman, I showed up the next day for my shift looking purple or something of that sort. My breakfast was a muffin and a bottle of Pepto-Bismol. Oh yeah… forgot to mention that Kelly was working for us now. She was pretty much running the show as festival producers did in those days. I never drank red wine with Glassman again. Just beer.

I was smug. More so. I was impatient with some of the staff and resented one guy coming in from out of town to do work. Guess it's a testament to the OIAF, but shit, man… so many people think they own the festival. I remember—sorry—Prescott Wright hovering over me all the time in the booth telling me what I should and shouldn't be doing. Annoyed the fuck out of me. Who the fuck was this guy anyway? I was later told, by him, that he basically invented the OIAF (untrue). Knott told me to ignore him, but fuck a duck, what was I to do? And man…the guy farted all the time. Between him, the projectionists and my hangovers, it was a funky-smelling booth.

I think *Wrong Trousers* won that year. Now I like that film a lot and it's a worthy winner, but, in my book, it's a safe choice. For me, the film of '94 was Filmtecknarna's hypnotic and disturbing black-and-white dreamscape, *Revolver*. Rumour has it that four

of five jury members wanted to give *Revolver* the Grand Prix. Because the lone member of the opposition was so steadfastly opposed to the Swedish film, the only other film they could agree upon was *Trousers*.

By this time I knew Knott was leaving the festival. Warner Bros was gonna hire him to recruit. I decided then and there that I wanted his job. I didn't know sweet fuck-all really, but I knew I wanted to be with all these people, even the smelly ones. Before Ottawa '94 was out, I was lobbying people to support me as OIAf director. What a schmuck. These people had no power do to nothing.

It was a strange year…and one that I only understand better now because I'm seeing one of our own staff members acting pretty much the way I did. I remember a moment. McSorley and I are sitting in the Oasis (ha). It was the cafeteria/restaurant we hung at every day at the university. Sitting with us was one Will Straw. He was THE prof at Carleton. Very hip guy who made Lacan, Foucault, and Bourdieu sound interesting and approachable. Will was the rock of the department. The guy who cared about his students. He organized trips to New York (with Mark Langer) and was always socializing with us. He was a real mentor to us all. We wanted to be like Will: smart, funny, hip, and cool. That day, though, Will looked at us and said that he was 40 years old and felt lost and unsatisfied with his life. It was a shock to hear this. How the fug could he feel this way? He was a tenured prof… all the students adored him… Christ… he had it all.

I didn't understand.

I saw the CFI and OIAF as deadbeat in those days. Everyone seemed tired. The CFI had been routinely dismantled since the mid-1980s and was down to just a handful of people now. Money was very tight. Because the place had been saddled with a massive debt thanks to a previous director, Knott was faced with the task of putting on the OIAF with very little money and a lot of debts to pay. I treated him like crap in those days. He frustrated me. I treated McSorley (remember…I was working for him during the off-year of the OIAF…managing the cinema) like crap. I treated everyone like crap. I thought I knew everything and saw these guys as deadweights… saw them as guys who'd been there too long and were crippled by fear. I figured I—the master of nothing—could rejuvenate the place. I got angrier and felt more and more stifled by the situation. If only I was given the chance, I could show them and everyone what I could do, who I could be.

(September, 2005)

The Beginning of the End of the Beginning, Part 3: The Tent

Well, you know the saying: be careful what you wish for… Things began to change in 1994/1995. First, the CFI president layed off some deadweight and I ended up inheriting the job of director of non-theatrical services. It meant more hours, money and responsibility. It was a joke really. The film rental division was sagging. Hardly anyone rented 16mm films anymore. We housed a collection for UNICEF and the National Research Council. Real dull science films. UNICEF eventually cut our funding, as did the NRC. I spent most days just going through the massive amounts of film just to see what was there. We had a lot of animation prints on 16mm (Hubleys and NFB stuff mostly)… but the real thrill was discovering these old 'educational' films from the 1940s to 1970s. I found so many that, with a friend of mine, Lee Demarbre (*Jesus Christ Vampire Hunter*) we ended up starting a monthly movie night in Ottawa (Reel Mondays), where basically we got drunk and showed off-the-wall films (and gave away prizes like chocolate ass balls from the nearby sex shop. As Lee said, "They melt in your ass, not in your hands").

Okay…so Knott left. That left me, McSorley and the president's son (who had been put in charge of the CFI). It was a very awkward time. First, the son offered me McSorley's job. As much as I wanted that job, I refused and told McSorley what had happened. Did this happen then or earlier? Can't remember. Not important. Do remember that I was made interim director of the OIAF in late '94 or something… six months later…I conned my way into the position when I pressured the boss's son by saying that I had to have an answer about the OIAF job 'cause I was gonna go back to school (actually… maybe it wasn't such a con)… so, having no other options, he gave me the job of running the OIAF. It was spring 1995. That gave me a year and change to get my shit together. In hindsight it was probably a stupid decision on the son's part. There were more qualified people (Kelly, for example!)…but so be it. I got it and, except for a drinking problem, fights, panic attacks, firings, and the office fire, things turned out okay.

Being director meant travel. June 1995. First trip abroad. Annecy. Kelly made me buy a suit (sorry, a blazer, she says). I was so naïve. Felt that the director should be dressed for the occasion. Hell…I remember in those days thinking how important ASIFA was. I was scared shitless of ASIFA and especially that grumpy David Ehrlich. I actually printed out about 25 copies of our report and budget to present to the ASIFA board. I really thought they were powerful and had an active role in our organization. What a laugh. That was my first airplane ride. Some charter flight with a lot of middle-aged Québec folk. I remember that takeoff. Holy shit, man, I thought I was gonna die. I was gripping the seat with all my strength… I was sweating… shaking… convinced we were gonna die (that ol' death phobia again). Fortunately…the free booze eased things up.

What a pain in the ass getting there (still is). I had some heavy-ass boxes and had no idea where I was going. We got into Paris and I had no idea where I needed to go. Fortunately, Michele Pauze of the NFB was there with some other NFBers and they guided me along. I had some nasty arguments in later years with Michele, but I'll never forget how sweet she was to me during that trip.

Annecy was overwhelming. I knew maybe 5-6-7 people. It was a scary experience. Fortunately, Knott and Alder and Simensky were there and they introduced me to some folks (including Rockin' Ron Diamond. He was telling me about some crazy idea to do some big animation 'website' for the World Wide Web… whatever the hell that was!)… It was maybe the purest festival experience I had. Because I didn't know anyone, I went to all the screenings. I hardly drank and went to my room early most nights (at least till I met a posse of Aussies—including Dennis Tupicoff—and Irish animators—then the nights got longer and blurrier). The craziest experience was getting lost in Annecy. The hotel was at least 1-2 miles away and I just kept making the wrong turns. It took me about an hour to figure it out. Ha…I remember Candy Kugel. That was the year that someone entered her room while she was sleeping. Freaked her out. Was also the year of the infamous Annecy closing ceremony that was totally disorganized and out of whack (ha…unlike the OIAF! Kidding.) Hung out with Maureen Furniss a lot. Went to see what's-his-name's films… Starewicz… really got off on those films. Dead bugs committing adultery!

Fast Forward

This piece is getting too long. My 2nd festival was in Stuttgart. This was really the 'satori' for me in animation. No suit this time, but did fly to Charles de Gaulle again. Had to spend 9 hours there waiting for the 2-hour or so flight to Stuttgart. Ended up dozing on a bench and missing the flight… so make it 3 more hours. Finally got to Stuttgart and passed out on the bed, exhausted. Next night I hooked up with Jayne Pilling. We were chatting away when this freaky-looking guy with shaggy hair, big glasses and a black leather coat took a seat with us. This was Gerben Schermer from the Holland Festival. I'd like to say that we hit it off immediately, but we were so pissed that I can't recall much…except that we sat around talking all night and then the three of us headed back to my room at the Maritim (the best festival hotel!) and drank some whisky. I passed out and spent the next 24 hours in my room trying to recover. Okay…maybe this wasn't the worst…but since I was in a foreign country…this hangover seemed like the worst. Oh god… I remember twisting, turning and vomiting…watching Jackie Chan films in German on TV… and then FINALLY venturing outdoors at about 1 am, where I caught a bit of whatever programme was on.

Things got much better. Met some Brits (ruth lingford, I think) and a real sweet Scottish girl. Ended up palling around with her all week. Met Peter Dougherty, the New York born MTV Europe Creative Director. Acidic sense of humour. Right up my alley. But beyond that…I remember one competition screening above all others. This was the year of Hilary by Anthony Hodgson, a film I loved so much (it ended up getting 3 awards in Ottawa)… and a

crazy film by some Estonian guy. My Scottish pal and I took seats in the balcony so we could drink our beers in peace. The Estonian film was first, I think. Man...I just remember being jolted out of whatever the moment that film started. Until I saw *Ring of Fire* and *Son of Satan*, it was really my big 'satori' in animation... I had NO idea what the film was about...it was just loaded with cinema references... a sarcastic British narrator...and really sloppy drawings. It was so smart, alive, funny and unpretentious. I had never seen anything like this film...and was just in stunned silence the whole time. Oh man...this was life...I just felt so good about life...I wanted to embrace people. I was buzzing with energy. This is what animation could be!! It didn't have to be so damn cute...or so cartoony...and perfectly drawn... of course... being a film studies major... I felt some comfort in the film... it was about, sort of, the history of cinema...there were references to Bergman, Godard, Truffaut...I really had no idea what the film was REALLY about (not sure I do fully grasp it today)...but whatever it was, it lured me right smack into animation...it gave me a home in a sense... a connection... I found my centre.

After the screening I saw Otto. I excitedly asked him about this film. He asked if I'd like to meet the filmmakers. Holy shit...yeah...that would be great. Later that night...or maybe the next night...we went to their room. They were these older guys, dressed in shirts from the film... They were just sitting around having some vodka or whatever hard liquor. They invited us in...I was introduced... "Chris, this is Priit Pärn and Janno Põldma." I'm sure I was like a kid meeting a hockey star. "I loved your film. I have no idea what it was about, but I just loved it. It was funny and smart...and just great..." Parn said thanks...and offered a drink. Before I left... Parn, like a hockey player giving a boy an autographed picture or free tickets, gave me a cel from the film. Oh man...that was amazing. I still have that cel on my wall.

Funny...during the closing ceremonies I remember seeing this young man with flowers in his hair collecting the Best Student Film award. He struck me as a bit arrogant. Only later did I realize that this was Andreas Hykade, who had won for a film I didn't see then: *We Lived in Grass*. Two years later that film would finally grab my soul.

The night after the festival ended, Otto, Priit, Janno and I went to dinner at a small German restaurant. It was, even now, the most memorable dinner I've had. The place (which no longer exists) was locally owned. We had, Christ, about 4-5 courses... and the rule was that you had to finish everything on your plate. Meantime...we kept drinking something or other—-real sweet, delicious, dangerous stuff. We laughed so much that night. I was finally learning to relax a little and be myself (whoever that was)... that was the night I earned a nickname that sticks today. This strange older guy who worked at the restaurant part time kept sitting with us and pouring us drinks... at one point he called me "Sepp." No idea why. But the name stuck. Until this day Otto and the Estonians call me Sepp. When Jarvis was born in 1998, it became Papa Sepp (if you look at the end credits in Parn's film *The Night of the Carrots*, you'll see a "Papa Sepp" in there).

For years I really had no idea what the name meant. Sepp in Estonian is like Smith...maybe Blacksmith.

Oh, and the film was called *1895*.

What's it about really?

A guy trying to figure out who he is and what he's supposed to be doing with his life. (Reminds me...yes...when I programme the OIAF, I pick films that I think are worthy...but it's also clearly subjective...and there are pieces that will undeniably reflect my life/concerns of that moment.)

My almost brotherly relationship with Gerben Schermer was born there and my long, long road down the path of Estonia started in that Stuttgart balcony.

That year in Stuttgart was when I, literally, entered the tent (I say literally because Stuttgart does have a tent!) Everything clicked. So many relationships that are important to me today (Pilling, Alder, Dougherty, Lingford, Schermer, Parn, Poldma, Hykade) all have some link to Stuttgart '96. I left Stuttgart with confidence. I could run the festival.

The downside? It was also the period that elevated my drinking habit. I was like a kid at camp. We had fun every day. There were films to watch, people to meet, sights to see. I was actually sad to leave Stuttgart. One of the only times I remember feeling that way after a festival. I didn't want the feelings to end. I wanted every day to be like the festival. So when I got home I started drinking more. For the next four years I became increasingly lost in the festival, in animation, in booze.

Last fall, when I was staying with Hykade, I asked him about the name. He told me it was like 'Joe,' but usually used to describe sort of a dim guy.

Ha, I was the village idiot.

(October, 2005)

Frolicking in the Tent

*Well, more than anything, it seems pretty nec. to let
the reader know I'm something other than the so-
called author of a given piece: I'm a fully formed,
fully flawed human being... penis warts and all. I
basically insist on eliminating any sort of protocol of
superiority for the POSITION of the author—his/her,
y'know, "status"—vis-a-vis the reader. I'm just, what's
a better expression, an "active entity" in the frolic.*
– Richard Meltzer, interview with author, 2002

During the 2004 Ottawa Festival we had a panel, devised
by Steve Dovas, about the state of criticism in animation. In my
guise as the Animation Pimp, I was asked to be a part of the panel
with Rita Street, Richard O'Connor, Amid Amidi and Mikhail
Gurevich.

I think there was some anticipation that the Pimp would let
go, unleash his venom LIVE. Maybe I thought that too. Instead I
sat there with nothing to say. Now okay, part of this was because
I was exhausted from being right smack in the fact of the festival
itself. I couldn't process much to get saucy about on two weeks'
worth of a few hours sleep. But in truth, I was silent because I
really didn't have much say. As I heard the others talking about
this and that technique and industry, and their critical strategies
etc.... I realized that I really didn't give a hoot, that I wasn't an
animation critic or a historian nor did I ever want to be one. I
knew this before and in fact I never sold myself as either. I've
always been an outsider in animation (yes... okay... I realize that
I do have a bit of power as the... as Plympton—the fact that I
can, say, refer to willie billie so casually is PROOF that I've got a
stake in this campground—once deemed me, "the tastemaker" of
the Ottawa festival) and what you've read over the years have just
been observations about many different things made by someone

who stumbled into this animation tent. I never saw myself as a permanent resident, just someone passing through. I mean... isn't that life in itself? I just picked things that I thought were interesting and, in particular, how these people, ideas or whatever they might have been, affected me as a person. And that was the key. You never really lose sight of the observer. And in that sense, you not only see this world of animation through the Pimp's eyes, but you are also seeing the essence of the person behind the Pimp.

The tales say as much about me as they do about the tent. And it wasn't just about what animation brought to me directly... it was never direct... animation came to me filtered by the world I'd experienced before and around the tent. So it was never about criticism or history, just a philosophical jaunt.

Nick and Dick

Even that approach is nothing even close to being unique. My own introduction to that personal gonzo style came through the 1970s and '80s writings of Nick Tosches and Richard Meltzer. So much of the free-form style that has dominated Pimp columns comes from Meltzer's influence. When he was a full-on rock writer in the 1970s, he reviewed records he never listened to, concerts he wasn't at. His work was dense, playful, self-centred and almost always funny. For whatever reason, one review ("Real Time, Real Demons: Bouncing with Bud '64") always stayed with me. Inside a Bud Powell CD review was a story about Meltzer's "first completely sexual relationship." For Meltzer the critic wasn't some objective, impartial deadbeat who just stood atop a mountain telling the readers what he saw. He was down in the muck with them. (Here's a link to an opera review called "Fuck My Childhood": www.angelfire.com/ny4/ungodlyvision/AtN/fmchildhood.htm)

Now Tosches... holy fuck... what can I fucking say about my first fucking encounter with grandmaster Saint Nick. He'd written a book about Dean Martin called *Dino*. I didn't really know or care much about Dean Martin at the time, but some prof at school had suggested it. It just blew me away... it was

41

profound and profane. I'd never seen the word 'fuck' used so poetically. I mean… one minute Tosches would be calling Jerry Lewis a cocksucker… and then he'd be referencing Dante and pre-Greek philosophers… and it all made sense somehow:

> He [Dean Martin] has heard of Dante and the Commedia, of the hundred cantos that rose towards a paradise of light, love and reason with the breath of a woman at their heart Pura Luce, piena d'amour. But what was all the light and love in the world compared to a single good blowjob? That was what women did to men, turned them into fucking pazzo poets. And what the fuck did Dante know about hell? Dante Aligheri and Jerry Lewis. Nine years of listening to that mortuchrist' wail and whine—then he really could have written a fucking Inferno. Fuck it all. Fuck all that love, light and reason shit. Fuck Beatrice where she breathed. Fuck the moon in your eye like a big pizza pie.[1]

Beyond that, there were passages of pure fiction where Tosches clearly made up dialogue and internal thoughts attributed to Dean Martin. It was the MOMENT for me… the moment when my writing and views took the stick out of their ass (or at least partially out of my ass). In the end, Tosches' hyperbole and references told us more about the essence, the core of who Dean Martin was (not to mention Nick Tosches) than any straightforward authorized biography ever could.

And, in both cases, these guys were interested as much in ideas as people. Tosches always placed his subjects in the larger context of the world they lived in. They weren't treated like people who lived above or around us, uncontaminated by society. In Tosches' case, he was interested in dark, unsung figures (Jerry Lee Lewis, Dean Martin, Emmitt Miller, Sonny Liston). Meltzer's work was more self-centred (and I don't mean that in a bad sense). When he writes about music or writers or whatever, it's first and foremost about how they fit or interact with his own life.

1. Nick Tosches, *Dino: Living High in the Dirty Business of Dreams* (New York: Dell Publishing, 1992).

Tent Pegs

When I started writing about animation I wrote formally, from a distance. Check out anything I wrote before say... spring 2000... and it's real straight-laced routine stuff. It reads okay, but you can see the stick moving around in my ass... trying to get loose.

And I remember that it was while writing about Priit Pärn and, get this, Alexander Petrov's *Old Man and The Sea*... that I could see the words and attitude becoming a little looser, a little more personal, a little less following what others told me to say or what I thought they wanted me to say.

But it was frustrating to be alone in a way. I'm not saying that I was Mr. Groundbreaker by ANY means... but from what I could see... no one in animation wrote with that subjective unapologetic transcendent gonzo passion that Tosches and Meltzer brought to music. Yes, there are many who are CLEARLY passionate about their subject... but they speak as if their subject is the centre of the world rather than a part of it. Look at mainstream film critics. They judge a film solely based on what came before it. They don't consider its time and place of creation.

Then there are the techno-fetish folks who judge animation first on HOW it says something. WHAT it says is always secondary. Take Chris Landreth's *Ryan,* for example. I keep reading all sorts of stuff about the innovative technology, but nothing about WHAT the film is about—other than the standard claptrap about Larkin's life.

This has been a problem in general. There is never any critical dialogue about a film. If it's bad, no one talks about it. If it's great, we all say, "Hey, that was great..." If we don't understand it, we resort to "It looked real beautiful... nice brush strokes and textures..." and all that assorted horseshit that's more in the realm of the wine connoisseur. Bottom line, I just never felt moved or motivated by anything I read about animation.

It was either a fan-clubby historical approach (Barrier and Beck—and I am NOT dissing those guys for a minute. I may not dig their style, but they are passionate about what they're doing); polished, technique driven (Canemaker—again... I may not click with Canemaker's writing style, but I admire the beans out of the man for continually seeking to give a voice to all those unacknowledged, unsung studio artists. Canemaker's like a cartoon homicide cop); or dense, academic and coded (sort of an inversion of the fan-clubby approach—speaking only to those already resting atop the ivory tower).

In the end, when I couldn't find any likeminded writers… I said fuggit and contacted Meltzer directly and just invited him to write. I figured that even though he had no animation experience, he had enough life and writing experience to easily be able to write about animation. I was right. (I'm still surprised that Richard even answered my email and agreed to write for the Ottawa festival).

The situation is starting to change a little (thanks to the Internet and the availability of more work). I admire the heck out of Amid Amidi for singing with such commitment, intensity and passion. Now if he'd only stop drooling over all things designiest so much! Dr. Toon has always been a fave of mine—even though he talks about mainstream U.S. animation too much—because he looks at tendencies, trends … all in a historical light. And I am REALLY excited to read Chris Panzner's work. As his recent pieces on AWN show, he brings a gonzo sensibility to otherwise dull (for me) industry issues. Panzer shows that he's not afraid to speak frankly about anyone or anything. And I think animation has always needed that.

What frustrates me the most though is the unwillingness of many of these people (above and beyond) to talk about NON-Hollywood films. We just keep seeing the same stuff being written about the same people and studios. Anyone who stepped into this 'tent' would think that animation is ONLY Pixar, Disney, DreamWorks, AMERICAN. It's like listening to some generic FM station that plays the same 50 fucking songs from the same 20 fucking bands. We need more writers to actively engage and champion those unsung films and animators.

That said… I don't feel the anger I once did toward writers like Barrier and company. They write about what interests them just as I do. How can I piss on them for that? I might think…

"shit... Beck... can't you take a gander out the window and see what's going on down the block...", but the same can be said of my own views. I even sometimes envy these guys for their passion and wish I could get all stoked about a Woody Woodpecker or Felix the Cat cartoon.

As for me... I'm just trying my best to articulate what I see around me. I've written about animators I felt a connection with... whose work... whose life... might help me unlock some mystery inside me.

My words are just a reflection of a life (faults and all) in process. That's it and yet that's all.

(February, 2005)

FESTIVALS AND THEIR DISCONTENTS

The Animation Pimp

Few years back was planning a piece 'bout (not boot) festival directors bein' pimps. Johns and hoes are interchangeable (e.g. Joe animator is a John looking for a hand-job from a studio and also a ho offering the studio guy/gal themselves as a whore/john, a tidy, quick piece o' meat). The whole shaaaaabang of them (whether Russian animators or California buyers) straddle the line. This was about '96, when festivals became a site of decadence.

Figured festivals were/should be galleries, museums, venues for artists to gather and share ideas, work and experiences. I hate galleries and museums. Damn stagnant receptacles for the glorification of the artist as GREAT (WO) MAN. Needless to say these artsy circle jerks didn't attract the public, who don't seem to understand the term 'animation.' Should we use 'Animation Film Festival' anyway? Maybe 'Cartoon Festival' is more public-friendly. Yeah…International Cartoon Film Festival. The (point) being that the festivals were elitist.

Then Big Bird convinced Siebert that cartoonies could in fact sell coolness and More Tittie Visuals were born. And so began the wallpapering of animation. Festivals changed. Suits started comin'. Students came to find jobs, not ideas 'cause ideas don't buy Nikes (i.e. coolness). Studios came to show their 'human side,' headhunt, steal new styles (ya ever notice that "Rugrats," "Duckman" and the whole Csupo look borrows a bit from a well-known Estonian animator who influenced the Ukes, who were lushingly lured to Hollywood?) and wank. Nuttin' wrong with that s'long as they payin'.

Same time governments turned right and figured that cartoons weren't no important t'ing to be payin' for so might as well let da' mouse cover it. Welcome booths.

Ottawa is not so bad I guess because Annecy has whored itself worse than any of us (Roy Disney! Give me a fuggin break). But hell, they attract a shitload of people and studios and sponsors so I guess maybe it's a good thing, but I tell you each year I plan the festival's programme with no freakin' idea how much money I will have. So maybe I'm just jealous (then again...Europe has more bodies then Canada).

The Ottawa Festival is a crapshoot. We plan the programmes, hire staff, invite programmers and guests, but have no clue if we will make enough money. "Yeah," says Terry American, "but you're government-supported up dere in your socialist country." A fallacy. Twenty percent of our budget is covered by the government: $24,000 (City of Ottawa), $90,000 (Telefilm Canada), $15,000 (National Film Board of Canada), $4,500 (Region of Ottawa-Carleton). Considering our size, history and importance in North America, these numbers are disgusting.

My demonic inner voice, while dropping the kids at the pool, yells, "IF WE WERE IN TORONTO!" Of course, the funny thing is that we work hard to avoid showing 'cartoons' and try to convince people that animation is an art form. This never works and in the end if we simply resorted to showing funny cartoonies we'd be on our way...media attention would flow in every direction. But then where are we? We've got press, but it's for all the big companies who are getting it already anyway...the independents and small companies are left in the dark again.

The media doesn't care about Andreas Hykade, Paul Driessen or Raoul Servais. They are more interested in some Ottawa schmuck who is inkin' dogs for some half-butt TV production.

Intermission

Whining aside, this is an OK job. I make my hours, travel around the world. I write.

Where am I going with this anyway? I think I was more in love with the title and trying to shock people than saying anything relevant or new. This year, Ottawa felt good. We maybe broke even.

Maybe I'm suggesting that the heart and soul of a festival remains in those dark spaces. Don't be fooled by the façades of the suits and the logos. This is just foreplay. The real down and dirty stuff lies within those silent, dark walls which come alive in a sensual play of light and sound that bring pleasure, pain, ecstasy, laughter, insight, shock, guffaws, grunts, groans. Within the shadows these sounds bring you closer to you and those around you. The rest is just whoring. So in the end me and my fellow pimps and pimpettes offer everything for the needy starved festival-goer. If you want quick, no bullshit solo action, we've got booths and rooms for you. If you want more intimate, interactive, in-depth experiences (e.g., group sex?), we've got a nice dark 969- (not shittin' ya) seat space for you. And if you just want to talk, that's OK too. But no profanity.

(December, 2000)

Annecy, Audiences, Art and Sandwiches

I've never been a big fan of cinema audiences. Within those darkened, shadowed walls you can't help but see and hear a world that is a little bit fascistic. You either laugh or cry or applaud almost entirely in unison with the other seated souls. Emotions are suppressed so as not to disturb the others. It's entirely inappropriate to mock a film or laugh when others cry, or boo while the rest applaud. I just hate it. You can never truly be who you are. Emotions are tailored to the tune of your fellow audience members. It makes sense really and explains a lot of this society, which carries the belief, "Rules say there is nothing more." We live in a repressed era. The genuine or authentic is replaced by the mechanical or virtual. We cannot even laugh (on our own) at television. 'Canned' guffaws do that for us.

For this reason I always like two types of movie theatres. The first is kids' films. This is a wonderful experience. All these crazy little voices shouting an endless parade of grunts, guffaws and basic primary reactions unmediated and unconcerned with those around them. The second is the Annecy Animation Festival. It's great. They boo. They applaud sarcastically. They whistle...throw beach balls around...and it's complemented by crazy closing ceremonies, generally poor film selection and, surprisingly, a general lack of 'taste.'

Contrary to the notion that the French have good taste, the audiences in Annecy seem devoid of any. They want bunny rabbits, ducks, farts and gag films. They loathe anything 'ambitious' or 'arty.' It's quite surprising given Annecy's roots, but reveals how far Annecy has strayed from those days of 'promoting the art of animation.' In particular I remember in Annecy '99 how the audience was merciless in watching Austrian artist Barbel Neubauer's abstract film, *Firehouse*. They whistled and applauded throughout her film and then she had to stand on stage after it. It was a terrible experience and she was deeply hurt by it.

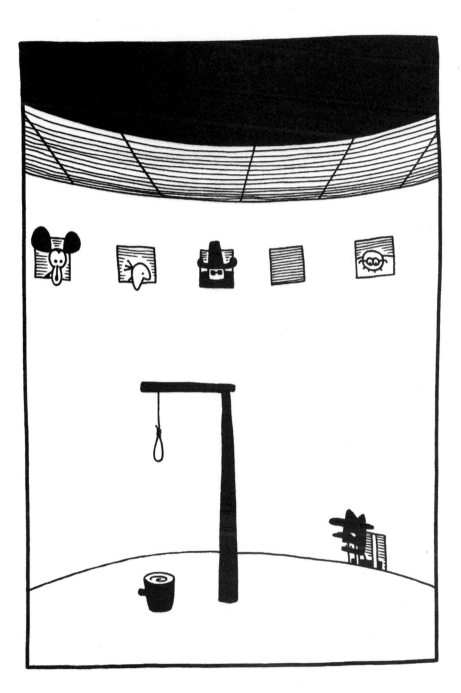

Fortunately, the jury consisted of more open-minded people and Barbel received a prize in the end. Justice.

Festivals are the last haven for stimulating animation, but even within these walls this is becoming a threat. Christ, in Ottawa, I keep hearing the same ol' complaints: "How can you choose *The Night of the Carrots* over great animation like *Famous Fred?*" What I loathe more than anything is that this mindset forces me to defend what is often an elitist group. When I became festival director I was eager to fight the apparent snob mentality of associations like ASIFA. For me, as long as a work stimulated me mentally, that was all I needed. I don't need to say this is ART and this is SHIT. But lately, I've found myself succumbing to the very elitism I loathe.

But hey, I may not agree with their taste, but I absolutely love this lovely crowd and wish other festival audiences would rise from the dead and respond. Animation festival theatres have become like the popular theatre of Brecht's time. He once said it was a world where the audience checked their head in at the door. The difference here is that the material being shown is usually high quality, provocative, challenging and innovative, but what we find is a case of over-polite, repressed audiences...and Christ, I don't know what life is like within commercial studio walls, but the independent crowd can be extremely conservative. It's part of this desperate attempt to project animation as a bourgeois art form. To applaud quietly and politely (like a golf clap wherein three fingers gently tap the palm of the other hand) and to cry over *Father and Daughter* is really about defining a notion of high art. To boo, heckle or applaud sarcastically is to reflect primitive, primate qualities attributed to low-brow culture (e.g., sports fans).

And, yes, animation is defined as entertainment and it needs to be more accepted as a stimulating form of expression. However these 'proper' artists (you know who they are) merely reinforce the very social injustice and inequalities they often critique. As another Frenchman said, by creating a high and low in art, you are merely reinforcing social or class differences. And this is often the problem (I've been guilty of it at times too). Too often we divide animation into a polarization of art vs. industry. Disney vs. McLaren, etc. We frown upon those commercial 'twits' who are 'unrefined' and lack sophistication, while we golf-clap a Frédéric Back, Raoul Servais or Yuri Norstein film. Yet, this very attitude only further distances 'artistic' animation from the general audience. No one wants to be told WHAT is proper. The high-brow enthusiasts have created a colony where we are told that to enter this realm you must understand proper etiquette or the 'delicate sensibilities' of a Renoir. Yeah...well, whatever. I'm gonna go and clean the shit off my shoes and make a sandwich... and ya know what? I'm not going to properly slice the sandwich into four pieces. Just gonna eat the whole friggin' thing. This colony of supposed sophisticates is a creation of those in power. It makes them feel better about themselves. It makes them special. It fills a bland materialist existence. Funny, but the irony of my bitching is that I had to go to university to learn that HIGH and LOW distinctions are silly.

We need to move beyond the extremes of art vs. industry. Yes, there are commercial craftsfolk who blindly reject anything with content, but there are also those so-called sophisticated folks who are just as blind in their assumptions. For example, *Father and Daughter*, *The Old Man and The Sea* and *The Mighty River* are considered beautiful, DELICATE, sophisticated works... in general...by the 'experts'...but, shit, *Father and Daughter* is a hollow effort. Yes, it's a beautifully designed film, but its story is sappy and emotional and really bears more resemblance to, let's say, *Geri's Game* than more provocative pieces like *The Hat* or *Flying Nansen*. Hell, I've seen episodes of "The Simpsons" and "South Park" that are more mentally stimulating and provide as scintillating a social critique as any Priit Parn film. It's like Charles Chaplin and Buster Keaton. Chaplin wanted to be a serious artist. Keaton wanted to make people laugh. In the end, Keaton made more profound works.

Okay...rambling a bit...what's my point? 1. Annecy screenings are the best because you can be an individual. 2. Annecy audiences, however, can be very unsophisticated. 3. The word ART and all the other slang associated with it (e.g., 'sophisticated') needs to be re-defined. 4. I do not cut my sandwiches.

This month's Animation Pimp is sponsored by the Royal Canadian Mounted Police and Quebec police: "Nothing says police state like tear gas, pepper spray and designated protest areas."

(May, 2001)

Proposal Modest A

first the at place took memories festival favourite my of One
We .1997 in Festival Animation Student International Ottawa
screened that *Cracks First* called programme a presenting were
John like animators established of variety a from films first
,Pärn Priit ,Burton Tim ,Judge Mike ,Lasseter John ,Kricfalusi
Around ,film Hébert's .Hébert Pierre and ,Griffin George
particularly was (film first his actually not was which) *Perception*
typical a ,eye lazy the to ,was film minute-16 This .memorable
to Needless .colours and objects flashing of full film abstract
and restless little a became audience student primarily our ,say
Jury .frustration in shouting and applauding ,whistling started
the and film the with impressed so was Holty Ellen member
screening special a have could we if me asked she that reaction
,mumblings hesitant of minutes few a After .festival the in later
result The .(jury the on also was who ,Hébert did as) agreed I
,stage the on danced People .anarchy joyous of minutes 8 was
first the was This...etc ,songs sang ,puppets shadow made they
and fast quite by went actually it and film the seen had I time
there ,surprise my to much ,Well .painless relatively it found I
the up speed to decided projectionists the :this for reason a was
unique a was It .performance the to contribution their as film
.performance

refreshing a was this ,screenings Festival Annecy the from Aside
-and-seat-your-in-sit ,ass-tight the from departure unique and
time rare The .screenings festival most of atmosphere up-shut
reaction in up spoken ever has audience the of member any that
not is itself in reaction The .film the with problem technical a to
,screams person The .fit shit a having ape an unlike entirely
booth projection the to runs ,seat their in down and up jumps
performance their general In .window or door the on bangs and
we'll film competition mediocre the from distraction nice a is

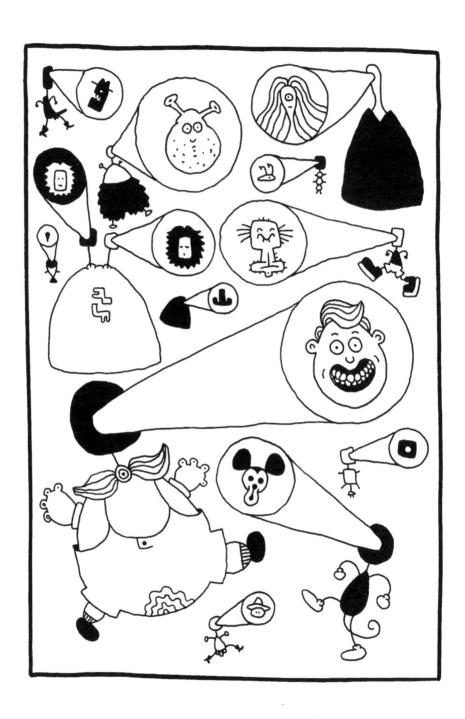

.forget soon

,booth projectionist the in manager stage a as worked Having
funniest the and acts ape these of few a than more seen I've
the inside from morons these watching are them of aspects
the on pound they as apes like look do really They .booth
making ,words incomprehensible mouthing ,door or window
all—side to side from tilting head ,gestures hand crazy
.ART of name the in supposedly

These .reality projectionist's the of ignorant are people ,Typically
few the) projectionists film feature ,part most the for ,are guys
far a is which ,(owners theatre by screwed been haven't who left
leisure of amount decent a for allows that job demanding less
screenings Festival .pace natural more a least at or time
is experience the and unique are (Ottawa in especially)
working they are only Not .projectionist the to new occasionally
short of barrage a with dealing also are they ,days hour -14 -12
gun automatic an loading from going like It's .videos and films
the at often are they ,Additionally. shooter-six old slightly a to
16mm a had we years for) equipment theatre's the of mercy
,that Beyond .(focus of out screen the half showed that projector
numerous ,problems sound ,listed ratios incorrect had we've
PAL accepting stop to decision our hence) issues quality transfer
.disasters unforeseen other many and (1999 in videos

during occurrence regular a not it's 'cause) sudden a of all Now
,pretentious some with deal to have guys these (films feature
door or window their on banging moron screaming
.(reason a for locked are ,cockpits like ,doors projectionist)
once—laugh projectionists the makes show ape the ,Generally
from them distracts also it but—bar metal the down put they've
these of Because .(can they if) problem the correcting actually
propose to like would I ,experiences ,unnecessary mostly ,many
You .festivals at films own their project filmmakers the that
and creation of process the Take .it project You .it made
writer's a to going Imagine) .duration full its to exhibition

(.words author's the read else someone see to festival

,screened be to film the for order In .out planned all it have I
a films 10-15 show we say Let's .there be to has filmmaker the
video a and 16mm a ,projectors 35mm two got We've .night
then and door the outside filmmakers 15 the up line We .deck
.station their at format each in filmmakers four first the up set
.etc ,level sound ,ratio ,loading ,splicing for responsible are They
,table the to film your take you ,finished is film the When
one...Meanwhile .booth the exit and can the in it put ,it rewind
is this While .film their started has competitors other the of
to filmmaker next the escorts staff friendly our of one ,on going
filmmakers the ,screenings the Following .projector 35mm the
.audience the of applause the earned having ,introduced are

(October, 2001)

Greetings from St. Helena

"Every festival organization should have the freedom to choose their options, philosophy and ideas which make the festival different and SPECIAL, exactly what festival visitors, filmmakers, buffs and fans are looking for! How uninteresting if every festival was looking for Annecy or Zagreb. It would not be worthwhile neither to participate nor to visit."
– ASIFA Board of Directors: Comments on the Toronto '84 Animation Festival

Yeah... sure... for the most part... the opinions of the Pimp are also those of the Ottawa Animation Festival's Artistic Director. I don't apologize for that. Although not many folks think I should, one rapacious crankbag blasted me (as festival director) in a (Pimp) comment space last summer because... umm... not sure why actually... I guess it was because her friends' films weren't being accepted into Ottawa competitions anymore and she felt that, as the Napoleon of festival directors, it was my intention to deprive her friends (whomever THEY are) of a screen in Ottawa theatres. I was flush with pride. At long last someone who sees the layers of empathy dripping from the pores of my flesh, a peasant who recognizes the power and sway of a GREAT festival director. Hurfugginrah! They actually believe that I have spent day and night carefully examining each of these so-called artists' films, while conducting extensive background checks into each so-called artist's psychological, academic, criminal and sexual history. Once I had carefully narrowed down the list of so-called artists, I then set out to find a feckless Selection Committee who would unconsciously succumb to my dastardly demands... or die. Failing that, I had Plan B: seduce them with liquor, opium, goat photos and whores. Once the committee was 'convinced,' these so-called artists would NEVER EVER see the light of the screens in MY kingdom!

Alas, 'tis a dream, a wonderful dream, but nevertheless merely a candy-coated imagining from the lands of pillows. In truth I am little more than a self-loathing, barely educated, poorly organized procrastinator whose idea of empathy, generosity and socializing routinely involves proper palm placement during self-loving to ensure maximum effect.

OK, enough. To the point: November was the 1st anniversary of the Pimp column. I was gonna try and form some thoughts about the selection process in Ottawa so that we could have it in print and move on to more important tasks like examining why the live-action artists are such fashionable arses... BUT then the world went nuts (more so)... there was that whole Giuliani thing, then the Bush thing, then the stolen lumber truck baseball contraction, then Mario's sore hip, then Patrick Roy pulled out, then my doctor called and said my cholesterol was high, then this girl called and said something about Daddy grade 10 mother was a cheerleader loose sperm, then there was the Italian crisis as I walked by the forum ruins and wondered why Italian animation SUCKS, then my brother called, he rarely calls, then Richard said the SD reader fired him, which is like Gretzky being cut, then I went to a GBV concert and couldn't hear for 2 days, then I listened to *Far East Suite* continuously for one week and, hell, the next thing ya know it was xmas and I had shopping to do, decorations to hang, cookies to bake, then came the new year and my annual enema. Soooooooooooooooo (whew!) finally... in the month of love and suicide, when I suffer from neither, I found a moment to articulate a few thoughts about festivals and specifically competition film selection for those of you who care.

Every year people bitch about the film selection; that's part of the game. I LOVE it when a 'rejected' entrant sends angry emails demanding to know what moron obviously missed the point of their film. I like that energy. You spent SO MUCH time with this child. You believed in it enough to make it. You SHOULD be passionate about it. What irks me is the ignorance of the process. "How could this film get in and not mine!?" "Everyone at my school thinks it's THE best film ever." "How can *Cybersix* get in and not *Father and Daughter*?" Stuff like that.

It's hard to get your film into Ottawa. There are six competition programmes generally running no longer than 80 minutes each. That's 480 minutes of film. We receive more than 1300 entries. Fewer than 100 are accepted. Annecy, as a comparison, receives the same number of entries, but offers at least twice the competition space. As such, me, my momma, her sister, her sister's cousin's uncle's neighbour's friend's brother's daughter's stepfather's ex-wife's dog with a blocked bladder has a decent chance of being screened.

Tick-tocking aside, folks forget about the categorization of entries. Entries are judged within their categories (e.g., kids' film, TV series, independent film, graduate film, commercial, etc...), so when you see *Cybersix* or *Celebrity Deathmatch* in competition and not the latest Plympton or Quay epic, it is NOT because the committee felt that *Cybersix* is a better film. Some ask, especially the folks from the old part of the world, why categories? Why not just judge everything on the same level? Well...films are not produced in the same conditions or with the same intentions (ya OK...I know that's a rather problematic argument in the end too—Why accept 'crappy' TV animation? Is it fair to have Iranian animators competing against NFB toonsters?—But a line must be drawn—get it? Heh heh heh).

Until this year a committee of international animation professionals selected competition films for the Ottawa fest. From the beginning of my tyrannical reign, I contemplated slicing the committee. We (hell...I) finally decided to do it in 2000. There were a variety of reasons: 1) It costs us almost $10,000 (CDN) to bring four people to Ottawa in the summer to deliberate and then back again in the fall for the festival. 2) selection by committee sucks. Invariably, because it's such a small community, the same faces begin showing up on different committees and juries (just take a look at Cinanima 2001 as a great example). 3) While peer assessment is a nice dream, invariably these animators don't have the opportunity to attend festivals to keep up with contemporary animation. So what happens when people aren't keeping up with the new stuff? They tend to make comfortable and familiar decisions. We all do that...but if you're not watering the noggin...

your taste buds are gonna stagnate. Hence...(and I say this as a first-hand witness) committees often pick films because of WHO made them or WHAT prizes they won, rather than the actual quality of the work. 4) Furthermore, there is rarely any detailed debate. More often than not, a simple 'democratic' vote ends all discussion: "next film, please." The result: animation festivals start to look the same.

Now...this is less a criticism of the people than the system. These four people spend 10 days in a room watching 1300 films. That is an insane task to ask of anyone (increasingly we found it difficult to even find people who wanted to do it). Often they are watching 100 films a day. They become cranky, hungry, tired and slowly begin to get on each other's nerves. Their patience diminishes, the vision blurs and their mental process tires.

In short...it's an unfair experience for the committee member, festival, filmmaker and audience.

Our solution, and it is by no means perfect, is to have selection done in-house under my supervision. It usually involves at least three of the festival organizers. As Artistic Director, I have the final say and naturally my decisions affect and influence the look and tone of the event. I make no apologies for that. A museum or gallery has a curator, why not a festival? In truth, there is nothing radical about this system. It is common practice at live-action festivals as it is with many newer animation festivals (Holland, Fantoche, Anima Mundi; Stuttgart has a combination).

There are a few critics of this system who throw out that tired line about democratic process. That's just an excuse for avoiding responsibilities (see 'democratic vote' above); an emergency exit that eliminates the need for thoughtful, impassioned discussion and provides a handy hand washing for those who really don't have opinions; besides, since when is democracy in the best interests of the people?

With our in-house system I have the advantage of knowing virtually all the contemporary films out there (not that THAT necessitates TASTE). Without the restrictions of a committee, we take at least a month to observe the films, leaving plenty of time for discussion and repeat screenings. Yes, I have final say, but I take the opinions of my colleagues seriously and rely on them to stop me if I'm perhaps being too lustful toward, let's say, an Estonian animation film. Besides, the process demands more than one judge.

We also have the ability to reconsider a rejected film or two if there is room. Why not? Why this formal OPERATIC procedure that sings: ALL IS FINAL!!! ? I ain't afraid to say it: We make mistakes, especially with the limbo entries. See...there are films that are VERY GOOD and VERY BAD. That's usually fairly easy to sort out...but that big pile in the middle is essentially left to a crapshoot. All sorts of important, but also trivial, influences sway selection of those films: Maybe they had to piss when they saw your film? Maybe the coffee was brewing. Maybe it was just before lunch after a long morning. Maybe they cut it off too early. Bottom line: Any festival that tells you that the system of selection is some pure, objective process of GODS is, as my friend Ronnie said, "Shitting in your mouth and calling it a sundae."

Now you know.

(February, 2002)

Via Slug's Saloon

One will be the more learned, the more one knows that one is ignorant.
— Nicholas of Cusa

Oh my god No fucking way Good story but same ol' same ol' Ginger can kiss my green grass ass Self-conscious hip Speaking of enemas Technique is unique but this is fucking boring Narration is weird disjointed intense Hey these animals are really cute Pushing the Canadian accents to extremes Fairly Hey a freak dog with three legs Cow cud with big balls Been there seen that Blah blah Bangles Eat me! I'd like to sock someone I'm feeling violent the clichés never end Disney has redefined bland nice bosom though pro-girl but of course she's umm…hot I like tea biscuits I smell monkey poo We are talking about blueberry chocolate confusions sometimes I think it's chocolate but it's blueberry Nice design Jerry Stiller bird I like blueberry tea biscuits I've had 2 cups of coffee Disney's answer to Powerpuff Design=Burton Jokes=lame I'd rather eat rice Pretty fucking obscure Really a series? Pretty funny Cleaning rooms is a no-go Winking is a no-no One bite of a cabbage and his wish will come true Suck my cakehole ya bad acting bitch Pretty original but I dunno kinda boring too There's that dog again A fart joke multiple orgasms hand in pants vomiting little hairy muffin Every lame idea becomes a TV concept it's like a fucking receptacle looks like an early '80s cartoon but would look bad even then A meccano dream here we go again first Elvis reference Belongs in heaven lame jokes poor dialogue Nathan Lane!? I've had better tales in my ass Cereal company doesn't but toys in box Igor's 'character' influence Not on tape Blow me! Annecy can keep it! Decent design mediocre script Pre Dickable Holy phuk. See "mimi"

Now THAT's animation! This music is making me thirsty No way Nice Mexican accent ya skinny phuck is a dog aware of his existence? Don't be greedy come and get it no its wrong here try some ge ya goin' real big fat albert

#1
my nose runs on occasion
there is a no in nose
I am a no

I hate elves and for dummie books die please light green has that 'overbeck' look red while circle dancers dance in a circle I was nice ONCE not again Stay there you're more boring than your boring city Ruined by coupling duck hunt They're shooting ducks s'like a fortune teller…eh HA HA HA Reindeers drinking stupid old broad Sometimes when I crap it's poignant Phuck U That rough raw style Fresh towels are fine Flutes should be banned Elastic band MAYBE just because there are three people and I am but one who said NON! Make the pain go away Great gag Bugs can't play drums 9-11 reference #1 How come the Penguin? I wanna work for Don Bluth, but Don Bluth doesn't work anymore either He's fucking dreamin' in pencil Hey…fran/ will Krause influenced! Thick line drawings slavery bit of Larkin influence Elderly schmelderly RRRRRRRRRRRRR Why is this animated? So much realistic detail Just shoot it LIVE! Maybe Can. Panorama It's NEVER Jules Verne? Character design is just silly Clitoris? It belongs in a hole St. inspector Nein This is one of the WORST entries ever cheese burger amiga man I feel like sleeping too A lo ghostbuster with a halo/belly button De la A La Nice bits poor pace at times not always clear something familiar Woody Allen Big eyed guy in cub sketchy style even worse then the Quays Nails cotton and things that don't move Great voice actors! I was out-voted so its maybe for panorama Frankenstein created turns on creator? I'm losing my mind on Day 2 I don't like my mummy bunny honey huuney strange atmospheric not THAT bad woman as oven max schrek that damn 2d look hey… that guy has no nose but he does have a trailer Oh dear now he's a bird Why? The new King! Softfocus No...but I do! Preachy but nice design so-so so-so mmmmm...hp sauce I don't like red landscape First we drink

#2
Frogs are green
limes are green
go away

#3
Sleep
I need Sleep
Dreams are good
Does anyone sleep WELL?

I can photocopy my hand too.

Genital issues hysteria is caused by wanking but what is caused by crying? Tape fucked and it's 11 min. Nein death sex birth go work at NFB we don't need to hear this song if they DO IT its in looks like found footage bla SWANSBBBITTTS Time frozen? We're into the 3d shit Raoul Servais is still alive big hats umbrellas tom tina maybe/no I say NO they say PANORAMA maybe for kids category? Very stylish it is done fat people bolero b/w subway NO NO NO NO NO NO NO NO NO NO NO NO do not enter test film credits longer than movie The loving was comin' WEEEEEEEEE....I'm floating Feathers, canes and cello Lighten Up! Curtain rises Please let us stop Fuck off creep I like RED!!! I like Red Sumo river phukker my stomach is beeping Soviet anthem! Yippee!!! Oi my head Already showed at Ottawa 76 Don't like lighting framing or the fucking dolls finger puppets suck I want to dance he's right Life is hard especially when I must watch pretentious stuff like this finale-mother-son Winks! No waste a No Speaking of Pärn Seven Sins and into the void it goes 2 men shoot their dogs "oh for something to eat" This one won't be on the menu Miles Davis robot Capture filmmaker and remove computer Pixar pool balls not enuff 'balls' Bosom

Wacky Unintended parody of surrealism Jesus Christ germans doin' Japanese robots This is fucking weird like snowshoes Nox3 ugly scary powdered film? They go dark Shadowplay Chuck Gamble black this/that Pärn/Krause "I'd like to take a crap on the tv screen" Spoons are good for big fuls of cereal wank

#4
Starlight
Starbright
Please be the last Star
Like This
I see this life
\

how much are we paying this education handcuffed to your dick poe was American I've seen toys in my nightmares…and then the scream came… Margaret rewind the tape please Whose Sam? Look MA! Sand on glass! Drink your tea and shed up No seeds! The horror! No classical guitars please Tumpkins I am not of the same opinion Baden has great hot springs but tuscania was much better by starlight Smut U my friend are an idiot Spiderman Whose to say what is not objective Whose to say what is objective Isnt objective subjective? Is my reality objective or subjective? I like bugs! No! I LOVE bugs!

#5
Burton, Tim
Elfman, Danny
Festival, no

Is that gum? Pretentious git is that a NO I smell? That best not be a tightrope meanwhile at the bar? Areba si signor I'm beggin you to SHUT UP I invented the door bell this child has the voice of a thirty year old Remove this 2 Kaks Was that a handjob? How many ways can I spell stooped. No whistling no whistling no ninjas either I don't mind her ass but the other 2 say "no" Not working umm…gosh stupido city as jungle flying turtles statues pyramids turtles flying around why me smile? HAHAHAHAH

AHAHAHAHAHAHAHAHAHAHAHAHAHAHA WHY? There must be a way to stop it What's with this accent? Atmospheric nonsense 1-2-3- NO! 3 mins of colour bars culture.

Je crash Pierre t'amitay I loved it just in case someone from Roman reads this Last minute is weak Disq condie comp animation Touch each other in funny ways NO! [I added a drawing] Sorry Pal but once again... This is not for tom and tina school...miscellaneous porn nookaleedookalee [drawings of spheres, tunnels, cubes] Do beans get gas? Tape damaged uses the ACTUAL Python track I'd like to like it more than I did I'm sad Best Acting! Entered before? Gak gak no spend less time on your logo This is really depressing Aussie narration must stop Make a film without dialogue and stop reminiscing about your damn cousins brothers uncles aunts nieces dogs cats cities and dads Accordians and fake French accents w/love are and have always been OUT The stupidest why even bother yet most truthful STOP OINKING! Speaking of nightmares disqualified parn/driessen most copied I just wanna say BYE heh heh Does this mean that if I reject your film I am intolerant? Poor singing if ya gee...asks me beetlejuice beetlejuice beetlejuice I'm running too! Speaking of sinking ships! Tina thinks its cheese another stork what a waste of a FINE poet disqual. Childrens categories not today! Everyone hopes that each tape is damaged now. Jarvis laughed when she ate the whole chicken

Disc jockey no I want to forget it all cut together

They WILL never know wankadoodledo some people think that non-narrative means no narration airport London melting ice kinda ol school collage trace it's a narrative! Bad mood tired easy to irritate always find someone to accommodate me my dad on a bender but with a rabbit narrative? I am to put an end to this... escape slow unclear not sure how interesting to caricature the faces of statues OH GOD Please make this end. I wish I blinded that guy in lear? Gloucester...oh hell...Oedipus'll do too. So umm...what is it with woman and cats why not dogs or birdies or vibrators ?

Every film brought excitement hope potential now its just an ache an arrogance "PROOVE IT BUDDY" impatience…films gone in seconds but how else? How much of the limited scenes are painted over how funny paist vs life logic/reason goes out the window senses take over TAPE SMASHED… speaking of gas pipes…where is the engraving pallice?

Friday [drawing of a head with a hat that then serves a boat in a drawing above with the sun and seagulls above] ONE OF US CANNOT BE WRONG oh yes…that is true and it is I who is not wrong this time What's with the 'Stephen Hawking' voices? Lego head as a bowling ball beating up al roker is good effective anti-smoking using who is the careless neighbour funny [more drawings] disqualified 'ite [drawing of spider] newspaper town matrix references are very annoying salt hahahahahaha Looting is the best dude
Damaged.

I don't get it.

Unedited Selection Notes
Written July 9-17, 2002
Ottawa, Canada
1670 films were entered
90-something were accepted

(August, 2002)

74

Rant

Let's be clear about this one: it's relatively trivial and, contrary to what some of you pugs think, i.e., that all Pimp columns are rants, this one IS a RANT. My turkey? Festival reviews. You know…you see them on AWN or on the ASIFA Website or in ASIFA newsletters or in that Korean mag *Animatoon* (*Animation Magazine* doesn't even bother w/festival content). Enough of them, OK?

These reviews are, in general, useless, lazy, so obviously work-for-hire-to-see-my-name-in print-even-though-I've-never-been-to-a-festival-before-and-didn't-go-to-half-the-events. These love letters are getting us nowhere. They don't help the readers, they don't help the filmmakers and they don't help festival organizers. Why is it like this? OK, well, first off… most of the reviewers are guests of the festival they're reviewing. They sometimes get travel and hotel, passes and meal tickets covered by the festival. Do you REALLY believe that these folks are going to give a wholeheartedly subjective POV? Who wants to risk not being invited back to a fest?

Two, what they write is usually just cut and pasted from the festival's own pr material, a grocery list of activities. See… it's not all that possible to attend EVERY event at a festival so the poor reviewer, already feeling guilty about the fee, hotel, pass and free event snacks, feels they've got to cover the whole shebang even if they didn't attend and what we get is a bland description of the event they didn't attend under the guise that they did attend.

Trois, perspective. Every animation magazine/newsletter is guilty of this and, YES, I understand WHY. No one has a budget à la BIG newspapers to send a reviewer to cover an animation festival, so they must rely on people they know or people they know who know someone who might be going to said festival. The problem is that in some cases they hire inexperienced people—now hold up. I realize that that can be a boon w/ the right person because its good to get the distant/outsider take on our little insular world—but unfortunately most times we don't get the 'right' people, so the perspective can be naïve and quite limited.

How are they going to know if, for example, Zagreb is any better or worse if they've never been there before? Maybe that doesn't matter? I dunno. I think it does, Zagreb has a long, rich history. Their organizers are quite passionate and active in the animation world. They travel to festivals, meet filmmakers, generally do what they can do make an interesting festival. You don't see that effort with a lot of festivals anymore.

(The following is a digression). There are so many damn festivals now being organized by people who have no interest, no connection, no awareness of festival history or culture and are solely creating an event so that they can promote their companies, shallow TV pilots and, heck, maybe they'll find some Dickens kids to exploit along the way.

Reminds me. (Digression #2) I just read a nasty piece in a Toronto paper about the Montreal World Film Festival (big live-action event). Some lady was moaning about the fact that only the public came to the festival AND, get this, that the festival showed too many films by people she'd never heard of. Umm… lady… the VERY point of having festivals in the first place was to showcase neglected, overlooked filmmakers who had few avenues for exhibition to a WIDER audience.

Animation festivals need to remember this. We are not here to lick the toe jam of industry. We exist to introduce new works by new/old voices to new/old viewers. The industry already has exhibition spaccs called, umm, the television or the cinema. The industry should be kissing festival toe because w/o festival films, they'd have no one to steal styles from (fortunately, concepts are safe).

My point? The same as always… don't close the door to the past. Festivals have a history, had a reason for coming into being and you, as a reviewer/attendee/entrant, should be aware of such things. And this is precisely why festival reviews need to be a little bit more w/ it. Or maybe you don't care about such stuff…if not, well, bully for you.

Four, rarely do they (reviewers) talk w/ other folks or even organizers. If I were to gripe about the ticket system in Annecy, the terrible opening ceremony at Fantoche this year, or the sometimes stupid projection in Ottawa, I'd first approach a festival rep and say, hey man, how come your ticket system is lousy? What's with that loser slam poet on opening night? Then they can give you some explanation and you can take it from there. Better still… just because you hated the ticket system, maybe others liked it. I'm not saying u need to be more critical necessarily.

Fest. organizers (except me) are not consciously trying to be evil, so why attack them in print? But at the same time, if there are some fundamental problems people are having at a festival, the festival people need to hear this of course. And, hey, just because YOU had a poor time because you lack basic social skills or didn't like one or two programmes doesn't mean that it was a bad festival or programme. Ask other people. Even if you liked it, ask the programmer why they chose what they chose. Ask other attendees what they thought of the tepid student competition. Also be aware of cultural context.

I read reviews by people saying… WHY didn't they do this? Why didn't they do that? Well… kids… festivals do not exist on equal playing fields. Ottawa doesn't get anywhere near the state support that Euro. Fests like Annecy or Zagreb or even Holland get and so sometimes we (for example) have to make decisions based on those economic realities. And this is where experienced goers are a pain in the ass. They go to Annecy or Hiroshima, let's say, and are treated in one way, maybe they get meal tickets or there are a lot of parties (i.e., free grub) and then they start expecting doggie bags everywhere. Hell…we even get people who call us asking if there are any parties…they don't apparently care about the films (this stems from 1996, when studios dumped a truckload of money on festivals, resulting in an orgy of parties).

Point, again, is that you cannot employ the same sweeping critical standards/expectations to all festivals. Why would you? This was the problem with ASIFA festivals of the past. Everyone looked the same. What's the point then?

Not to contradict myself, but there are also dangers when experienced people are reviewing. Take Pat Raine Webb's Annecy 02 review in AWN for example. Pat (a former ASIFA board member) is a good person, goes to animation festivals every year. Problem is that she goes to the same ones all the time and has a particular fondness for Zagreb (perhaps connected with the free hotel and passes that Zagreb provided ASIFA board members for many years). On the whole, Pat's review is fine. She briefly talks about some highlights from competition, but it's the last few lines that got my goat.

"If you want lots of action and don't mind crowds and queuing and more screenings then [sic] one human being can handle, then Annecy is the festival for you. But if you want to find the true spirit of animation you have to go to Zagreb!"

I've nothing against Zagreb, "nothing against Pat," but it irks me that she makes this GRAND SWEEPING statement about Zagreb w/o EVER ONCE visiting, not just Ottawa... but more importantly, Holland, Fantoche, Anima Mundi or even Tough Eye (granted a young festival). And why hasn't Pat visited these festivals? Because they didn't pander to ASIFA board members? Pat's a respected figure and it's asinine to make such a myopic statement. Maybe I'm overreacting, but the downside of the ASIFA system that existed for so many years (and Ottawa was one of the big beneficiaries of it) is that other festivals that did not seek out ASIFA approval got neglected, pushed aside, ignored.

Holland has been around since 1985 and I'd argue that it's FAR more relevant and true to the spirit of animation (whatever the fug that means) than Zagreb is today. And let's not forget Stuttgart, a very underrated, well-programmed German anifest. A fest that was largely ignored by ASIFA as well.

Do festivals even need these reviews? They're written right after the event. Sure, I can throw it in the reports that we send to the government funders, but do people actually use these reviews to guide them the next time the festival comes round in a year or two? (That's a question.) Oh, and I guess a glowing review earns the reviewer some points w/ the festival organizers. But really... given that most of these reviews are so sort-of superficial, are they really helping the festival improve itself? If not, then what is the point of these reviews beyond being 1,500 word advertisements for a festival? Magazines need to re-think why it is that they are reviewing a festival and what it is they are trying to convey through these reviews. Meantime... kids... at least write honestly.

One road is to give us an honest reflection of your experience at the festival. I mean you can't properly sum up the whole experience of the event, so at least give us yours... and that doesn't mean what you saw...but everything... give us the whole kit, baby... the hangover, breakfast, what was on Croatian TV? Do they still have hard-core porn for free there? What about the local liquor? Is masturbation more exciting in a foreign country? Did you screw around? Was it your first festival? Were you shy? Did you stay by yourself, maybe only going to screenings because you didn't know anyone? Give us the truth, man.

How was the flight? Did the festival peeps meet u at the airport? Did you spend a whole day just sitting round the Bonlieu shooting the breeze w/friends and colleagues? What about the city? Did you check out the thermal pool in Baden? Walk along the river? Festivals are not just about films. They are social and cultural experiences, a chance to meet new people and gab about life. All these things are part of a festival experience.

Or make it gossipy... a sort of Michael Musto-type thing about star sightings, who was being a bitch to whom, who was stumbling drunk. (OK, I know animation is so humble and down to earth that there really is no star system... but hey... let's create one....) "Who was that young girl linking arms with Oscar Grillo?" "What was said during that tense conversation between Kucia and Schwizgebel?" "Does Griffin really have a foot fetish?" "That Dutch festival director was drunk BEFORE breakfast, again." "Did you see that Estonian animator getting it on with that Swiss lamb? No, really, I mean a lamb." Now this approach wouldn't be overly useful perhaps, but it would sure as heckles be entertaining.

Or hey...say you ain't into that stuff 'cause you didn't do much but see films, exhibitions and attend panel discussions. Man, you're dull; you're probably an academic. OK then...still...

I know an academic sort, crazy kook, who wrote what initially seemed like a bizarre, nothing-to-do-w/Ottawa review of Ottawa. Part of the problem was language. English ain't his first. Anyhow... after I re-read the text for the 5th time I realized he'd written quite a thoughtful little piece that expanded beyond the Ottawa festival and embraced the whole of animation. What did the films shown at Ottawa say about the current situation in animation? And he went on to theorize about this, quite passionately, even getting into comparisons between animation and other arts (imagine that!) I didn't agree w/his takes on stuff...too-turn-of-the-century, elitist romantic for me...sort of guy who believes there is REAL art and NOT REAL art. Yeah... OK...buddy.

Anyway... what I did like was how he attempted to examine the festival on a larger socio-cultural blah blah blah level. Animation was taken out of its self-imposed cage and introduced to the real world (OK...maybe not 'real'... or here or now... but at least ANOTHER world). AWN commissioned this review, but in the end they didn't print it because the writing was not very clear or comprehensible in places and it would require an intense and hefty amount of time to re-work this piece into shape. It's too bad, 'cause I think that overall it was one of the VERY VERY few useful/meaningful festival analyses.

AWN has published its share of gimp reviews (e.g., check out Kelly Neall's review of the Tough Eye 2003 festival. Has she even seen an animation film before?). Worse still... check out the blowings (book and festival reviews) of that SUPERSTAR of animation scholars Giannalberto Bendazzi. This guy is a show, baby. He gushes about EVERYTHING he writes about w/o actually giving you any evidence? Look...that cartoon encyclopedia is fine and dandy, buddy...but umm... it does not warrant these incessantly hollow dribbles. It's time to start earning your keep and cease with the wanna-please-everyone hallmark drippings.

At the same time though, AWN has also published some of the more innovative festival reviews. In 2001, AWN asked animator and all-round good guy Chris Lanier to write about his experiences as a competition filmmaker at Sundance. Lanier wrote a thoughtful, intelligent sketchbook/diary piece about his experience. Or check out Don Duga's wordless review of the ASIFA-East Awards told entirely through sketches. Not a big fan of the sketches per se but I sure do like the idea. AWN has also composed photo scrapbooks of festivals. These are perhaps not as effective, but it does give you some visual sense of the environment.

Perhaps AWN's finest moment was Dan Sarto's review of SAFO 99. In it he writes about the festival's director:

"Chris is no stranger to controversy; he can be outspoken, and his straightforward manner doesn't always sit well with some of the crusty veterans on today's animation scene. One thing, however, is clear to me—he knows animation, and he knows how to put on a dynamite festival." What's not to like about those four lines of poetry?

Some other standouts reviewers are Czech writers like Stanislav Ulmer. You can find some of his reviews on asifa.net. He often provides a very thoughtful, in-depth analysis of a set of films that stood out for him at a festival.

What are some other ways to improve reviews? Maybe mags should invite a quartet of people from diff. backgrounds to contribute their POVs on a festival, or just set up a festival forum discussion group where people can chat about what they saw, what they liked/disliked, problems, etc... Actually that'd be a damn good idea.... Maybe even invite a festival dir. to do a chat w/people so he/she can get their feedback directly. Then again... I've tried this a few times on the AWN café and Animation Nation and I find that when you actually turn things around and ask people what it is that they want from a festival, they haven't the faintest idea. How can a festival be good/bad if you don't know what the heck you want from it?

OK... well... s'bout it. A pretty insignificant and maybe insular rant, although I dunno... if you're in animation and don't care about animation festivals then maybe there's a problem w/ you...or them.

(October, 2003)

How To Avoid Pissing Me Off or...
Ottawa Festival Entry Tips

A few tips for making the life of festival organizers and entrants a little easier.

Fill out the entry form
Do not send tapes in unmarked envelopes unaccompanied by an entry form or letter of introduction. No entry form, no entry. They get tossed.

Read the Rules and Regulations
Ottawa does not accept an entry unless the entry form is signed. If it's signed, we are assuming that you've read and understand the rules.

Check your tape
You've sent a blank tape. There's nothing on it. That hurts.

Cue your tape
That means that you should rewind your tape to the beginning so that we don't see the middle of some Belgian TV movie of the week. It also means that we do not want to see color bars and black screens. There's nothing more annoying than being blasted by that fuggin color bar BEEEEEEEEEEEEEEEEEEEE EEEEPPPPPPPPPPPPPPPPPP sound and THEN having to wait for an eternity as a smooth cloud of silent darkness lumbers by to ensure that your entry is tossed out faster than a gob.

Rejection
a. Nothing personal
You didn't make the cut. Don't take it personally. We don't give it personally. I'm not a fan of competition to begin with. Festivals are a collection of personal opinions, nothing more. Please don't

send angry letters telling us we're uncultured swines.

b. Don't ask for detailed feedback

And also… please don't ask me to give you some feedback about what you can do to improve your film. What I dislike about your film might appeal to someone else. What I like might (very likely) be abhorrent to someone else.

c. Have some perspective

I know it's especially hard for students… but we get a lot of responses saying: "But my parents, friends, teachers and classmates all loved my film!" Look… I'm sure some of them did, just as I'm certain that some of them just don't have the gonads to tell you they thought it sucked. But beyond that… remember that you're making these films inside a little room… Imagine animation as a big apartment (i.e., flat). Everyone is working away in their own little space… own little world… often oblivious to what is going on in other rooms near or far from them. Your film might very well be the best in your school, co-op, or studio, but you are just ONE little room among 1,700 or so other rooms filled with people all thinking the same thing.

d. Don't brag in defense

And PLEASE (I've written this before somewhere) DO NOT start harping on about your film being accepted at the Golden Squirrel Short Film Day in Portland, Ontario. I'm not trying to slag these festivals but they ARE NOT getting the same pool of animation that we are getting. Same goes for the big live-action festivals. That's fantastic that your film got into Montreal, Venice, Cannes, etc.…but these festivals again receive a limited number of animation entries… so don't get all huffy and puffy because you got fondled at Cannes and rejected in Ottawa (or Annecy for that matter).

This invitation is NOT transferable

Congratulations, you made the cut.

When we send invitation letters to competition filmmakers, we

bold, CAPITALIZE, and <u>underline</u> THIS INVITATION IS NOT TRANSFERABLE. We are inviting YOU, the person who created the work, not your cameraman, producer, girlfriend or uncle. I'm not really sure how much clearer we can be about it. You don't even need to read the rules this time 'cause it's right there big and bold on this one-page sheet. So please, stop asking.

I can't afford to ship my film, can you pay?...

And when we say we cannot pay, said filmmaker gets quite belligerent. This suggests that you are not following Tip #2. If you did, you'd see that while we do pay for return shipping and are always willing to forward your film to another festival, we do not have the means to pay for the shipping of your film TO the festival. This goes for Panorama and Competition films. Think about this before you enter. If you ain't got the moola to ship, then don't enter.

Beta transfers

A minor problem... but again we make it VERY clear that we cannot accept PAL system Beta tapes (sorry... I didn't make up this ridiculous region system)... yet every year we get blasted for not accepting PAL (suggesting, again, that Tip #2 was overlooked). In a lot of cases we do make transfers, but they cost us about $70 (CAD) per five- to 10-minute film. It's not just an issue of money. When we make a transfer from the PAL tape you send, you're losing a generation during the procedure. So your, let's say, 40-year-old Pops comes out looking 50 with 10 extra pounds. And you can guess what happens next... this unable-to-pay-for-a-tape-but-able-to-pay-for-an-international-flight filmmaker shows up at the festival and gets all heated when his/her film don't look so good up on the screen (and hey... we have damn good video projection, so don't go there, pallie.) Bad situation all 'round.

A little sugar, baby

We're generally pretty proud of the films that win at Ottawa. Every year we try and organize Best of Ottawa programmes that tour around North America and, sometimes, Europe or Asia.

These tours are a MAJOR pain in the rectum to organize, but we do it because it promotes our festival and we're trying to ensure that short animation gets seen by as many folks as possible. But ya know what? How about a little return on that? How about some of you winners listing your Ottawa award (or any other animation festival awards for that matter) on your festival poster, press sheets, videos, DVDs or even a film print?

Some of you animators are sluts. You'll love animation festivals like moist whores until you get your film into a live-action festival and then suddenly you tighten up like a nun. All that matters now is Cannes, Venice or Berlin. And yeah... I get it... you just want to be accepted period... not just within the realm of animation. You wanna be loved by everyone and not just treated as one of those retards from that "special" world of animation.

Animation festivals EXIST to show your films, and the least you can do is acknowledge these festivals if you win an award. Why aren't you putting that Grand Prize from Ottawa, Annecy, Stuttgart, Holland, etc.... on your posters? If we're not good enough for you, then why the fug are you even entering your film in our festivals? You owe it to you and us to show your award off. It helps you. It helps us.

That goes for studios too. If you win the Best TV Show award in Ottawa or Annecy, I wanna see/hear you telling people about it. A motley crew of international animation folks from wide and diverse backgrounds are judging you. If they've chosen your show... that's a pretty high compliment. Take it, embrace it, flaunt it, lick it.

I know that you spend a lot of time and money making stills, videotapes, film prints, paying for postage and posters etc.... All I'm asking is that you take more care when you're sending your films to festivals. Certainly read the entry forms, but also find out more about the festival you're submitting to. Don't just go to their Website... 'cause you ain't gonna find anything objective there. Post questions on discussion forums, ask other animators, do a Google search, see if there are some (ha ha) past reviews of the festival. There are a lot of festivals appearing and disappearing each year and you owe it to yourself to take better care of your work. I mean, you spent all this time and energy on it, so why wouldn't you care more about where it's being shown?

As a writer, I send out articles and manuscripts. I make sure that I read the requirements of the magazine/publisher carefully before I send anything. I also check out what they published before and keep track of every place I've sent my material. This IS pain-in-the-ass work, but, folks, it's part and parcel of the artistic process. The work does not end when you finish the film or manuscript… that's just the beginning.

P.S.

Before SAFO 03 we had maybe two to three Panorama filmmakers decide VERY late in the game that they were not going to send us their film to screen. That's an INCREDIBLE pain in the ass. Not only are you screwing up our programme, but, more importantly, you've just taken away space that could have gone to a fucking filmmaker WHO WOULD HAVE APPRECIATED THE SCREENING TIME.

A few (not many) of you seem to think that being accepted for Panorama is a slap in the face. How's that? You're being shown in the same venue as the competition films and being seen by the same audience. So you're not gonna get a chintzy prize or small amount of cash… big deal… neither are 95% of those in competition.

In fact, most folks I know actually prefer the Panorama screenings and often go there looking for overlooked gems.

(November, 2003)

From Quays to Krays?

I used to joke with staff and friends about how I was certain that I could grab a quartet of Mission dwellers, install them as pre-selectors for the Ottawa festival, and have no one notice the difference between their tastes and those of so-called animation professionals. Sure, they'd make some strange choices… but hey… so do the 'pro' selection committees. And, hell…we sorta did it one year when we invited former NFBer Ryan Larkin to participate (he lives in the Old Brewery Mission in Montreal). OK… but as I said… I was pretty much just having a laff.

I just visited the very fine Fantoche animation festival in Baden, Switzerland, where this journalist from Parnu, Estonia (beautiful seaside town) told me about an experiment an Estonian festival tried last year, using an ex-con as a member of the selection committee. After I rolled my eyes and said… "yeah… right… ya drunk phucker," he pulled out a copy of this festival's catalogue and, sure enough… there's the committee page, including the likes of Estonian animator Priit Tender (*Fox Woman*), a Finnish journalist, a Russian academic (Mikhail Surevich), a Latvian animator (Nag Emist), and this noted Estonian criminal Ülo Voitka (who, along with his brother Aivar, formed the famous Voitka Brothers). I couldn't stop laughing as I looked over the page, which not only featured the guy's mugshot, but also this detailed biography of his, umm, accomplishments. But this is all very serious, part of an attempt to help criminals reintegrate themselves into Estonian society. Apparently the festival receives funding to do this.

They also save a bit of money too. A local policeman is used as the secretary of the jury and, each night, the soon-to-be-released criminal is returned to the local jail (saving the cost of a hotel). As absurd as it all sounds… it really does make perfect sense on so many levels. First and foremost, it's a useful humanitarian gesture. This also brings a lot of attention to the festival and animation because you know that the media will cover a story like this. It also provides a fresh perspective on animation films. Gone are the same converted faces and voices.

Can you imagine the jury meetings? Who would argue with this guy? In fact, the journalist told me that the guy did in fact snap during one session. This Russian egghead, Surevich, kept going on and on about the use of light and texture in the Brothers Quay film *In Absentia*, and Voitka lost it, ran at Surevich, wrestled him to the ground, all the while screaming about how he was gonna get those "faggot twins." (Voitka later calmed down when told that Surevich said that it was made by the Quays, not the Krays. In fact, Voitka was impressed to learn that beneath what he called their "faggotty cocksucker smugness," they were actually from South Philly, USA.) Fortunately, the cop was there to cool things down. Surevich wasn't hurt, but he did resign from the jury.

OK... clearly there is the potential for some problems here... but anyone who's been on a jury with animator Mike Smith knows that animators can snap too. Still, I'd like to take it one step further and have a full jury made up of international criminals. There's no need for hotel or meal expenses, as they'd all be in prison. We can use a prison guard or policeman as a jury secretary. And they could have their meetings in those jury rooms with the glass screens. Of course... they'd watch the competition films with the audience. They'd be escorted in before each screening, handcuffed to the chairs, and surrounded by about half a dozen uniformed police, including their cop secretary.

Can you imagine the atmosphere at the screenings? One thing competition screenings have lacked at animation festivals is anticipation, tension or even excitement. Well, you can be damn sure there'd be some tension at these screenings. Will a prisoner try to run for it? Will there be a hijacking of the screenings by one of the cons' buddies? Even the usually apathetic-toward-animation general public would be lining up for tickets.

And what about the jury meetings? Can you imagine these guys trying to discuss the films they saw? Kucia? Driessen? Gratz? Priestley? Pappo? What would happen with four to five soon-to-be-ex-cons deliberating? Can you imagine the threats? The good thing is that there'd be no bullshitting. These guys would be very clearcut about what they liked and disliked. We'd be free of those rhetoric-laden jury comments that accompany each prize winner. Instead, we'd probably get short, concise, blunt statements like "'cause it rocked, fuck" or "it made me laugh."

The possibilities make me dizzy. Not only do festivals get a ton of extra money and exposure, they'd never have problems with fuckwit sponsors bailing on them at the last minute or weasel sponsors running out on their bill... 'cause our new buddies would be all too willing to help get our money back—or maybe know people who know people... ya know what I'm saying?

And of course, we'd have exhibitions. But instead of Caroline Leaf's art... we'd get, say, Weegee-type photographs of the crime scenes and maybe have an archival show featuring textiles and materials from each crime scene (weapon, blood-stained clothes). I mean... in a sense... the criminals are artists... whether they murder, rob or rape. So why shouldn't we get to see their work? I bet they'd sell more of that art than that Kovalyov sketchbook crap. During the Meet the Masters sessions, they can then meet with festival attendees and describe the motivation behind their work (e.g., drug money, passion, "pissed me off") and what they plan for the future.

Hell...this experiment might even have a long-term effect on the types of animation films being made. Might give the animation community some balls. Animators might think a little bit harder about making their next film knowing that soon-to-be-ex-cons are judging their work. Maybe we'd finally see less artsy-fartsy pastoral ceramic crap and more hard-hitting street work like Chris Shepherd's *Dad's Dead*, or that crazy Villard's *Son of Satan*.

I bet even Andreas Hykade would finally get the kudos he deserves. These guys would love *Ring of Fire* and *We Lived in Grass*. I imagine these guys probably wouldn't like festival animation in general though. Too white, airy, self-righteous, pristine and middle class for them. They'd likely prefer classic Bugs, Daffy and Tex. Something funny... something that makes them forget (remember *Sullivan's Travels* by Preston Sturges?). Can't blame 'em.

Down the road, maybe this can lead to animation workshops in prison. Priestly and Gratz (who collaborated on a prison film) could be the first animators to go. They can head over to the local Portland prison and do once-a-week workshops, show some films, get the guys working. Maybe even make it a week-long workshop and make the visiting animators stay in jail, give them a taste of real hardship, not the mental-emotional stuff they find time to moan about in their own often perspectiveless lives.

So… yeah… I like it… I've got to talk to our board and managing director, but I'm definitely keen on trying this out. As absurd as this whole idea seemed to me when I first heard it, it actually makes a lot of sense and is a win-win scenario for everyone.

(December, 2003)

ASIFA-East Festival. May 16, 2004. Manhattan.

I'm supposed to get an award tonight. Figure it's a prank being pulled by one Hayden Mindell, a former OIAF employee who was the victim of two nifty jokes in L.A. and Ottawa. The last one occurred about two to three years ago, but I keep waiting for that day when Hayden has his revenge. And hell, I'm so accustomed to being called a retarded asshole by some of you Justice League freaks that when someone wants to celebrate something I've done, I figure that there's got to be a catch.

The award will be the last thing of the evening. Fuck me. My heart is pounding all night. Yes… I've no problem hosting every OIAF or SAFO screening or introducing filmmakers… not a problem at all… but when the spotlight is on me… I get flush, eyes down, heart races. If someone yells at me or pushes me… well, that's easier. I can always slug them or hurl insults. But a compliment… Shudder shivers and shits. "Thank you" seems unsatisfactory and cliché. Maybe a good ol' "FUCK YOU" would liven it up.

Okay… but that's not why I'm writing. As I'm sitting here nervously watching the proceedings, I discover something very disturbing. First, let me give you the setting. The ASIFA-East festival presents awards by category: student, commissioned, independent. There are about three to four awards given and then the films from that section are screened. There's a lot of applause. I'd say four rounds of applause per person. Applause when they go to the stage, leave the stage, film starts, film ends. That's a lot of applause. It's too much really, when you consider that the applause BEFORE and AFTER the announcements always falls short.

Not one winner made it to the podium before the applause ended, nor did they return to their seat before the second round of clapping collapsed. In both cases, the winner, betrayed and

abandoned by the audience, was left walking alone in silence. So, for example, Karen Aqua went up to get her experimental award... but as soon as she hit the stage the applause had completely faded, leaving her with a long, uncomfortable walk across the stage. You hear the crickets. The return home was even worse. AS soon as Karen reached the floor, she was faced with a long walk down the aisle in silence. It was like everyone else had moved on. She meant nothing to them now. "Yes, dear... you got your nice piece of paper, but be a good girl and hurry back to your seat, will you. Time's a-wasting. We need to move forward."

Okay, so I'm freaked out now. I do NOT want to walk across the stage in front of a silent audience. I mention the problem to my two ex-RISD wingnut seatmates, Fran Krause (*Mr. Smile*) and Jesse Schmal (*Sub, Kids Next Door*). After a few more announcements, they too notice the problem.

We discuss the drawbacks of applause, specifically its superfluity. Why four rounds of applause? It seems too much, especially in light of the front-/back-end shortage. But if we just have applause when the winner goes up... he/she is then left with a very awkward and LONG walk back to their seat. If anything, we need more front-/back-end applause. Maybe people are saving it up for the films. A long round of applause during the announcements would tire their arms (remember the crowd is comprised of people who make a living with their hands).

Okay... so let's focus on the films. Applauding before a film is just wrong. How do we even know it's any good? No one applauds before a film at festivals or in cinemas. 'Course some would argue that we should applaud the person just for making the film to begin with. Perhaps, but what if the film promotes a value you find reprehensible? PES's new film promotes urinating in the ocean. I prefer lakes. How can I applaud his film? Can I now turn my back on that film after I've already applauded it? Seems a bit deceitful to me.

Okay... so we can certainly knock off pre-film applause. No good can come of it. No one will be hurt by its absence and, most importantly, it will give the audience additional strength for the announcement applause.

Now… the end-of-film applause. We certainly need it—although not everyone will like the film and so some additional energy is saved through an absence of applause or by the use of the energy-efficient, half-assed golf clap that involves the fingertips of the right hand lightly tapping (or even brushing) the right palm. But wait, Fran asks a brilliant question. "Has anyone ever made a film with pre-recorded applause at the end?" Who said Americans were the special-ed folks of the world? Genius, Krause, pure genius. It makes perfect sense on both ends. It eliminates the need for the audience to waste more energy applauding and the filmmaker doesn't need to worry about what music to use during their end credits. The post-film applause is often made more out of habit than passion, so why waste your time and energy when the film can do it for you?

This is good. I feel that Schmal, Krause and I have potentially saved and radically altered the future of cinema.

But this doesn't help me tonight. How the fuck am I going to deal with the inevitable audience betrayal that awaits me? Perhaps I could just remain seated, oblivious to their applause when my name is called. They'd eventually give up. That would show 'em. Give 'em a taste of the treason they've fed everyone else. Then after they stop, I'd hop to my feet and walk to the stage. Surprised, the audience would be forced to give me an additional pre-award round of applause. Still… it would probably fall short again before I hit the podium.

What the hell am I going to do? It's getting closer. My heart thumps like wet flesh on a bare ass. Sweat appears (on my brow). And fuckanutbutt… Drew Carey is in the crowd. I haven't felt this way since the Yankee game this afternoon when I was FORCED to rise for the seventh inning rendition of "God Bless America" as americanwingnutpatriots shouted TAKE YOUR HAT OFF all around me. What the fuck is it about the hat, boys? How is removing a piece of cotton made in China from your head—a device that these days is saving you from cancer—a form of respect?

I, of course, refused to sing. I was always told that God Blessed

Canada. To sing otherwise would be treason. Still... wasn't quite as scary as the Japanese businessmen—complete with accents—singing the U.S. anthem. That was damn funny. Forty years ago the Americans and Japanese try to annihilate each other, but when they smell dollar, all is forgiven. Ba ha ha ha. Okay... sorry... not gonna go there. Where was I? Okay... I'm freaking out. I WILL NOT BE ABANDONED LIKE THE OTHERS.

Linda Simensky announces my name. I hear the applause and calmly walk down the aisle. As I hit the stage, I sense the clap collapse. I will not let them leave me. In a flash, I sprint across the stage and reach the podium just as the applause shatters into a smattering of claps (Krause and Schmal, I figure) before falling completely and utterly into silence.

I made it. Relieved, I'm hardly aware of what I'm saying. Too excited to speak. Muttered a few shout outs to the Virgils, joked about pranks and dreamed a dream of a "Quincy" reunion. For a moment, I felt certain I saw Drew Carey—a man who has seen first hand the very darkness in the souls of whom I speak—give me a proud nod of the head. As if he was saying, "You did it kid, you did it. You showed those "Friends"-loving bastards whose line it REALLY is."

Overconfidence envelops me. I strut across the stage, applause swimming in my head. But as soon as I jump off the stage, I feel a slap of silence. BASTARDS. They've fucking betrayed me too. Forgotten. My pained eyes look across the rows, but their eyes ignore me and look forward, awaiting their next victim. I pass Carey's row, praying for his sympathy, but he too has gone; feigning fatigue, his head is lowered into his hands. GOD DAMN YOU DREW CAREY.

Accompanied by no one, no thing, the walk home is long and lonely. Lapped, clapped and spit, I fall into the shadows of my seat, swallowed by the darkness of yesterday.

Other No Less Disturbing NY moments
O'Connor's discussion of chocolate milk, blood and puss.
Plympton's love.
Bob Sheppard.

Dilworth standing across from me adorned with neck scarf, Hawaiian shirt and cigar.

Olivia Ward's brother who, despite being awakened by phone at 2:00 am, INSTANTLY knew and hummed the "Quincy" theme.

Pat Smith's unwavering devotion to "Friends."

Urine-drenched hallway in Tribeca.

(July, 2004)

THE AESTHETICS
OF
ANIMATION

In Search of STUFF, Part 1: (F)art

The Word proves those first hearing it as numb to understanding as the ones who have not heard. Yet all things follow from the word.
— Heraclitus

I am a scientist—I seek to understand me.
— Robert Pollard (Guided by Voices), "I Am A Scientist"

Okay, bear with me. I'm a little behind with this whole Art thing. Everyone seems to know what art is; I hear the words thrown about with ease. I mean I always figured that there was a difference between For The Birds and Breakfast on the Grass. Seemed damn simple enough: one evokes emotions, the other challenges the mind. For me, art challenges the mind. Sensory perception is fine and dandy but it doesn't explain WHY. As Homer once said, "Why me laugh?"

Art for me is like a good dump. The natural release/reaction to what your system has experienced during the day. I like creative works that leave a stink, the natural breath of the creator. To smell is to be. Even if they stink, they're human (e.g., Ed Wood) and that makes them better than that other stuff we call Hollywood (which I use quite sweepingly here), which ain't nothin' but a manufactured piece of plastic poop. Can't smell nuttin' (hence no SENSE/CAUSE). 'Tain't art. Pretty easy. Done. Finito. Ka......... PUT. And hey...to put the nail home, there's the client/self split. How can anything client driven be art? How can anything personal NOT be art?

So all's going along well in my head until I'm reading Homer's Iliad and discover that it's pretty much just a Hollywood action movie. A MASSIVE war starts because of a fight over a gal and then we encounter passage after passage of gruesome violence. So what's the difference between Homer and Homer? But back to me...why can I embrace the highfalutinESS of Faulkner and George Griffin and just as quickly run out and rent Booty Call or Big Daddy and then laugh my ass off at the stupid jokes?

Maybe I should just relax and let it go. Who cares WHY things are, they just ARE...right? Just go wherever my senses lead me... Sorry...it's not enough to know that Bubblicious tastes good, I need to know WHY it tastes good (childhood flashbacks? Specific flavour that is NOT in Hubba Bubba? Present chewing location?).

Last week while watching "Murder, She Wrote"—the early seasons are great because Lansbury was willing to let her annoying character have the piss taken out of her by other characters—oh yeah...so been reading a lot of Greek philosophy and turns out that Plato and Aristotle were saying some things about art and one of my sortofpals recommended Nietzsche's Birth of Tragedy. I decided there and then—while watching Jessica Fletcher—that I would try to find out just what ART is.

Plato's Take

Okay I'm back. It's a day later. While I was gone I finished the rest of Plato's *Republic* and wouldn't ya know he's got a few not so mild things to say about art. Plato was quite a moral fellow and believed in a divine order to the universe. The pursuit of wisdom and knowledge was for him the ULTIMATE goal. So he pretty much shunned art because it is imitative and the only works to be permitted in his ideal state would be those that honoured the gods or famous guys. Why? Well because imitative art produces merely a semblance of reality. As such it is false—see NATURE was itself a semblance of the DIVINE reality (or for us non-believers...we could say that NATURE is the reality and HUMAN nature a COPY and then Art a copy of that copy)—so if I paint a picture of a man—it is two notches below reality/truth—whereas if you paint a nice fine picture of the big man, you're I guess a notch from truth and that's better for everyone.

But no cold chump he, Plato breaks down and admits that he'd still allow imitative art in his ideal state because of its charm and sensual pleasure—now hold on—doesn't this upset the

WHOLE damn book since Plato is constructing an ideal state and if you start letting a few bozos in—sorry that's for another time.

Hey...speaking of the senses, I'm being overwhelmed by Jerry Lee Lewis: *Mercury Years, Volume Two 1969-72*, some scorching country/gospel/rock tunes that are imitative of no one but the devil himself. Check it out.

So yeah...Plato's view of art is limited but he clearly allows that there are two aims of art: emotional and intellectual. So that's good news for you Hollywood fans.

Aristotle Has Some Ideas...

Okay. Next. Aristotle.

Another day has passed. I finished Aristotle's *Poetics* and an overview of the man in Coppleston's *History of Philosophy*, Vol. 1 (you should be reading THIS nine-volume series instead of that damn hotel drawer fairy tale). Aristotle's got a bit more to say about art than Plato, but again I guess it's important to remember that these are less theories of art than reflections on the art of the time; as such *The Poetics* is MOSTLY just a "How To Make Poetry/Drama/Comedy" (the comedy part was lost) book. Outside of a few bits on the origin of poetry and the idea of universality, *Poetics* don't help me much at this stage of the game 'cause I'm trying to figure out what ART is and why we do it.

Aristotle touches on some good stuff in *Poetics* about the origins of mimesis (imitation) and expands that in *Metaphysics*. Buddy boy says that we long to KNOW. As children we learn (via our senses) through imitation. This is indicated through the reaction of our senses. The eyes (especially) produce recognition and recognition helps us to differentiate between things (e.g., trees from water). Through repetition we become familiar with the world. Familiarity brings pleasure 'cause we ain't so out to lunch no more. The key to this is memory. We learn from memory. From memory comes experience. Experience CAN produce knowledge and skill. Skill comes from many experiences. A general assumption is formed. For example, I have a headache. Experience tells me that by taking an aspirin I will relieve myself of the headache. However I do not possess the skill to explain WHY the aspirin achieves this effect. Skill involves knowing WHY. In short...experience knows THAT but not the BECAUSE. Skill or *tekhnê* (Greek for craft or art) grasps the BECAUSE.

SO...art is a sort of expansion of what we experience and is produced for necessity (a bed, plate, cup), pleasure (a picture, toy) and knowledge (mathematics, philosophy).

Nietzsche's Two Thoughts...

Let's skip ahead in time to Mr. Nietzsche. In *Birth of Tragedy*, the little pastor says that we can divide art into two streams: Apollinian and Dionysian. The former is a subjective individual approach that seeks beauty and a higher form (i.e. how the world SHOULD BE), while Dionysian is a more objective form that shows "the incompletely intelligible everyday world" (which... umm...is still a subjective viewpoint). So certainly we can see how the Hollywood system strives for the Apollinian form of harmony and order (EVERY Hollywood product is based on a classical narrative system that gives stability-disruption-resolution-closure or what is the Aristotelian notion of completeness), whereas some like Phil Mulloy and Ryan Larkin are slightly more Dionysian in that there is no sense of completeness, harmony, but more a concern with showing the world as it IS. The audience is left ALONE to figure out the "incompletely intelligible."

Yet this system doesn't quite work because animation is by very definition limited to the boundaries of its technological infrastructure (material of film/video/digital, camera—and the speed, aperture, framing—and projector—and projectionist). Thus no animators are truly chaotic and wild. Certainly cameraless animators are (to use the Plato ratio) a step or two closer to the reality/disorder but they still rely on film. Of course, with that hardcore logic...painting, literature and music have SOME whisper of a structure. The only truly free arts would be speaking, singing and dancing. Cha Cha Cha!

It gets more confusing when you see that Nietzsche says that individualism is commonly Apollinian whereas the loss of self into oneness is Dionysian (like when you're stoned) BUT clearly the Hollywood system in fact diverts the individual into the illusion of a form of oneness through its production of films that it thinks will reach a UNIVERSAL audience (as opposed to the particular—although it relies on the illusion of the particular/unique experience to sell merchandise) and through its use of tragic/comic models seeks to EVOKE a general emotional reaction from the audience. Whereas the Dionysian reps like, say Ryan Larkin or David Ehrlich, make films from an individual perspective for the pleasure of the ACT itself (i.e. little care for audience). Furthermore in showing the world as it IS, the Dionysian artist is seeking an understanding of this state while leaving the audience to do the same individually. Some would say this is self-absorbed but clearly Hollywood does not REALLY give a shit about the audience (as individuals) whereas MANY (not all) of these apparent Dionysian folks DO actually care about individual perspectives.

Soooooooo the way I see it...Apollinian offers universal types to present the world as the Artist thinks it should be using examples of BETTER or WORSE, which then evoke emotions from the audience and give them a feeling of oneness. Whereas the Dionysian shows the world as the Artist thinks it is, warts and all, and leaves the audience to sort it out for themselves.

A-ha! Kant Has A Point

Let's see what that pissant Kant has to say. In the *Critique of Judgement*, he talks briefly about what Art is. First, he separates it from nature (art is work, nature is effect) and ESSENTIALLY says that art is work by man (which means that ALL humans are works of art—except that grade 9 French teacher who wanted to touch me in odd places). He then distinguishes Art from craft and science. Science knows. Art can know. (What about science films like *Haemorrhoids*, a 20-minute film depicting the removal of IT from someone's hairy red ass? Is this science or art?) Art is Free Art. Craft is Mercenary Art. (Ah...hold up...now we're getting somewhere!) Mercenary Art is a disagreeable occupation that attracts someone mostly because of the pay cheque. So could we not say that MOST kids who go to school to LEARN how to be a big studio artist are in fact NOT artists (but craftsmen) because they have a specific purpose—to make money (check out those discussions groups where some youngin' asks, "How much should an entry-level animator make?") and gain recognition (e.g., being ACCEPTED in a school and then a studio)? In Free Arts, the artist creates for the sake of creating. Fame and fortune are secondary. The primary pleasure comes from the act of creation (oops...sorry...production). THEN again...the free artist seeks grants, subsidies and has screenings, readings, openings...so is that not tinged with fame and fortune as well? And anyway... from what I've seen, the kids at Pixar (for example) are MIGHTY content whereas I've encountered a lot of 'free' artists working in miserable/disagreeable conditions.

Immanuel breaks it down further. He says that within Free Art, there is mechanical art (making an actual object, like say a bicycle or car) and aesthetic art (seeks to arouse a feeling of pleasure). Within aesthetic art Kant locates fine and agreeable art. Fine art "furthers the culture of our mental powers to (facilitate) social communication." The pleasure of fine art stems from reflection rather than "mere sensation." Agreeable art seeks to provide merely enjoyment in the moment...and does not serve as material for future meditation or quotation.

Now initially I thought I'd found a home for Hollywood...but clearly this category doesn't fit either because one thing Hollywood does not want is momentary un-meditative enjoyment. They want the audience to remember through quotations, merchandising, repeat screenings, etc... It's a system that feeds off our tendency toward unreflective sense prioritizing: "It made me laugh (or cry). I want to laugh again." It's still very much in keeping with Kant's claim that agreeable art only provides "agreeable noise" that keeps minds in a cheerful mood (sort of like Prozac). But hey... whatever the make-up of agreeable art, it's quite clear (sort of) that superficial or otherwise, it is art and ANYWAY a boatload of make-work academics have reflected on Keanu Reeves; so much for the moment.

Let's stop there. We've pretty much got a sense now of WHY we make art (imitation/improvement) and WHAT art is (virtually anything made by humans including you, me and your Grandma). Despite my assumptions, *Monsters Inc.*, Hot Wheels, bobbleheads, Britney Spears and IKEA furniture are ALL Art. Hollywood may be a robotic assembly line, not to mention a technological based medium, but these systems were designed (and accepted) by/for people, so THEY be Art too. You are what you eat, so I guess we get the system we deserve. Hey...s'good enough for me 'cause not only is "Murder, She Wrote" art (which makes me feel far less guilty), but so am I.

Okay...everything's art...but this doesn't explain why we love and loathe. I guess judgement helps us differentiate between Plympton, Pixar and Pollock (alliteration...heh heh. Is that art? Guess so). But what is judgement (and taste) and how is it formed? Well...as they used to say on "Hammy Hamster" (is that one notch below truth in so far as it uses ACTUAL animals—if so does that mean that all real animal and nature films are in fact the highest forms of art?)..."That's another story."

(March, 2002)

In Search of STUFF, Part 2: Yummy and Yucky

Last month we checked out some philosophical takes on what art is and why people do it. Now that we've determined that basically anything made by humanity is art, we can turn our attentions to judgement and specifically how we determine what we like and don't like.

We are always judging STUFF: I don't like this. I don't like that. Thumbs up. 4 stars. This tastes like shit (a strange statement because it implies the classifier is familiar with the taste of shit—and even then there are different types—man, woman, child, dog, cat, bird). This is beautiful. This is ugly. These are pronouncements of taste. Taste is subjective. Feeling and Knowledge are taste's guides.

What is Judgement? (Kant)

Brain = thinking/feeling/desire

Thinking = understanding/judgement/reason

Understanding = Halle Berry is a woman. Women are human.

Reason = I see Halle Berry + my penis rises = I find Halle Berry attractive.

Judgement = Halle Berry is a hottie.

Judgement = reflective and determinant

Determinant = Halle Berry has boobs (particular) = Halle Berry is a woman (universal)

Reflective = Halle Berry is a hottie (particular) = Women are hotties (NO universal) = what is a hottie? (Need to find a universal)

When u judge u go through 4 processes or "moments:"

1. Detached - You don't "lose yourself" in the movie but still find it pleasurable.

111

2. Universal - I expect you to share that belief.
3. Multiple meanings - Walt Disney wanted to tell a love story. I like the design. You like the story. Halle likes the acting.
4. Necessity - I want to convince you philistines that my judgement is right.

Detachment + Universal + Multiple Meanings + Necessity = Common Sense

Common Sense = Common Cognitive Reactions (e.g., "Check out Tex Avery's *Magical Maestro*, you'll laugh your ass off.")

\ experience of art = experience of life = ethics?

What Does It Mean To Have Taste? (Bourdieu)

Pierre Bourdieu (in his nice little scribble, *Distinction: A Social Critique of the Judgement of Taste*) says that our tastes are not, as Kant seems to think, some "gift of nature," but rather closely tied with our education (quality, duration) and social origins (i.e., family, friends). These origins generally dictate the manner in which we consume culture.

Consumption of culture is an act of communication that requires deciphering. So a work of art (whether it is *Sleeping Beauty* or *Flying Nansen*) is only going to be interesting to those who have the code that can decipher the work. Those who don't have that access will be limited to superficial chaos. For example, "That Eddie Murphy sure is funny in *Shrek*." This person will be stranded (according to typical ART views) at this superficial level and be unable to identify the "stylistic properties" of the work. When we ask this person why they think Eddie Murphy is so goddamn funny, they might not be able to articulate a response and instead say, "I dunno...he just makes me laugh...there's something about him."

When Mr. Pop encounters a work it is almost as if he applies the experience of life to art, whereas Mr. Pure (i.e., intellectual) actually breaks with the ordinary experience of the world and detaches himself from WHAT is represented. Bourdieu suggests that those detachers are, in the process, distancing themselves

114

from all that is human. Mr. Pure rejects the common passions or emotions that we invest in our daily lives. Mr. Pop revels in empty involvement or vulgar pleasure. In short...Mr. Pop is willing to lose himself in a film, while Mr. Pure detaches himself. As such, Mr. Pop goes right in the face of Kant's four moments because he obviously does show interest.

"Taste classifies, and it classifies the classifier," says Bourdieu. We judge each other by the choices/judgements we make and this is unfair because we are not all playing from the same level playing field (education/social origin). Some tastes are 'tastes of necessity.' Mr. Pop eats filling, economical food (McDonalds) out of necessity. Mr. Pure fine dines, notes presentation, serving and etiquette because he's got a 'taste of liberty.'

What does all this mean? First, Kant's notion of taste as something natural is a load of cow chew because, as Bourdieu suggests, it is tightly connected with social rearing. Secondly, taste becomes a means of social control because it serves the interests of power and distinction due of its emphasis on individuality and rivalry (i.e., academics are notorious back- stabbing status seekers). In short, taste (and its rejection of natural enjoyments— low, coarse, vulgar, servile) is a word those in power have created (consciously or otherwise) and defined to keep us slugs in line.

But hold up here...we're only talking about THOSE twits who DENY Mr. Pop (i.e., not all), there are plenty of us who appreciate both the vulgar and the refined. And what about the reverse? What about those who ignorantly lash out at/reject the world of Mr. Pure and denounce, for example, McLaren, Quays or Breer as self-indulgent wanks? Is this not just a reverse form of discrimination on the part of Mr. Pop? If we understand Mr. Pure's rejection of Mr. Pop as a denial of sameness, is then Pop's refusal of Pure a rejection of difference? If so, what does this say about Mr. Pop's ethics? Is his rejection of non-narrative, experimental, abstract or foreign art xenophobic?

(April, 2002)

In Search of STUFF, Part 3:
Fear of a Non-Narrative Planet

in one of phil mulloys films see a man running back and forth on a train track between 2 brick walls when he comes to the end he bangs his head against the wall at one pt he trips and stumbles off the tracks as he gets up he sees a forest of trees startled he rushes back on the tracks and runs back and forth again unknown inability to articulate fears thoughts into language miscommunication misunderstanding fear anger violence socrates laughed at those who feared death not an ounce of understanding or knowledge yet we avoid fear loathe it narrative films provide patterns stabilitydisruptionresolution nonnarrative follows no route no centre noTHING to grab endless always being freefloating some say wanky selfindulgent shit is that the case or fear of unknown being wrong fear that presumes a right nonnarratives personal unique challenge assumptions we are so in tune that apparent lack of melody is alien life 9 5 day night open close time constrains us being set according to pre-defined clocks controlling time cannot be tamed look at the days as cycles not single entities days weeks weekends history divides by decades as if actions of time can be neatly summarized despite that we don't control time our life is not a narrative escape escape from what escape from time is escape from deaths not possible beginning is end is beginning is end is beginning is end is end over means over end being in not for moment like sex orgasm intense moment process is richer reward lifes not summarized in one moment neither should art the pleasure of nonNARRATIVE is sensual cognitive maybe confused but a feeling moved disgusted don't run see it again and again until its system becomes familiar acceptable understood education alphabet addition once other now familiar narrative taught everywhere commercials newsprint radio television internet always wasn't western industrial phenomenon homer greeks asians scattered multilayered narrative jumps time space people assume one is rightwrong disneydickwilliam schuckjones always right but theyre just 1 language articulation possibility among many too many take 1 to be truth its like english language we me expect other to learnaccommodateund erstand mean we right they wrong tribalism close to home what you know know yourself doesn't mean stop stagnate end no more knowing living process always experiencing flexibility respect of other views like like like with boxing started in sept quickly discovered I couldn't skip worth shit hated doing it looked like a fool within a few weeks found myself getting it now I can rotate my feet doublejumpcrossovers coming basic skipping is familiar fear is gone worked at understanding led to confidence new perspective but to just do basic skipping becomes tedious mind/body needs challenge its why I cant understand those who keep laughing same jokes hollywoods fine once in a while nice to have some certainty resolution emptiness but after time same ol character music story dialogue tiresome like paint by numbers cant eat big macs everyday die unhealthy fat no taste me thinks this rejectionfear of alternative forms of narrative might reflect some culturalreligiouspoliticalrace xenophobia rejection of japaneseestonianpolishrussianchinese film a refusal of other possibilities interpretations realities everything we experience is subjective everything we inhale intake is but a possibility tough though mediaeducation prioritizes tribe rarely get other eye voice too much work easier to stay near tribe but as jagger said ya gotta move yet same time get miffed by those non-narrative pure art fugs who reject shakeheadlowerbrows at my your right to enjoy spongebob simpsons south park as valid as man who planted trees tale of tales both tribal need empathy not sympathy sure taste of necessity is real but taste of liberty is possible dont mean u need to book a flight to Tallinn cause I got the solution to this fear of nonnarrativeabstractexperimentalotherdifferencethem see was watching American pie 2 and this guy was learning tantra so he could get real deep and spiritual with his friends mom seems to me you we could do worse than to give tantric shaggin a try taint goal orientated tis in the moment and teaches ya to step into the other shoes and all the while raises your consciousness of the inner outer world within around you so next time you bitching griping about some lameass artfukkfilm with dotscirclesquares orsquigglylinesabsurdplotssymbolicoddshapedprimitivelydrawn characters head to the bedroom with someonething you love or could and let the tantric meat dance begin might not clarify your bewilderment over the latest art film but ya just might have the best sex of your life bottom line kids just cause your house has four walls don't mean u need to

Conclusion

OK...well that concludes my STUFF trilogy. Here's the STUFF I learned.

1. Everything produced by humans is art, even me
2. a) Judgement is a mediator in our mind between our understanding and reason
   b) Taste is a bullshit distinction that reinforces social differences
3. Industry and Indies need to come together for some goalless tantric sex
4. My appreciation of Booty Call, "Murder, She Wrote" AND Hubert Selby Jr. is normal, balanced and healthy

(May, 2002)

Aural Allochezia*

In general, music today is a piece of shit as r its anoiac†
listeners. The Top 40 has always been a stinking pile of fumosities
but there was a time when you could find The Kinks, The Who,
Big Joe Turner, and other semi-legitimate musicians. Today, it's
a combination of blatantly manufactured boy/girl groups or a
sad series of minstrels disguised as genuine reps. of black urban
experience. Bull cud, all of it.

Naturally (naturally because corporations have horizontal
integration now—owning film studios, music labels, television
stations), music in film, and specifically animation, reflects
the cud quality of the Top 40. In fact, music has become the
canned laughter of movies today. Movie music has always been
pretty bad, but when used properly, as either diegetic material
(part of the mise-en-scène) or as an integral component of the
film (e.g., Warner Bros, UPA, or John Hubley), it can set a tone
or mood without overdoing it. Today, music is in a sense the
motherboard of most movies. It doesn't just suggest a tone or
mood, it pinpoints EXACTLY how you should be responding to
a scene. Hey maybe U enjoy this. Not me. When I go to a movie
I'd like to have the option of figuring it for myself. I don't need
to be told when I should laugh, cry, hurt, shit, and sigh. It's bad
enough that I have to endure this canned laughter nonsense on
television. "Umm...just in case you forget, we're hoping you'll
laugh right about here." It drives me INSANE. Needless to say
(but I will), the music produced in film is the sort of bad noise
(there is GOOD noise) you're gonna be listening to in the 7th
circle of hell alongside that toe-tapping Riverdance asshole.

But hey, forget about me; think about yourselves. Movie
music is the BIGGEST slap in YOUR mug. Soundtracks are not

* allochezia (al o KEE zee uh) n. Defacation from somewhere other than the
anus. Also, defecation of something other than feces.

only telling you that you are stupid, but they are also controlling your reaction to their product. There's a long line of suckers who, moved to tears by a Stink song in Emperor's New Groove, rush out to the nearest mall and pick up the soundtrack in order to recreate that plastic feeling they thought they felt in the theatre.

On a strictly financial level, soundtracks are an ideal way to generate some extra moola for a failed piece of cinematic shit, save some asshead's career (see Elton John, Stink, and Phil Collins), and get mom and pops into the mix. Timmy and Susie won't know Stink and the two fat guys, but eternal hipsters Mom and Dad will remember them when they were 'cool' (heh heh heh... right) and rush out to re-live their lost youth which would never have been lost if they'd just avoided Disney films, organized religion, and alcohol-inspired unprotected sex to begin with. You are what u eat I guess. This is perhaps THE 2nd major problem with animation soundtracks. They're trying to sell the music to the parents. Look at Iron Giant ('50s soundtrack) and Shrek (John Cale!) and those ultimate pseudo-hipsters, Klasky Csupo. Just because you get the B52's dickhead, Patti Smith and other uncool visions of what makes COOL to sing in The Rugrats does not make it any better than Stink and the others. Anyway...if Patti Smith were COOL she'd never have agreed to it in the first place (btw, she was NEVER cool).

Targeting the parents has probably done the most damage to the overall quality of the music. I mean...while it ain't Robert Wilkins or Bud Powell, earlier Disney films (Winnie the Pooh, Jungle Book, Aristocats) had some catchy melodies that kids and adults grooved to. The closest any film's come recently is Toy Story. Yeah...there's some annoying mood music and that weepy Jessie/Sarah McLaughlin interlude, but they got Randy Newman (who was and sometimes is cooler than Patti Smith) contributing a slightly not so terrible song, "You've Got a Friend in Me" (although why do I sense that one of those NAMBLA sickos uses this as a theme song?*) and Riders in The Sky do a decent ol' howdy doody stylin' for "Woody's Roundup."

* Just in case it's not clear, I think that NAMBLA and anyone associated with it should be fustigated.

And hey, bad scores are not just a 'commercial' problem. Let's take The Old Man and The Sea (sorry...I'm always picking on it), Father and Daughter and The Night (Regina Pessoa). The adaptation of Old Man is bad, but the music is even worse. Father and Daughter is a decent enough film, but when the old broad dies and runs to her father (becoming a young girl again in the process), the music reaches this icky crescendo that destroys the simplicity and authenticity of the rest of the film. The culprit in both cases is Normand Roger, but I doubt it's his fault. Dudok de Wit, like Petrov (or maybe Pascal Bland) lost confidence in his ability to simply convey emotions through his images (picture = 1000 words).

Another film that irked me was festival fave The Night. A young girl is having trouble sleeping because of the shadows and sounds she imagines in the night. Pessoa (the director) creates a really creepy atmosphere and boosts it with the sounds of doors creaking and other house noises...but, feeling this isn't enough, we get a "UMM...I JUST WANT YOU TO KNOW THAT YOU SHOULD BE SCARED RIGHT NOW" soundtrack. Pop...there's goes the tire on this baby. Another flat.

And hey...even my man Priit Pärn suffers from the occasional lame soundtrack, but in his case it's not the use of the music, but the cheesy synth. sound.

Conversely...take a look at the films of Igor Kovalyov. Until Flying Nansen, he'd never used music in any of his films (and even in Nansen it's very brief)...and yet his films convey so much through movement...the movement of the characters, the camera and the editing.

In a strange sort of way, the commercial reasoning for damaging our aural senses is understandable: they're trying to sell cds. While the kids are playing with their Atlantis toys and porking out on Atlantis happy meals...mom and dad can enjoy a nice little number from that ex-punk rocker Stink. But what's with Petrov, Dudok de Wit, and Pessoa? They ain't selling soundtracks. Hell, being impoverished indie animators, they could have saved some bucks by avoiding music altogether.

Aside from the greed element, the OVERUSE of music shows

how utterly unconfident the image-makers are. They're supposed to be visual-visionaries and yet NONE of these modern dipshits seems to understand the power of a silent image. Before they spend their money on music, maybe some of these ARTISTES should take a walk to the video store and pick up a Buster Keaton film or, better yet, Carl Dreyer's *Passion of Joan of Arc*. Watch. Learn. Listen.

(August, 2001)

SEX & DEATH

"Long Live Tits"

Yo, yo, yo ladies.
Da pimp is here
makin' wit da mouth.
Ya know what I am sayin'.

Been hearin' some yappin'
'bout couple o' films:
Ring of Fire
and *Night of the Carrots.*

Seems you honeys be
thinkin' they be crappin' on ya all.
Making da' ladies look bad.
Ya know what I'm sayin'.

Dat makes da pimp mad.
He don't like no rain from da honeys.
Less it involves cork poppin'.
Rather be mackin' than yappin'.
Ya know what I'm sayin'.

Okay…y'all listen up.
Carrots got a few ladies:
that salivin' elevator button,
a big titty waitress,
a yappin' German egg
and da fat kid's mom.

Don't understand da problem ladies.
All da men be biscuit-arsed smack-offs.
They be huddled away in rooms with nothin' but fantasies.
What u see of da ladies is nuttin' but views through

the eyes of cavemen.
Ya know what I'm sayin'.

Seems dat feminism gone so far dat no one be 'lowed to say shit
'bout no woman.
Don't seem right if ya ask me.
'Sides...how many fuggin German-speakin' sister eggs do ya
know?
Ya know what I'm sayin'.

Da imagined, desired world ya all are dreamin' of, don't exist.
Not sayin' it shouldn't—'cause da pimp got nuttin' but lovin'
for all ya sweets—
but ya all be dreamin'. Dis here film be showin' da world for
what it is, not what it should be.
Da men all be IDIOTS. Don't hear da men 'plainin.'
'Sides...there be stupid MEN and stupid WOMEN.
Ya know what I'm sayin'.

Main man Diego don't do nuttin'. Bloody fool dat's all.
Time ya hardboileds stop confusin' your reality with da others.
Ain't no one reality ladies and be time ya stop t'inkin' 'cause just
ain't so.
Ya know what I'm sayin'.

As with the Fire film.
From da get go, this guy Hykade is da BOMB.
'Side the Uke and Estonian, he is king of da cartoons right now.
Ya know what I'm sayin'.

Okay...da film. Listen up.
Two guys headin' to some fuggin Fellini with Dante world o'
bends.
Is it hell? Dunno...seems plenty nice ta me.
These two fellas just be trying to bone and get their groove on.
Ya know what I'm sayin'.

Turns out though that da man we be callin' HERO,
ain't nothin' but a low-down lady-beatin' mutha' fuggah.
Da man we usually be laffin' at à la Walter Brennan be da real
    man.
He be lookin fo' da love like Chef, not Ike.
Ya know what I'm sayin'.

Man who be treatin' da ladies right get himself some love and
    some bustin'.

'Gain not sure what da problem is.
Some dancing women.
Some chicks waxin' on each other messin' with da tongues.
A chick munching anuther.
Why sex be sexism?
Merely a view within the minds of two lost souls.
Ya know what I'm sayin'.

Ya all need to open up...
Some pages of dat dead bald French guy's book *The History of
    Sexuality*.
No pictures. Won't be gettin' ya off.
But damn if it don't help all ya repressed folks understand da
    ways of sexuality.
Ya know what I'm saying.

If sexism be defined as the objectification or oppression of a
    gender by another gender,
then don't see how these 2 films fit.
If anyone bein' objects it's da crackers.
They ill-defined, fugged-up creatures.
Sure...the waitress, egg and elevator button be re/op-pressed
But shit, if ya axe me, everyone be messed up.

Ya know what I'm sayin'?

(February, 2001)

129

Shrekxxx

I didn't plan on writing more about sex, but after seeing *Shrek* last month, I knew there was more to discuss. This is a film that critiques superficial beauty. It attempts, like its ancestors *Freaks* and *Terror of Tiny Town* to celebrate the fringe folks of society (e.g., ugly, short, fat, talkative, and all-round dysfunctional). *Shrek* suggests that true beauty is found on the inside, far from the exterior scars of the body. This is pretty radical stuff for an animation feature.   Unfortunately, *Shrek's* 'treatise' on beauty is as superficial and hollow as the beauty it attempts to define. Hmm…it's all kinda ironic when ya think about it.

"Beauty is skin deep," the film suggests. Really! Well phuk a duck! Never heard that one before. Much-pilfered film theorist Laura Mulvey once noted that the film protagonist is our substitute. He/she represents us during the film. Sounds good to me. In fact, this adds an element of subversion to *Shrek* because, while Hollywood traditionally asks us to identify with the rich, good looking, and cool, *Shrek* gives us a butt-ugly, misanthropic ogre. Not since *Marty* (and, recently, *Julian Donkey Boy* and *Gummo*), has a film asked us to identify with two-drink minimums.

But wait a minute, let's look beyond the cinematic surface towards the actors: Mike Myers and Cameron Diaz. Now I dunno 'bout you, but I bring certain expectations to a movie with these actors. We are able to accept this grotesque figure because of Mike Myers. Myers represents a harmless, nostalgic comic style (Wayne Campbell, Dr. Evil and Austin Powers) that relies ironically on false appearances. It's much easier to accept the ugliness of Shrek knowing that nice guy (hey…he's Canadian) Myers is behind the body. It's the same with the princess. Cameron Diaz is a hottie. Her characters are fun-loving, a little quirky and a bit sassy. We KNOW that Myers and Diaz can do no wrong. What's not to like? Consequently, when we glance at the screen we are looking at ugly folks, but seeing our modern-day fairy tale heroes.

The film's ending is a cop-out. The princess maintains her undesirable appearance. I want to see the ugly guy get the hottie. We all do. I mean…what?…ugly folks are instantly attracted to other uglys? Is the film suggesting that freaks should stay with their own kind?

Herein lies da paradox: While the uglies stick together, the donkey (Eddie Murphy) and the she-dragon are on the verge of getting it on (hmm…didn't Murphy do a transvestite?). That's just fugged up. One minute the film is promoting quarantined love and, in the next, bestiality.

OK. Fine. You don't buy this theory. That's fine, even dandy… but there is no denying, lying, ironying, or getting 'round this sad truth: in order to discover her inner beauty, the princess must receive a kiss from her true love. Umm…this sounds like *Snow White* syndrome all over again. A man is necessary to this woman's existence and identity. The princess is nothing until she gets a peck from the pecker. Seems to me…she'd be better off doing a Loreena.

The sexual politics of *Shrek* are mighty confusing. Like *Toy Story*, we've got two fellas who grow to learn, understand and respect each other. Pretty much what love should be don't ya think? But no, once again, underneath this supposedly liberal surface (and hey…isn't a liberal just an active conservative anyway?), we have the uniting of a man and a woman. Viewers just aren't ready for homosexuals yet. But hold on a second! What's this? The dragon is coming on to the donkey! The donkey, initially uncertain, returns the admiration! OK…so basically it's better to promote bestiality than homosexuality. It's OK for a donkey and a dragon to mack, but not two men (cartoon characters at that).

I'm NOT on a crusade for homosexuality, what I am on about is this bloody need for a COUPLE to begin with. Why must every film end with a formalized union? It's all marriage propaganda, which in turn is Christian nonsense. People…*marriage is not a given fuggin truth!* It's an ideological system. A system of belief. As Philip Roth's character David Kepesh whines: "Coupled life and family life bring out everything that's childish about everyone involved. Why do they have to sleep night after night in the same bed? Why must they be on the phone to each other five times a day? Why are they always WITH each other? The forced deference is certainly childish. That unnatural deference." So there.

Fukwad had it right. Exiling fairy tales would sure as hell create a lot less chaos in the world. People might even come up with their own dreams. Imagine that.

(July, 2001)

Animation to Get Off To?

Okay, I'll be nice this time. Unless you're very liberal—and I don't mean liberal as in voted for Ralph Nader—I mean liberal in the sense that you: like "Mr. Show"; appreciate the humour of Tenacious D; don't necessarily like, but don't really have a problem with, handballing; and/or don't think getting a massage with a "happy ending" from a Vietnamese masseuse is a bad thing—you probably wanna…umm…bring down your favourites page and go visit one of your super groovy bestest Websites like www.ivanfarberspeaking.com or my friend Hayden's favourite, www.schuminweb.com.

Festivals (Cardiff, Annecy, Stuttgart, Spike and Mike) are always showing so-called erotic animation programmes. Not really erotic per se: the mating habits of animals (*Beastly Behaviour*), Betty Boop, the Avery redhead (*Red Hot Riding Hood*) are not erotic to this here cat. And *Buried Treasure*? That ol' perverted black & white film about the guy backdooring barn animals and chasing his wee-wee around the farm is DEFINITELY not erotic. This is typical, given the G.W. Bush dressed as A. Gore reality of the animation community. These sex programmes are damn tame, my friends. To me erotic means I will be aroused…But hey, okay, so they're not erotic, they are called sex programmes on occasion. And who said sex has to be erotic? Still…I beg to differ here because these so-called sex programmes are like non-cable TV porn, just a lot of tease…a series of corny, obviously-faking-it tableaux—hell, correct that…you don't even get 'faking it'…'cause faking it involves two people and few of these programmes ever show two beings doing it, let alone faking it.

So I figured there must be some pretty hardcore work out there and I called up my friend Lee and sure enuff he had three full cassettes of animation porn. I vaguely recall that he and I did a porn cartoon night at a local bar years ago, but I was too drunk to remember the details which I hope is why he has three volumes of animation porn, OTHERWISE...

Settlin' Down For Some Good, Ol' Fashioned...

First film is called *Bungle in The Jungle*...native theme. *Fucks Pause, Faux Pas and Fox Paws*. (Who finds cartoon bestiality erotic? Not me.) *Buggery on the High Sea*...This one's got, let's see, a bunny, pig and mouse on a pirate ship. They see an island of...you guessed it!...hotties. But before they can say land HO, some other band of devious cat pirates are already diggin' for oil. So a fight ensues and the pig's crew thrashes the cat pirates and boy, it's nasty! Some sharks bite YOU KNOW WHAT off the cat pirates. Meantime the pig and his pals take a stab at the gals—who don't seem to care who they're dancin' with...

Bowery Boys Meets The Bimbos. Oh boy, get a load of this technique. It's silhouette. Looks like a lost Lotte Reiniger film. This is almost festival worthy...and I swear that one of the "Mr. Show" cast members is doin' a voice here.

Arabian Delights: a sheik has, gee, a harem. Not only does this momentarily arouse me, but it triggers the rest of the harem to pounce on the sheik. Oh damn, gee, that's terrible. Happened to me during my first dance at 15. The tent's collapsed. Okay so he sees a doc, who gives him some tonic. HA HA HA. He's growin' boobs. Oh dear, he drank the wrong potion. Now he finds the male drink, gulps it down and goes nuts...

For, umm, whatever reason, the film has cut off and now we're watching *Sexrise in the Orient*. The animation is so bad I think I saw the transparencies moving like in that Coldplay video, but accidentally (and I bet that Coldplay video didn't even USE cels to begin with). MEANWHILE my brain is startin' to go numb. Memories of Ottawa selection. I'm not getting aroused at all from this and it's almost giving me a headache...making me dizzy...everything happens so damn fast.

This toon sex ain't for me. Too cold and weird. Even the worst live-action porns at least TRY to create a friggin' story line to get you all hot and lathered and anticipatory...but hey that's OK...if 'you' wanna get off with this stuff, that's cool... some folks like sharing spit with animals, food and inanimate objects...so why not animated versions? And heck there seems to be a lot of this stuff out there, so surely more than a handful of people are INTO it.

The Point Is?

So why aren't the festival programmers getting off their place that ain't their mouths and showing this really outrageous stuff? Even Spike seems to ignore hard-core ani-porn, although he doesn't mind hard-core ani-violence.

But hey...Smut duck. It's all part of animation history...these contributions are just as valid, legit, REAL as legit soft porn like *South Park, Beavis and Butthead, Ren and Stimpy* and Plympton, or even artsy-fartsy artists like Wayne Traudt, Suzan Pitt and Erica Russell. All of these works (from *Fucks Pause* to *Buggery on the High Sea*) are legitimate forms, expressions, reflections, imaginings from REAL guys and gals like me and 'you.'

I'm guessing this part of animation history got brushed aside PARTIALLY because of morality and taste (and let's not forget that these ain't films you're gonna find in the *Whole Toon Catalogue*, so this requires a historian to delve into the secret, lurid world of ADULT ENTERTAINMENT) and that seems to be an illegitimate excuse, given that I can argue that some of the stuff that the current group of historians lapdance over is quite politically and socially, to use the original meaning of porn, "disgusting and obscene."

E.g., Karl Cohen's book only really deals with lurid underground films in the context of the 'legitimate' world—which is important—but we need someone to go down into the sewers and find the stuff that doesn't surface. And what about ol' Bendazzi... How can he justify excluding the makers of *Bowery Boys Meets The Bimbos*? Why aren't these German creators in his encyclopaedia?

Where are the historians uncovering the Golden Shower era? Who made these films? Who distributed them? Why do these films exist? What does the creation of, and apparent need for, these films say about 'our' view of sex? Was there a stag party circuit? Did these toons play before live-action porn features?

Let's not limit our definitions of unsung and overlooked figures in animation history to storyboard artists, voice actors and layout men 'above ground'…'cause that's cow chew…that's just another case of blatantly subjective and repressive readings of history.

That being said…what I SORTA don't get is why someone wants to spend so much time creating this sexual world—whether writer, painter, etc…? I can understand an artist wanting to capture the essence of some great lay they just had…but isn't it easier to go and meet someone…or hell…it's prolly cheaper to BUY someone. I guess film-video-digital is a better long-term investment, but just seems kinda sad 'cause there's no real human. Not touching is like living inside a bubble or being a writer. 'Course if we didn't deem aspects of sex between consenting adults IMMORAL, unnatural, yadda yadda yadda, we wouldn't need porn and advertising (isn't that just 'soft' porn?) in the first place and we'd all prolly be a lot happier and satisfied. And who the hell wants that?

(September, 2002)

"And Never Die... And Never Die..."

Touch wood. No one close to me, except a dog and maybe a cat or two, has died. There was a sort of momentary grade-nine gal who I tried to ball once whose family and best friend kicked it in high school. When Alzheimer's took over my grandmother, I was devastated, but she's still, technically, alive. Death scares me to no end, less because I'm at HOPEFULLY the half-way mark (35) than because I'm a parent now and I want to make damn sure I'm here for my son until he's ready to go it alone. Just writing that makes me quiver with fear. Naturally there's an element of arrogance that's connected with the rise of the industrial age and the shift from state to individual control. And the notion of NOT being assumes being is essential—important. Every once in a while I slip into BAD FUNKS. Standard dark stuff…that often involves an INCREDIBLE head-buzzing PANIC that I could die at any moment. The last time it hit me was mid-June. And right in the middle of the damn death funk…this St. Louis baseball player goes and dies. He's 33. Clogged arteries. FUCK. I slept so poorly that weekend. By Monday I managed to crawl out of the dark, demons momentarily gone, back to writing…then later that week I hear that The Who's bass player, John Entwistle, died (ironically, his few song contributions often dealt comically with death). It's silly to you, but The Who were the bible of my youth. (I felt better when I later learned that despite a heart condition ol' Thunderfingers was snorting coke) So…right back into the dark. Now Socrates helped me a bit. As he was about to drink poison, he talked about death and the stupidity of fearing what you don't understand. Hey, a valid point, but maybe it's a fear of losing what we have/are. Then again…hopefully…it'll be so quick that it'll be a moot point.

Violent Toons
Meantime I was watching this new Justice League movie from

the Cartoon Network and suddenly noticed that despite guns, villains, ships, bombs and all manner of crazy violence, there was an absence of death...and ya ya ya...I KNOW, OKAY...'tain't nothing new. That's the nature of Hollywood...all the MEANS without ENDS...all the CAUSE without the EFFECT. Just do it. It was the same thing with *The Powerpuff Girls Movie* (another Cartoon Network production). The girls violently and swiftly destroy an entire city (with apparent pleasure), but miraculously they manage to avoid murdering anyone. And okay sure...it's probably some latent adult release via the creator, but these movies are made for and aimed at kids. Ironically, the films of Plympton and Don Hertzfeldt, which regularly feature pretty gruesome violence, at least SHOW the results (hell, they slobber over it!) and are probably BETTER for kids than these other hypocritical cuds.

We seem to have devolved into a world of fuggin TOYS (bizarre, given the "oh, people like us do die" reality of September 11th)...I cannot remember one action animation series (let alone live-action—and as a chum reminded me—remember those A Team shows where Murdock would fire a huge bazooka into a jeep and not manage to kill anyone!?) where people are shown dying—the natural friggin desire/result of firing bullets AT people. Now mark this down folks, 'cause you won't hear it often, but I've always respected Disney for *Bambi* and *Dumbo* and even *The Lion King*, because death is at least addressed, confronted, out and open. Beyond animation..."Homicide" had a brilliant episode with Robin Williams all from the p.o.v. of a family who've just seen their wife/mother gunned down while on vacation. And hell...even "Buffy" dealt with it (according to my gal). Okay, it's one thing to have Daffy, Bugs and Elmer beating the tar out of each other with no cause...clearly these are caricatures, exaggerations, dark comedies (for KNOWING adults)...but this action-hero nonsense is set in the 'natural' world.

Consequences DO Exist

Now I don't give a hoot about the issue of entertainment-influenced violence (I grew up playing toy gun related games and have YET to kill anyone). This isn't a so-called bleeding heart liberal call for the reduction of violence in entertainment. I got a brain and two hands, I can turn the damn television off...no... what I'm baffled by is the utter lack of common sense/logic. I'm talking mindset/philosophy here. It's not just cartoons...remember all those pretty greenish bombs dropping all over Iraq back in the early 1990s? Man, they were beautiful. Do you remember the images of the results of those bombs? The decapitated heads of children? The burned women and men? Of course not. Because we are never shown this material. Even after September 11th...the truly graphic images were, THANKFULLY, not shown (although I did watch that ABC documentary by the French guys and I'll never forget the sound of the 'thumps' as bodies fell).

I'm not saying we need to see all these corpses...but, then again, maybe we do? Maybe that's a way of driving into the heads of many of us that firing guns, dropping bombs, gutting, slaying, etc. actually have CONSEQUENCES, that is, DEATH, loss of life, pushing up daisies, ground ZERO. Aside from the planes... I remember the image of the lifeless fire dept. priest and that AWFUL AWFUL medium shot image of people at the windows/ ledges of the WTC building after a plane hit. But we don't see it. All we see are tears, dirt and U.S. flags. That's not enough. And hey, let's turn to Afghanistan, Sudan, etc., where the U.S. has killed hundreds of innocent people. How many reports did we get about lost families? Did we hear from any heartbroken wives over recent lost husbands? Did we see any footage that suggested human loss? No, of course not (at least in the mainstream news), 'cause that might actually make us question the actions of our countries.

(After I wrote this section, I heard an incredible story on the news that some Canadian police were asking kids to turn in toy guns because they felt that not only were the guns looking more realistic, but more to the point, they were contributing to a gun culture mentality. That is an astonishing and courageous thing for a cop to say today.)

Take A Serious Look

Now there have been some interesting takes on death in animation—but naturally it comes from the indie side. Caroline Leaf's *The Street* (taken from Mordecai Richler's book) addresses the death of a grandparent from a kid's p.o.v. Pierre Hebert's *Souvenirs of War* is a blunt depiction of the deadly results of war. Estonian Heiki Ernits made a funny piece called *Jacob and Death* (1994) in which a man convinces death to let him live forever, only to find that when everyone else dies and the world changes, he finds himself very alone. In the end, he virtually begs death to end his life. And boy, the Aussies are obsessed with death. Check out *Uncle*, *Dad's Clock*, Sarah Watt's film...I can't remember the title...but it's about losing a child... and, specifically, Dennis Tupicoff's heart-wrenching films *The Darra Dogs* and the recent *Into the Dark*.

There's just so much blatant hypocrisy going on here: violence without responsibility, violence without effect, denial of death.

Why on EARTH would these producers/executives permit such extreme displays of violence in "Batman," "Superman," "Justice League" and "Powerpuff Girls," BUT not permit ANY hint of the results of these actions (beyond destroyed buildings), especially considering the HUMAN damage we saw done by the relatively recent destruction of three buildings in REAL life? How is this justified as RESPONSIBLE? Is this to ensure that children grow up continuing to believe that guns are cool so they remain easy prey for Armed Forces recruiters? I don't know about the U.S., but before almost every feature in Canada, there is this stylish, fast-cutting Canadian Armed Forces ad that claims that it's all about responsibility, technology, learning and teamwork... As my Asian friend Arnold once said, BAHAHAHAHAHA.

A Dose of Reality

Well, writing this ain't making me feel a whole lot better about the prospect of not breathing anymore. At least with all this mass media nonsense, I can use my brain and hand to just switch the television off. Sure it bothers me to come across the asinine shows or to see my four-year-old suddenly fixated with the war toy section, but hey, I got a choice. If producers, creators and executives ain't gonna pull their heads out of their ass/wallet, then thankfully there are logical parents who can actually speak with their kids and explain the consequences of these 'toys' and that particular cock-driven alternative lifestyle choice. Ya know what? Why start or stop at toys? Go get the kid a real gun, take him hunting or to the firing range. Let him fire off a few rounds at a frog or the family pet, or better still, if there's a terminally ill (or close to it) loved one around, load her up and let the kid give granny or Uncle Charlie their peace (and yours!)...or lower the enrolment age for the armed forces. Ever see *Ivan's Childhood* about the kid soldier? That was great. They're small, flexible and unmarried. Sure they can be a bit undisciplined and wild, but, once potty trained,they're pretty low maintenance. Best of all, I bet they're phenomenal with guns 'cause morality ain't really creeped in yet...and heck, given recent events, some of these kids are gunnin' to go so there's very little emotional baggage involved. Plus, lots of other countries are doing it!

Death was-is-will be. No amount of denial, repression or cinematic rejection is gonna change the fact that we're gonna bite it. Thinking/talking/showing death ain't a bad thing because you are at least acknowledging its existence and in doing so are better stirred to get off your ass and live the life that gives you pleasure before you don't have that choice.

(October, 2002)

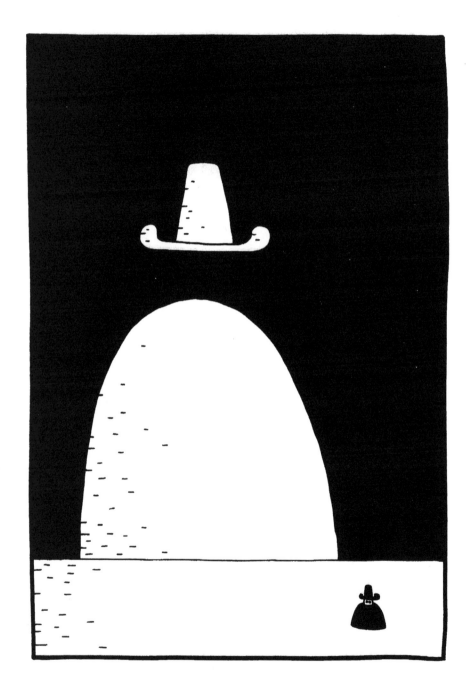

Father Who Takes the Darkness Away

Fathers of Night
My dad once told me...
My father taught me...
My father used to tell me...
My father used to say...
Sweet fuck all.
Nothing.

Two fathers.
One grandfather.
No Virgils.

—

Animation Films to Watch This With
Dad's Dead
Son of Satan
Into the Dark
Dad's Clock
Drawn From Memory
Flux
Home Road Movies
The Hat
Ring of Fire
We Lived in Grass
Family and Friends

Background
Father #1: Born fatherless.
Father #2: Grandfather till age five or so.
Father #3: Not Really My Pops. Cop. Abusive. Split.

I was supposed to write about *The Street* today. Instead I saw my first dead person.

Forget that "they look asleep" stuff… no… this guy looked BEYOND sleep, looked like the breath had been sucked right out of him… remember the way that bounty hunter at the beginning of *Attack of the Clones* got all shriveled up… well… it was something like that.

This once-man was my grandfather.

Everything stopped, and didn't.

Meaningless Memories of Unlikely Foreshadowing #1
Just before my uncle left the night before he said, "don't go anywhere."

Relatives arrive. Smiles. Daze, haze and craze. Everyone looking for distractions so we remember to forget.

Grandfather Always Used to Tell Me
"Your grandmother always considered you her son."

Meaningless Memories of Unlikely Foreshadowing #2
I left about 12 hours before he died. As I was leaving, I saw that his watch had stopped.

Uncle Once Told Me
During the 10-year exile from my grandparents,
I later learned, they used to drive by my schools
just to have a look at me.

Charlie Chaplain
Chaplain arrives. No one wants to speak at the service. Baffles me. How can you not want to SAY something, ANYTHING about your father?

I don't really WANT to speak, but need to.

Funeral Tip #1
If loved one dies in relatively normal way (all parts intact),
see the REAL dead person, not the waxed-up
funeral home action figure.

Funeral Day
Shaking like a dry drunk. Keep it together before I speak by pretending that the organist is playing hockey arena ditties.

What's with the God stuff? Grandpa hated religion(s). All of them.

My turn. Already? Told my cousins to make faces at me or pretend to pick their noses. Got up there and couldn't look up. Didn't want to see those grieving faces.

Still, I heard them.

"Abide With Me" was way too long. Last week I found a 52-sec. version by Thelonious Monk.

Childhood
I don't remember anything particularly clear about those early days, just an assortment of snapshots, most of them happy and almost all of them involving Grandma and Grandpa. I remember a lot of happy faces. Always being surrounded by family.

Funeral Tip #2
Always make sure SOMEONE who was intimate with
the ex-lifer speaks at the service. Nothing more cold
than leaving it to a stranger.

Pallbearer time. All us grandkids. Don't have far to go. Cold and heavy:

It was all show. Too cold to bury him. I figured that the hearse—which is the symbol of transference and closure—was going round the block, might stop at Tim Hortons first for a coffee, and then head back to the funeral home and put gramps back in the freezer.

Reception at uncle's place. He's a great guy. Wish he was my pops.

Post-funeral was maybe the hardest. We'd all been weaved together for the last four days, day and night. It kept us from truth, from solitude, from cold, hard sorrow. Maybe we also feared the death of the family. Gramps was the train station to our trains. Where we gonna go without a station?

While the choice is still ours, we return to our homes, families, lives.

In death we found life and love, but for how long? How long before we slip, fall and forget?

Post-Funeral Tip #1
Grief never goes away.

Since then
Friday, January 30, four days since the funeral. This is my first attempt at anything beyond grief. For some reason I figured I'd be fine the day after the funeral. Nope.

It feels like the ultimate breakup except that there's no form of appeal. No letters, calls, begging 'cause there's no one to perform for. OK, I guess church folk would say that I could pray to God.

I did go out and buy the bible. Figured it might be a good read.

You know how when you turn the TV off you sometimes see the outline of the previous image lingering on the screen? That's precisely how I feel right now.

January 30, 10:00 pm: A late night drive to my grandparent's old place, where I was born. Just sit in the car watching that old house, remembering and creating. Didn't stay for long. The house was sold last fall and I quickly realize that a strange car idling in a lane for 10 minutes is not normal.

Post-Funeral Tip #2
Do NOT watch Tim Burton's *Big Fish* after
the death of a loved one.

Music to Grieve With

When the Man Comes Around by Johnny Cash (the entire
CD, especially "Hurt," "In My Life," and "We'll Meet Again")
Time Out of Mind by Bob Dylan (especially "Not Dark Yet")

Objective

Private guy. Had trouble with emotions. Short tempered.
Didn't have a sense of humor. Distant sort. I guess he just
couldn't articulate all the stuff in him. Didn't matter.
We knew. He was always there when folks needed him.
What more?

Next Time You're in Ottawa

Apparently if you go to the airplane museum here in Ottawa,
you can find evidence of him on a part from the famous
Avro Arrow plane. When they were dismantling it, lines were
drawn on the plane with the words "Cut Here." Apparently
my grandfather authored those words. Guess that's where
I got my writing blood.

He started dying in 1996 when my grandmother had to be
placed in a nursing home because of Alzheimer's. He was
heartbroken. He emptied the house. Had a family fire sale.
House became creepy, empty, ghostly. He'd visit her every
day. Soon he was nursing her. He became part of the staff
in essence. But he let the rest of his life stop. He hated that
house. He barely slept. Last July he moved into the nursing
home. We knew something was up.

Vegas 1997

Kelly and I got married for him. We'd been together for five
years, but he was always asking (but really suggesting).

Post-Exile

When I finally found my way into their lives again some 10
years later or so, they welcomed me as if I had never left.
But it was strange because I was nine when I was taken, and
18 when I returned. Even though we were together the last
18 years, I still felt a little distant, a little bit like an outsider,
like I wasn't real family. Probably connected with the
fatherless birth too. It wasn't them though. It was me.

Satori in Ottawa?

Without me really looking, without me having any clue what the process was about or where it was going, I sorta solved the whole father thingamajig. Ya see, no matter how far I drifted into a world of darkness and hate later on in my life, the roots of my grandparents' love was always there as a series of abstract emotions, a faint beacon. I lost sight of it a few years ago when I became obsessed with finding my biological father. I tracked him down in 2000. I wanted him to accept me. I wanted him to make up for being a deadbeat dipshit. No go. After that failed, I tried to see if there was something with not-really-my-pops, but we were nothing but bad roommates in a real fiery house of hate. There weren't no love to be found in those fellas.

Why did I need this? I turned out relatively okay. I can't really explain it. Maybe it has to do with being a father myself. How the heck can I father w/o having been fathered? I guess there are times when you just want the comfort, the guidance, the experience of a father.

In writing the eulogy, I realized not only how much I loved this man, but also how much he loved me. This love uncovered an inner strength that I didn't even know was there. He was my father all along.

My grandfather's death led me back to my family, my roots and for the first time in a long, long time made me feel like I was part of something. Through his death, I found something like a life.

Guess it's time to get back to *The Street–*.

(March, 2004)

STYLES OF
RADICAL ANIMATION

Pierre Hébert and the Work of Animation in the Age of Digital Reproduction

WHEN I FIRST THOUGHT OF THIS MODEST PROPOSAL TO ELIMINATE FILM PROJECTIONISTS A FEW YEARS BACK, IT WAS FOR THE MOST PART, A JOKE. I WAS TAKING A MILD POKE AT THOSE ANIMATORS WHO—HAVING FAILED TO READ WALTER BENJAMIN WHILE STANDING IN LINE TO BUY AN ASIFA MEMBERSHIP—WERE CAUGHT UP IN THAT STALE BELIEF OF THE ARTIST AS GOD AND ART AS SOME PRECIOUS THING. WELL SORRY TO DISAPPOINT YOU FOLKS, BUT YOU AIN'T AS PRECIOUS AS YOU THINK, ESPECIALLY WITHOUT THE TECHNOLOGY NEEDED TO MAKE YOU SACRED CARTOONIES. AND IF YOU WERE A GODDAMNED GOD YOU'D HAVE NO PROBLEM BEING EVERYWHERE AT ONCE. AS SUCH, PROJECTING YOUR OWN GODDAMNED WORK WOULDN'T POSE MUCH OF A PROBLEM. THIS BRINGS ME BACK TO PIERRE HÉBERT, THE MAN WHO INDIRECTLY MOTIVATED MY PROPOSAL. SINCE THE EARLY 1980S, HÉBERT HAS BEEN DOING SCRATCH ANIMATION PERFORMANCES. SOMETIMES, HÉBERT PERFORMED SOLO, BUT OFTEN HE WORKED

WITH MUSICIANS. BY THE MID 1980S, PERFORMANCE ELEMENTS BEGAN TO APPEAR IN HIS FILMS (LE METRO, O PICASSO) AND IN 1988 HÉBERT MADE LETTRE D'AMOUR, A FILM VERSION OF A MULTI-MEDIA PERFORMANCE. IN 1999, HÉBERT LEFT THE NATIONAL FILM BOARD OF CANADA AFTER BEING THERE FOR OVER THREE DECADES AS AN ANIMATOR AND PRODUCER. SINCE THAT TIME HE'S CONCENTRATED ALMOST EXCLUSIVELY ON THE PERFORMANCE ASPECT OF HIS WORK. THROUGHOUT THE LAST TWO YEARS, HÉBERT HAS TOURED HIS SCRATCH ANIMATION PERFORMANCES AROUND THE WORLD.

THE PERFORMANCE GENERALLY INVOLVED LIVE SCRATCH ANIMATION WITH A MUSICAL COLLABORATOR. EACH PERFORMANCE WAS UNIQUE AND CONTAINED A LEVEL OF ENERGY NOT OFTEN FOUND AT A FILM SCREENING. THE RESULTS WERE MIXED (INSERT MILD GRUNT AND CASUAL SHRUG OF THE SHOULDER HERE). NO GRUNTS HOWEVER FOR HÉBERT'S LAST PERFORMANCE PIECE (WITH AVANT GARDE MUSICIAN BOB OSTERTAG) BETWEEN GARBAGE AND SCIENCE. FOR THIS HOUR-LONG PERFORMANCE ABOUT THE DISPOSABILITY OF CULTURE, OSTERTAG IS EQUIPPED WITH A MAC POWERBOO

K. ON IT ARE A WIDE ARRAY OF SOUNDSCAPE SAMPLES THAT OSTERTAG CAN MANIPULATE THROUGH A PROGRAM CALLED MAX. HIS LAPTOP IS CONNECTED TO HÉBERT'S POWERBOOK WHICH HAS ABOUT FIFTY IMAGES STORED ALONG WITH A FEW QUICKTIME MOVIES (PRIMARILY NEWS FOOTAGE). LIKE OSTERTAG, HÉBERT CAN MANIPULATE THE PACE, TEXTURE AND SEQUENCING OF HIS MATERIAL. THIS MEANS, FOR EXAMPLE, THAT HE IS NOT REQUIRED TO PRESENT IMAGES AT 24 FRAMES PER SECOND. BESIDES THE COMPUTER, HÉBERT HAS A DIGITAL VIDEO CAMERA AFFIXED TO THE TOP OF A PORTABLE HOMEMADE ANIMATION STAND. THE CAMERA IS CONNECTED TO HÉBERT'S COMPUTER SO THAT HE CAN MAKE AND INCORPORATE LIVE ANIMATION WITH THE ARCHIVED MATERIAL.

THE MOST ASTONISHING ASPECT OF THE PERFORMANCE, FOR OUR PURPOSES, IS THAT NO PROJECTIONIST IS REQUIRED. IN FACT THE ARTIST CREATES AND PROJECTS THE IMAGES SIMULTANEOUSLY. WHILE NOT ALL FILMS WILL BE IMPROVISED, IT IS CERTAIN THAT WITHIN A DECADE WE COULD BE SEEING FESTIVAL COMPETITIONS PRESENTED IN THE SAME MANNER. FUTURE COMPETITORS CAN TAKE A SEAT, OPEN UP THEIR LAPTOPS AND PERF

ORM. HURRAY! HURRAY, I SAY. THE DAYS OF LUMBERING TECHNOLOGICAL PROCESSES ARE OVER. NO MORE PROJECTIONISTS (I WILL MISS THEM)! NO MORE APE SHOWS (I WON'T MISS THEM). NO MORE 24 FRAMES PER SECOND! HÉBERT'S PERFORMANCE ASKS US TO RECONSIDER THE WAY WE CREATE, PRESENT AND EXPERIENCE ANIMATION. THERE IS NOTHING REVOLUTIONARY IN THIS. MUSIC HAS BEEN DOING IT FOR YEARS. HOLLYWOOD HAS ALREADY MADE A DIGITAL FEATURE FILM. BUT IN TERMS OF INDEPENDENT ANIMATION, WHAT HÉBERT IS DOING IS UNFORTUNATELY QUITE RADICAL. I SAY 'UNFORTUNATELY' BECAUSE THESE TECHNOLOGICAL DEVELOPMENTS COULD HAVE BEEN EMBRACED EARLIER.

ASIFA IS PARTLY TO BLAME. THEY WERE FOUNDED TO PROTECT AND PROMOTE ARTISTIC ANIMATION, BUT INSTEAD CREATED A MONSTER. ASIFA QUICKLY BECAME AN INSULAR GROUP OF INDIVIDUALS WHO, NAMELESS AND NEGLECTED, FORMED THEIR OWN OLYMPUS WHERE THEY COULD BE GODS. IN THE MEANTIME THE WORLD MOVED ON: THE POLITICAL, SOCIAL AND CULTURAL LANDSCAPES SHIFTED AS TECHNOLOGICAL DEVELOPMENTS EMERGED. BY THE 1990S, ASIFA HAD GONE , LARGELY UNAWARES,

FROM
OLYM
PIAN
GODS
TO
CAST
AWA
YS ON
GILLI
GAN'
S
ISLAN
D.

IT'S
TIME
TO
GET
OFF
THE
ISLAN
D.

(October, 2001)

Why is it Not Done?

Saw an interesting programme at the Holland Animation Film Festival in November (2002). It was called "Not Done" and was put together by a Belgian chum of mine, Edwin Carels. The three-part programme consisted of films and videos (by the likes of Martha Colburn, Stan Brakhage, Michael Snow and Leslie Thornton) that challenge the notion of what is and what is not animation in terms of both content and technique. What I found more interesting was Carels' accompanying text where he asks: "Why does a medium in which virtually anything is possible, in which the imagination has free reign and the laws of physics don't apply, so rarely shock its viewers?" And in particular, he takes animation festivals to the carpet for contributing to this stale situation by: not seeking out filmmakers in the experimental, avant-garde or art gallery world; not showing more performance-based work from animators like, for example, William Kentridge; not being a forum for serious debates about animation.

This is not the first time I've heard this complaint. In an article in the 2000 Holland Animation Film Festival catalogue (which was reprinted in the Spring 2001 ASIFA magazine), Canadian animator Pierre Hébert was critical of the current state of animation, suggesting that it had become a recluse unwilling to open its doors to new possibilities.

Conservative and Homogeneous

Although Carels is attacking my bread and butter, I tend to agree (in principle) that animation festivals have all become fairly conservative and homogeneous. No one really cares about animation festivals as a forum for serious discussions. They are primarily a forum for buyers, recruiters, ASIFA members and drunks. From retrospectives to competitions to jury decisions, everything is relatively peachy keen. Sure, some folks mildly bitch to their friends about this or that decision, but rarely is there any sort of loud, meaningful debate about a film or a programme. Even at Ottawa '98, when we got into trouble for showing this apparently racist Polish film called *Black Burlesque*, it wasn't the animation community that yelled and screamed at me, it was two Canadian Jewish associations.

And despite all the talk about experimental and cutting-edge animation, festivals are not actually showing anything overly radical. We hear that Robert Breer, Stan Brakhage and Martha Colburn are animators, but when did you last see their work at an animation festival? Rather than rely on the same old crowd of independent, student and studio animators, festival programmers have got to attend mixed-media and experimental festivals, art galleries, video shows—i.e., the other cinema. We can kick animation in the balls and awake it from its decades-long drool and bring in some fresh voices.

And as Carels suggests, why limit presentations to traditional film-video screenings? What about installations, dance performances, theatre? Artists like Pierre Hébert, William Kentridge and Kathy Rose all merge animation with performance arts. The problem here however (at least from an Ottawa Festival perspective) is that a single performance costs significantly more than a regular film screening. So, you know…what can I say… I'm copping out a bit here, but do I spend thousands of dollars for a one-night performance that's going to attract half capacity and leave me with no money for any other programmes JUST to win the respect of assorted intellectual-artistic hipsters?

But It's Not So Simple

Then again, what is a groundbreaking work? In this post-MTV age we've appeared to have seen it all? As John Waters sorta said…can anyone make something that is groundbreaking or shocking that doesn't involve sex or violence? In Holland, for example, I went to this difficult Japanese experimental screening and then went to a screening of commissioned TV animation (commercials, music videos, IDs, etc.). Aside from artistic intention (one sells a philosophy, the other, shoes), they both seemed stylistically similar. With the proliferation of mass media and the need to fill airtime, yesterday's avant-garde is today's Nike ad.

Besides, much of what we show in Ottawa is already considered 'out there' by both the local public and even portions of the animation community. Furthermore, we're not some free-floating entity; we are government supported and receive most of our money from animation studios, schools and software companies. We have to answer to the needs of those who fund us.

Nevertheless, I think competition and retrospective programmes can (and should) be easily shaken up. There are many works that straddle the lines between animation, video art and experimental, and in most cases animation festivals shy away from these works. As Carels suggests, there is a tendency in animation, more than in any other art form, to focus on craftsmanship. Animation folks are obsessed with the quality of drawing and animation. WHAT is being said is generally less important than HOW it is being said. I remember some Animation Nation loser saying that Priit Pärn films were poorly drawn...as if there is some set standard of drawing! Or how about those whiners who keep saying *Waking Life* isn't animation? I mean...first off...Shut the fuck up, it IS animation. 2. Shut the fuck up and THINK for two seconds about the content. Bunch of Disney-*Star Wars*-Tornado-Norstein weened Wankers. Not to keep harping on *The Old Man and The Sea* (I could also use the puppet films of Barry Purves, the works of Frédérick Back, any post-*Creature Comforts* Aardman production or Martine Chartrand's *Black Soul* as examples), but while all sorts of animation folks saw this gorgeous, beautiful animated film that used a painstaking fingerpaint technique, I saw a crappy, sentimental film that oh-so-poorly adapted one of Hemingway's few decent books. And then there's the computer. Every goddamn year I am asked why there are not more computer films in competition...well I'll tell you why, because they suck. The animators are so busy whacking off on whatever cool software they have, they often forget to come up with an actual idea (or at least one that isn't ripped off from some combination of *Star Wars-Star Trek*-Anime). I kid you not, the computer entries we get (and it's the same crop as every other festival) are so embarrassingly stupid and riddled with clichés that our decision process becomes that much easier.

Currently there are too many animation festivals showing too many of the same films, all being judged by the same voices. It's become too cozy and familiar. We need to hear from new voices. We need to get animation artists (and more specifically open-minded animation teachers—like Stephanie Maxwell—who can introduce their students to something beyond the typical animation canon) together with musicians, poets, digital artists, experimental filmmakers, so that these worlds can introduce themselves to each other with the long-term hope that something new and inspiring will emerge. A lot of people in animation bitch and moan (including me) over the fact that festival animation remains this hidden little secret...well, given that we've been sitting in our house with the windows and doors locked and the blinds pulled down...is it really that surprising?

(February, 2003)

Clinging to a small piece of nothing in the middle of nowhere

It takes a shallow grasp of history to believe that solutions exist to most international problems. Often there are no solutions, only confusion and unsatisfactory choices.
        – Robert Kaplan, *Warrior Politics*

Between grief and nothing, I'll take grief.
        – William Faulkner, *The Wild Palms*

Everybody's hoppin' just a boppin' just a boppin'.
        – Jerry Lee Lewis, "High School Confidential"

"I don't care." There I said it. I don't feel a damn bit of shame either. The U.S. has done what it said it would do and I don't care anymore. Same goes for animation, the part of my life that earns cash. These days I'm more concerned with my dog's limp, my book deadline, what we're going to do for a new venue for Ottawa 2004, the endless e-mails I keep getting about penis size (I don't know 'bout you...but I got over that whole thing when I was about 14. I mean are there really any women out there who believe that a BIG PENIS is everything? If so...please write c/o address below), and the NHL playoffs. I know, I know. What a petulant, self-righteous spoiled s.o.b. Well hey, la dee da. At least I'm not a self-styled polygamist. (Sorry, I just really wanted to say that phrase.) Maybe you're right, but what do you want me to do? Maybe it comes with tossing the bottle or having a kid or hitting that Dante age. You step back, slow down and actually think things through. All I know is that I find myself sitting atop a couple of fences at this moment.

Up 'til about December, I was pretty much lefty. It was

easy…just quote Nader or Chomsky, wave your fist, go to a few protests, visit alternet or common dreams, go see *Bowling for Columbine*, forward a few emails and you're done. Barely a sweat, but man do u feel good about yourself. Well…I got called to the mat by my friend Hayden. He lives in Toronto. Big deal. During the month of January he and I started discussing the war. I'd just finished (almost) this book called *The War on Freedom*. The book argued that the U.S. government basically knew and allowed the 9/11 attacks to happen. This had left me thoroughly depressed because how do you fight something so complex and jamesbondingly evil? Well…anyway…Hayden and I started gabbing about Iraq. He took the centre of right. I took the left. By the end of it I realized how daft I'd been. All the lefty stuff I was spouting: 9/11 was a conspiracy, Bush is an idiot. It's all about oil. Killing people is wrong. It was all empty rhetoric. It wasn't that I became an anti-abortionist Negro-hating redneck…no it was that I came to understand that the left could generate the same impotent verbal crap that also drips from the mouths of Bush, Rumsfeld and the rest of the boys' club. This really wasn't new…I was always annoyed by those drum-beating Communist hippies. They always struck me as so bloody intolerant of difference. They were morally superior, above it all and ironically almost sort of fascistic to a degree ("You're either with us or against us!" Hmm…). They could all quote Chomsky, Biafra, Rollins and assorted lefty pop stars. Worst of all, like Newt Gingrich, they had NO SENSE OF HUMOUR. Man…I once wore this T-shirt I got from *Bust Magazine* that said, "Feminist chicks dig me," and you should have seen the scowls. Anyway, all these gals pushing strollers and wearing those hats…sort of circular…kinda thing a lame-ass jazz musician might wear (my friend Andrea calls them NGO hats)…anyway…these broads confronted me and said they were offended by my shirt. I told them it was obviously a joke…but umm…they weren't laffing. Can u imagine what they'd do if I wore my T-shirt with Bin Laden wearing an "I Love NY" T-shirt? Shiver me timbers. And hey…just look at their poster boy, the self-righteous tattletale Noam Chomsky: "Well…the U.S. did this and this and then they

did this and this…oh…and that too. That was really bad…and I think they should be spanked." Chomsky apparently lives in an error-free, perfectly knitted (like his sweaters) world. I was part of some lefty e-mail groups and they'd always annoy me, but now they did so more than ever. Again they seemed humourless, ignorant and downright childish—like the hippies in the Beavis and Butthead episode "Animation Sucks." (You're purple! You're green! Yeah…but we're both red inside.)

Now okay…I'm picking on the extreme left here. Not all of the left are this cartoony…but hey…ya know what? That's true of the right as well despite what television tells you. It's easy to mock Bush. He's not an articulate man. He's a recovering alcoholic. He believes in God. His daughters like to tie one on. Hell…he wasn't even elected to office. But really, come on…do you really believe he's a Jerry Lewisesque moron? What is being served by reducing Bush and his administration to cartoon characters? (Yes…I realize that Rumsfeld is doing a cartoony Clint Eastwood of late.) These people are not morons and the sooner you come to grips with that, the closer you come back to reality. And please protesters…stop forcing your not-yet-hippie children to carry "War Kills Kids" banners. War kills men too ya know.

In the end, I'm stranded in a hailstorm of confusion spewed forth by the rhetoric of left and right. The task of discovering the cold hard truth becomes that much more difficult.

Still with me? I bet you're wondering how all this ties in with animation. Well…it's like this… Animation, for my money, continually falls short as a meaningful social art form. Like politics, animation seems dominated by extremes: the ballcap-wearing guns-ablazin' bodies-a-tollin' kill-everyone world of video game animation, or the just-short-of-it world of "Powerpuff Girls," "Justice League," and all those violence-without-effect films I prattled on about last year, or any number of phoney baloney films like *Spirit*, *Trumpet of the Swan*, *Treasure Planet*, OR (huff huff) on the other side we get the trite preachy wishy-washy let's-hug-and-forget-our-troubles-with-a-nice-cup-of-Ovaltine (oops…sorry…can't do that…they employ 14-year-old retarded midget giraffes from Kokomo) visions of, gee…pick a card, any card: Jacques Drouin, Bratislav Pojar, Stormin' Norman McLaren, Raoul Servais, Paul Driessen, Karen Aqua, Joyce Borenstein, Ishu Patel (*Divine Fate*...ugh)...and assorted do-gooders.

I don't know if it's just the nature of animation, the fact that it takes so damn long to do (although that's increasingly false) or that it's always been a more personally oriented form of expression...but animation just seems more and more out of touch with the surrounding world. Norstein, Back, Dumala, The Quays, Tilby, Kovalyov, Kucia...the list goes on...are among the leading animators...the voices that apparently matter, and yet sometimes I think they're just speaking to themselves. And before you start calling me a fascist...this isn't about the denial or repression of individual expression. It's about urgency, passion, and communication. Where are the outraged animators—either left or right? These be some pretty fucked-up times, kids...with terrorism fears, Iraq, Korea...and who can even begin to tell what the attack on Iraq is going to lead toward. In these times...hell... most of the time...we turn to culture for some guidance, some suggestions, even comfort...and I can find relevant (past and present) voices in writing, music, live-action, painting (and all those new-fangled media arts), but what about animation? I was originally planning to have a look at protest films in animation, but ya know what? There aren't that many and those that do exist are so cloyingly naïve. Where are the voices (past or present—not including propaganda films)? Aside from the ASIFA-East 9/11 project (most of which, unfortunately, included many smug and spoiled "how could this happen to us" responses)...there seems to be nothing out there beyond Flash animations—and even then most of these animators succumb to limitations of caricature.

Who cares, you ask? Exactly. This comes back to what I wrote about in February: No one gives a damn about animation outside of this little community. Aside from newspaper articles focused squarely on new technologies and jobs and all that industry stuff...no one talks about what animation is saying. Why? Okay...you can fall back on that old pegleg, lack of exposure... but ya know what? Animation gets as much exposure as short experimental film/videos and yet they seem to get talked about.

Maybe the answer is simple: animation says nothing interesting or relevant about the world. In Priit Pärn's film, *1895*, there were lots of jokes about what useful careers people might have had had they not become filmmakers…and you have to wonder about animators in general. It's almost like we've got too many Ingmar Bergmans and not enough Godards. Too many self-enclosed artists isolated from society. What would have happened if McLaren hadn't hid in his room playing with abstract musings all that time? Imagine what Norstein might be doing if he hadn't wasted the last 10-20 years with this bloody *Overcoat* project? Same with Dumala and his romantic schoolboy obsession with the existentialists, or Kovalyov and his land of selfish paranoias. And whatever happened to George Griffin? What about Priestly? Aqua? Borenstein? Leaf? The list goes on. Priit Pärn is one of the few animators (a slight nod to Pierre Hébert and Phil Mulloy as well) to really try and grapple with the complexities of history, politics, technologies and identity. Maybe the fact that he is so unique is what makes him so problematic for many animation artists. Animation needs to undo the noose and live a little. Stop treating the world as some precious jewel to be cloistered away in a glass case. We need trash. Trash is life. Trash has been eaten, chewed, swallowed, shitted, wiped, jerked off into, dropped, embraced, beaten, broken. Animation, odd as it is to say, needs more realists and less idealists. Animation has no Hubert Selby, Jack Kerouac, William Faulkner, Nick Tosches, let alone a Jerry Lee Lewis, Robert Pollard, or a Jackson Pollack. Animation has lots of Wayne Gretzkys, Tiger Woods, Michael Jordans…but you need grinders to win, those guys who give 110% game in/game out, who play with raw intensity, embracing every shift as if it were the last. Animation seems to lack that rawness, the reactionary GOTTA SAY IT OR I'M GONNA BUST nature that others have. Even the improvised scratch animators like Barbel Neubauer and Richard Reeves are often missing that fire that every artist MUST have. Martha Colburn, JJ Villard, Andreas Hykade, are among the few animators whose work excites me. Everyone else seems to go about at a nice leisurely pace, taking 4-5-10-20 years to make a film. That's something I really can't understand or respect. If it's not burning to come out, then maybe it don't need to come out. And maybe that's just a problem inherent in animation. Maybe that's why animation will forever be seen by some as the pottery of the art world.

Just a small dose of pragmatic realism would give us some balance and, ironically, take us beyond the limits of our current imaginings. Yoda was right…it's about balance, kids. Just like that German toon tells us…we need balance to have a level perspective of things. Without balance, we'll end up like Duck Dodgers and that Martian, clinging to a small piece of nothing in the middle of nowhere.

(May, 2003)
(Original title: "Leftovers, B-Sides and Outtakes")

Chillax

To sit around a bottle of rancid grape juice, speaking
of delicate hints of black currant, oaken smoke,
truffle or whatever other dainty nonsense with which
nature is fancied to have enlaced its taste, is to be
a cafone of the first order. For if there is the delicate
hint of anything to be sensed in wine, it is likely that of
pesticide and manure. How could so sophisticated a
nose fail to detect the cow shit with which this most
celebrated estate in Bordeaux fertilizes its vines?
    – Nick Tosches, *The Last Opium Den*

I've been glancing through some of the animation forums, and if they're any reflection of the animation industry, then I'd say a lot of people are freaked out by the Nostradamussed words of some no-name Disney exec who'll be a fart down memory lane faster than you can pass the beans. Anyway, the Disney guy essentially told a bunch of Disney drones that computer animation was the wave of the future.

Yeah... that's it, that's all. But all through the world of animation forums—a wonderful social tool where people gather under false names to connect and communicate with other people who also use false names—there was horror, panic and anger. You'd think there'd be bigger worries... you know endangered animals, rainforests, orphaned war children, who will win "American Idol," how that Jenna chick won "Survivor." (Did they fix it because of her mom's brain cancer?) I say, calm down people. Overreactions on all sides. First off, umm...it's a business. You can call it art as much as you like, but you'd be wrong. Profit comes before art. It always has. Computer animation is cheaper. Less time, less people, less money. Naturally this Stainton guy is a bottom-liner. On an ethical level, he's probably a twit, but in this context he's making an astute and very logical BUSINESS decision. And why is anyone surprised? Are you gonna tell me that you didn't see it coming? Well… gee kids… get ready… 'cause this is just the beginning of the end of what you think animation entails.

Animation as we know it will be dead by the end of the century anyway, absorbed by live-action features. It's already happening. *Twister*, *Spider-Man*, *Star Wars: Attack of the Clones*, *The Matrix*, and *X-Men* are all animation films. With mainstream animation dangerously obsessed with some slanted take on photorealism/naturalism, would it be all that surprising to see animation and live-action fused together? Actors will go after that, replaced by 3D characters and maybe down the road even 3D created voices. This is just the beginning, folks.

It's nothing new though. I'm not a cheerleader of the history-as-progress line nor do I think that every technology that comes along necessarily improves our lives. But hey… that's the way some of us wish to approach the world. It's a philosophy that's not limited to animation, it's always been connected with art, and almost always motivated by money. Writing has gone from stone, bone, ivory and metal to Indian ink, quill pens (they lasted the longest of any writing instrument so far), fountain pens and ballpoint pens. Along the way, the typewriter arrived around 1866 followed by the word processor (good ol' Wordstar) in the late 1970s. The tools have changed, but you'd be hard pressed to tell me that the changes in technology have led to a decrease in the quality of literature (it's just led to MORE bad writing perhaps). My eyes roll when I hear, for example, a writer talking about how he misses those days of purity and wonder when he had his old Olympia typewriter. There was nothing sweeter than hearing his fingers tap a little Gene Krupa on the keys. One of the funnier examples is Marv Newland. I love Marv. He's funny, smart and GENUINE… but he's got this thing about not having e-mail, YET he does type (using a typewriter?) on paper and fax it to me. It always makes me laugh. He won't use the damn computer, but he'll use a fax machine!? The typewriter and fax, once feared modern tools, are, like the record player (or is that gramophone?), rotary phone, and Atari, now just precious relics from a time gone by.

It's the same with cinema. Oh la la... le cinéma... it is magique, magnifique, c'est si bon. First there was apprehension about the technology itself, then there was all this fuss about sound, then color, then video, now digital. Oh the HORROR that we will lose that special, umm... what's the word?... oh yeah... NOTHING.

So do you really believe that animation will be any worse for wear if it dropped drawn animation altogether? Yeah... sure to a degree... we can haggle about the senses, the lack of touch, rhythm working with a computer... but even then you'll create a new rhythm. I don't have a problem finding a rhythm when I'm pounding on a laptop. But let's be real here, kids... yes... *Bambi, Fantasia, Sleeping Beauty* and *Pinocchio* were real pretty films... and so were *Iron Giant* and *Osmosis Jones,* but we were also forced to endure *Black Cauldron, Fox and the Hound, Spirit* and Don Bluth. Meanwhile, I think PDI and Pixar, among others, have done a pretty decent job. *Toy Story 2, Shrek, Monsters, Inc., Antz* and *Finding Nemo* aren't the cream, but they're as entertaining and visually interesting as any of those drawn classics. All of the aforementioned films were made to entertain and, for the most part, they do their job. Yes... something will change... but that's all... it'll just be different, not any better or any worse (and remember this is coming from a guy who generally loathes computer animation).

So hey, kid, relax, I ain't worried. In fact, I'm pretty confident that computer animation will be able to maintain the same level of character, story and music quality that we've come to expect from feature and television animation.

(June, 2003)

Andreas Hykade's Great Balls of Fire

You shake my nerves and you rattle my brain.
Too much love drives a man insane.

Forget Lacan. Forget Freud. Jerry Lee Lewis knew the truth about desire, greed and lust, and how it fucked you up. He knew it was bad shit, but his body ached for it. Check out Lewis's '64 Starclub performance. Made not long after his young son died, the concert is a violent, drunken, frenzied testament to desire, pain, anger and hate. It's raw. It's honest. In life he maintains the image of the Dionysian spirit, a hard-drinking, hard-fucking, don't-give-a-crap-about-nothin' man's man, but in art, the pain, anguish and uncertainty seeps through every note of his music.

Andreas Hykade ain't no Jerry Lee Lewis, but his films breathe the same polluted air.

———

Animation has too many scientists. Too many technical masters making cold, polished, certain films. They create within the calculating sanctity of a sanctuary. All the furniture has been replaced, the bodies removed, blood mopped up. Hykade is different. He's a raw, faulty, honest poet in the vein of Nick Tosches, Hubert Selby, and, yes, OK, Charles Bukowski. I'm not talking some macho hardboiled nonsense either; I mean a man torn between sin and salvation, good and evil, one who struggles to cope with the redeeming power of humility and weakness.

———

Hykade has given us *We Lived in Grass, Ring of Fire,* an assortment of TV stuff including a nifty young kids' series called "Tom."

I watch Hykade's beautiful, troubling films and remember that I knew some dandelion girls. When I was six, I pushed her into a brick wall. When I was 15, she dumped me. I was heartbroken, wouldn't let her leave the locker bay. Then I shoved

her and pushed her down the hall all the way to first class. I think I saw her put her head on her desk and cry. I followed her the rest of the day.

I don't remember this.

She reminded me last year.

—

I think it was the former Toronto Maple Leaf winger Busher Jackson who said, "Hey, Primeau, there's only trouble and desire." Ain't that the truth, fella. Always chasing time instead of livin' it. What happens when the now suddenly vanishes? You're confused, angry, and lost. You don't know where to turn because you don't know where you are. You're not prepared. You get angry and lash out. You want to hurt what hurt you. Isn't that why the boy burns the dandelion girl, the cowboy beats the angel, the ape goes crazy when his TV goes out? That guy chasing the clock, he's nowhere. Why this burn, burn, burning desire?

Lacan said it was all a ruse. When we're little pissers we think we're at one with the world. Then we see our mug in the mirror, see that we're separate from everything around us, and spend the rest of our lives trying to become one again. 'Course, along the way, it's also being ingrained in our noggins that we're incomplete. First came the church, then came the advertisers, dirty, soul-sucking con men (themselves doin' the deed just to preserve their own desires) telling us we're no good without God, the Bible or a bar of fucking Dove. Meantime they're snorting and guffawing as they guzzle the holy water and thrust their lust sticks in places they don't belong. We all have the beast inside.

Good. Beauty. Truth. Value judgements, all of 'em; given meaning and relevance only by us. To further the myth we create fictional characters to back it up: God. Jesus. Santa Claus. Ricky Martin. Icons of perfection. Flawless truth and beauty. Good God. Bad Devil. Beauty Ugly. Life. Death. You can't have one without the other. Ying yang. We also created icons of imperfection too. Dean, Monroe, Manson and Elvis. Lost souls and all that shit. No in-betweens. We're hell-bent on living in one of these either/or states.

Hykade's work, like Lewis's, Tosches', Selby's, etc., tries to sort through the extremes, to come to terms with the fact that there is no pure good or evil, just faulty liner notes to get us by. Snoozers like to ridicule assorted macho 'misfits' like Hykade for romanticizing violence, lust, and all the supposed essences of masculinity. They got it all wrong. These guys are ridden with guilt and conflict, trying to come to terms with the fact that there are no absolutes, yet being driven toward them all the same. It's not that they won't believe, it's that they can't believe. It's as if they know and see too much; yet not enough to extinguish the fires of alienation and desire that isolate them from world.

—

This isn't about dandelion girls, cousins, whores, cowgirls or even Beatrice. Hykade, like the rest of them, is seeking the father. The father of night, day, darkness, love, and pain—the whole kit and caboodle. Wasn't Jesus just lookin' for pops? Did the boy burn the dandelion girl because he believed his father or because he lost his father? Revenge for bailing on him. The sins of the father…

Fatherless fathers. I had two of them. Both were dicks. Real one came (nudge, nudge) and went. Fake one was violent, scary and nasty. I hated him most when I became him. I'm a father now. I want to forgive my fathers. Why is it that I blame them for the bad days and don't thank them for the good ones? They were too busy looking for their fathers to be one. Fucked up fatherless-fathers; boys being asked to emulate something that isn't there to begin with.

—

As some 15th-century Italian poet told us, to find heaven, you have to go through hell. Ya gotta stumble before you rise. If you ask me, and you didn't, too many animators, too many people, wanna skip the bad to get the good. That's bad (heh heh). Ya gotta know the bad to know the good. Hykade, a new father, uses the dirt and darkness of the past as compost to fertilize a future of light, darkness, and hope, not to mention a bit of bread with honey and jam on it.

(August, 2004)

Scratch Fever

Well I don't know where they come from
But they sure do come
I hope they're comin' for me
And I don't know how they do it
But they sure do it good
I hope they're doin' it for free
> – Len Lye (to friends near the end of a
> family function in New Zealand, 1925)

I'm not out to get Annecy. Things just happen this way. Opening night, Annecy 05, there was a special film that parodied experimental/abstract films. Purportedly made by Bill Plympton, the film poked fun at 'circles and squares' films. Annecy's Serge Bromberg was in on the gag too, introducing the film as a long-lost document. The audience loved it. It was all in good fun. No harm done.

Later on in the festival during a 'meet the filmmakers' session there was another moment of anti-abstract shenanigans. This time, Serge Bromberg grilled Canadian Steven Woloshen about his cameraless pieces. Bromberg admitted that he just couldn't understand these films and that it seemed as though Woloshen was making the same film over and over again. Strange words from the creative director of the world's largest animation festival, especially considering that Woloshen was a guest of Bromberg's festival. But, hey, no problem. Serge was honest. He didn't take the film, his selection committee did.

Anyway, this isn't about Annecy. Annecy audiences have always more hostile to experimental animation than other festival crowds. What interests me about these two incidents is that they reflect common responses to experimental animation (especially cameraless work): "it's all the same," "just a bunch of dots and circles," "narcissist wanks," "I don't get it." Etc.

Look, I'm not gonna fight to the death for non-narrative animation, because often it is cold and wanky, but so is a lot of narrative work. Still, I think the hostility towards these 'circle and dots' films brings up some interesting issues.

First, cameraless/scratch animation is all said to look the same. "It all looks like Mclaren." That's nonsense of course... we can go on and on about the uniqueness of rhythm, textures, colours, tones.

The problem, it seems to me, is less with the filmmaker than with the viewer. People don't know how to react to these films. They think it's a riddle, that there's a deep dark mystery to be uncovered. In some cases, sure, that is true...but if you take a look at, for example, the work of Woloshen, Richard Reeves, or Theo Ushev's moving new film *Tower Ballihr*, these are films about making you feel something. They convey the jumbled-up emotions of their creators.

Steve Woloshen is a guy I hold in high regard. He works for no studio. He gets no government funding. He works (or did) by day as a driver on Hollywood feature films. When he's not working, he makes films in his home. He has rolls of films in a closet. When he feels like making a film, he pulls out a roll and goes to it. The results are simple, passionate films bursting with energy. When I see Steve's films, I feel good about life (no small miracle!). I can feel his happiness seeping through the frames. He often uses familiar pieces of music (e.g., "Take Five," "Get Happy," and, most recently, Hendrix's "Voodoo Chile")...but he brings something special to the music. He makes it his own. (For those of you going to Ottawa this year, just wait till Woloshen's image explodes on the screen alongside Hendrix's opening riff at the beginning of competition 3. It's something special.) *Curse of the Voodoo Child*, for example, uses the Hendrix song, *Curse of Frankenstein* Super 8 footage, and snippets from a cheesy melodrama to tell the story of the birth of Woloshen's daughter (Voodoo Child). It's not a complicated film. Woloshen (like Reeves) isn't out to confuse and distance you, he simply wants to evoke emotions. You don't need to seek out deep mysteries, you just need to shut up and let the images and music take you over.

Even the hardcore abstract stuff isn't all that different. It may provoke and anger you, but that's still a sensory reaction. Seems to me people gotta take it easy, stop overthinking, just FEEL these films. Woloshen's films are really no different (on a base level) than classical narrative films like, say, *Gopher Broke* or *Boundin'*. Woloshen's films just want you to FEEL good, happy, alive, while *Gopher Broke* wants you to laugh. Last time I checked, laughter and good feelings were sensory emotions.

The big difference is that Woloshen and his posse are not making paint-by-numbers films. There are no laughtracks. No obvious cues and familiar gags that *Gopher Broke* and its ilk rely too heavily upon to get you cheap at Wal-Mart prices. *Curse of the Voodoo Child, Linear Dreams*, etc... try to reach a deeper feeling of happiness. They want you to FEEL with all you are. It's an infinitely more satisfying (at least it should be) and individualized sensation than the Pavlovian tendencies of many linear narratives like *Gopher Broke* (a film we *took* for Ottawa this year—just in case one of youse is about to email me a rant).

Kinda like the difference between a really good Italian dinner and eating at Wendy's. Both will make you feel good while you're eating, but only one will really leave you full and satisfied.

(August, 2005)

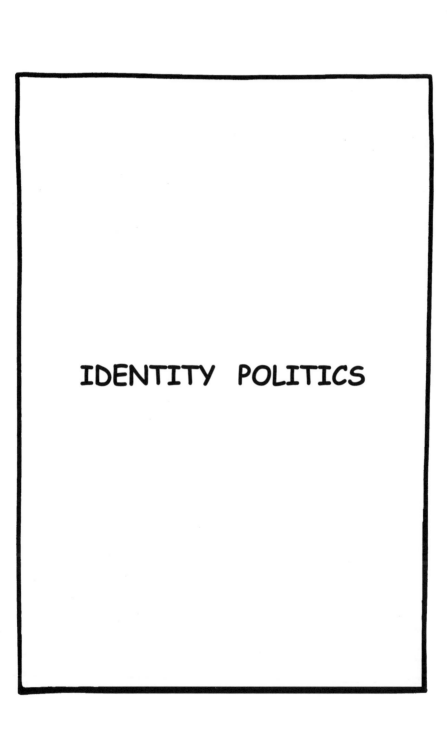

IDENTITY POLITICS

Just Like Us?

In general, I don't like cops, army folk, bible swallowers, or anyone whose primary function in life is to make, sleep, eat, dream, or shit money. I don't like fools, even when I'm being foolish. I don't like elitist/pretentious/holier-than-thou fugs especially when I'm being a self-righteous prick. I even lose it with those close to me. The dog, kid, wife, and EXSPECIALLY, the woman I emerged from. In general people who aren't doing something for me at the moment I want something done for me. In short, I can be a pretty self-centred intolerant jerk. And that's why I'm the ideal person to spot those same traits in others.

I dunno when it was, a few months ago maybe, but I noticed a lot of talk about Cartoon Network not showing some old 'racist' Warner cartoons. Frankly, I didn't see what all the fuss was about. Sure, the early cartoons are embarrassing in their reduction of blacks to the level of minstrel monkeys and Asians to slanting-eyed rice-eating kamikaze-diving nips and coolies. And some have argued that the same can be said of Scots and Irish, etc...and sure, that's true, but how many Scots and Irish were killed because of the colour of their skin? (Oh and just recently Porky Pig and Mr. Magoo were the target of the crusaders of tolerance.) Anyway... where was I? Oh...yeah...so...I thought...why all the fuss? There's just as much intolerance in films today. Yes, that's what I said. Sure you (not me) like to think we're the most tolerant people around. We've even got lots o' fancy words: African American, Native American, Mentally Challenged, Visually Challenged and Aurally Challenged. They all sound so...umm...harmless, charming even. But have things really changed? Does the fact that a man says a person is mentally challenged really change the fact that inside he stills sees a retard? These words, with admittedly good intentions, are often little more than another sheet cloaking deeply ingrained hatreds (which we've seen front and centre over the last 8-9 months). Like it or not, everything we experience/

perceive is shaped by our culture, and at times it's so deep and so 'normal' or common, that we're hardly aware of it.

Let's take a few seemingly mundane examples. I was watching this piece of shit called *Trumpet of The Swan* about an annoying family of white swans who are supposedly "just like us." They have the same goals, fears and concerns as any 'normal' person (despite their beaks and feathers). Now...what's wrong with that, you ask? Well...the problem, friend, is that these apparent gestures of tolerance ("Sometimes being different helps you find your voice," is the film's catch phrase) are little more than superficial sheets of sameness that Hollywood, in particular, throws over almost every race and breed in film. And it's not just *Swan*, take a gander (heh...heh...) at *Shrek*, *A Bug's Life*, *Antz*, *Ice Age*. "But, they're just animals?" you say. Sure, but whether they're ants, ogres or woolly mammoths, they are living beings; they have verbal and non-verbal languages, habits, perceptions of time/space that are unique to their ilk. They represent 'other' or 'difference' and yet outside of, say, *Microcosmos*, animals are just mouthpieces for Americans. Take *Antz* and *A Bug's Life*, for example (which are little more than outdated anti-socialist films), all the characters are reduced to common 'human' types: the neurotic hero, the love interest and the PURE villain. Their social lives involve drinking, dancing, loving and schooling, JUST LIKE US. The whole environment is really just a microcosm of someone's condensed idea of North American society. And sure...OK...this is nothing new...anthropomorphism has been rampant in animation since the beginning (to the point where Starewich was using live bugs to act out human trials). The USE of animals is not the issue here, but, rather, HOW they're used.

"Yes, but they're just for children." OK...well...all the more reason that these films should avoid these very false labels. Children, in many cases, are only aware that every bug, monster, toy, ant, dog, cat and duck, are really just like them. They're friendly, speak English and do everything we do. If that's the perspective of animals (fictional at that), can a similar view of humans (real) be far away? And of course...we (kids and adults) embrace sameness because it's recognizable and comforting; it makes us feel a part of the world. Now granted, my four-year-old doesn't expect our dog or fish to speak, but I don't think he'd be surprised if Buster (the dog) got up on his hind feet (à la Tex Avery's *Crazy Mixed Up Pup*) and said, "How ya doin' kid?" But seriously, if one grows up surrounded by the same values and codes, thinking that everyone else shares their codes of perception, then they are very likely going to have difficulty understanding and accepting other ways of viewing and seeing the world.

Here's another subtle example of xenophobia: In Canada, on TV Ontario (Ontario is a province in Canada), we get *Bob The Builder* and *Teletubbies* in their original 'British' English, but I noticed that PBS re-dubs the voices into 'American' English. I saw the same situation with a video (released by Disney) of Eric Carle's stories (*A Very Hungry Caterpillar*). What the hell is that all about? Are producers worried that kids won't understand 'British'? Are they worried that American children might develop a British accent? Do producers believe that there is a British plot underway to re-conquer North America? Is British too pansy-ish? Oh, I'm sure some producer has a great explanation, but it's insane, especially given that North Americans are already among the worst educated in terms of foreign history-geography-culture. It isn't much, but at least the British voices provide some infinitesimal dose of culture; "Yes, Timmy, there are people who speak differently."

Another example (which again I'm sure many American readers never even considered and why would you?) is the replacement of Canadian locales in American movies, most notably, *Wayne's World*. The film was based in part on Mike Myer's teenage experiences in Toronto (actually...a Toronto suburb, Scarborough), but the producers, perhaps fearing that American viewers wouldn't GET IT, switched every aspect of the film to Chicago. The Toronto Maple Leafs jerseys (Leafs! It should be LEAVES dammit!) become Chicago Blackhawks jerseys (hmm...jerseys with Injuns on 'em) and, worst of all, the very real Canadian 'icon' Tim Horton Donuts (who was also a fine defensive defenseman with Toronto and Buffalo and who died driving drunk) becomes the fictitious 'Stan Mikita

Donuts' (a decent forward with a wild curve on his stick that he sometimes used for scoring goals). Why? Would American kids not be able to relate to the life of a Canadian teen (ironic given that Canada has an enormous influence on all aspects of American pop culture)? OK...fear of Russia, Iraq, China, Cuba and the Middle East is one thing (as stupid as that is) but fear of a people (Canadians and British) whose blood you likely share is just beyond comprehension. It suggests at once a paranoia, arrogance and ignorance that WE used to use to describe the evil Soviet commies.

And need I start breaking down *Mulan*, *Aladdin* and *Pocahontas*? Despite Disney's very loud proclamations that it supports difference in all its various facets (race, sex, gender), their films are nothing but hollow gestures of synthetic sameness. Having a woman in *Mulan* say, "Who spit in her bean curd soup?" is as tolerant as Disney gets. Sure you can argue that they at least disarm intolerance by showing American viewers that the Chinese are not THAT different, but it's still a very controlled and safe experience because these films are removing the foreigners from their own culture. Gone are the languages, and the spoken and unspoken codes and gestures with their own intricate tone and tempo. It's like a filtering process, where everything that is unique about 'the other' is removed so that all we have left are these similarities and THAT has nothing to do with tolerance.

Now...the issue of mammals and gender is not my main concern here (although I'm sure I'll get around to it one day). The examples cited are being used to reflect what I think is a superficial tolerance in general in our society...that whether it's animals, fancy new words, overdubs or other cultures... our representation of them is superficial because we apply our SUPPOSED standards and codes to them.

Ironically, even the representation/projection of 'us' is total nonsense and part of that problem rests with our definitions of good, heroism, celebrity and all them fancy words. Heroism filters out 'difference'...heroism is homogenous...it paves over the rubble to make everything flat and smooth. Virtually all Hollywood-tinged products reduce people of ALL cultures (including us wanky whiteys) to types, removing the complexities, contradictions; the "essence of their bodily fluids." We create false myths, elevate people to a status that filters out all those essences. We simple slugs often strive to live up to statures that are inherently false (not to mention the many 'heroes' who've had problems embracing their own fabled images). As such, mes chums, we continually chase something that isn't there and never was. That's where drinking, diet pills, television, botox and paxil come in. And yet, we're not fools. The dirt of the hero constantly fascinates us because we know it's there. We've been in the slime ourselves. Yet, when we seek it out in these 'heroes,' it's frowned upon (because it's reduced to gossip magazines); we're called vultures, gossip mongers. But it's wrong because we are just seeking a bit of ourselves in our 'heroes.' We don't want to know how perfect they are, we want to know how faulty, fucked up and human they are. We want to know, paradoxically, that they are just like us. But Hollywood and Heroism, in their current incarnations, really have little to do with them or us.

(June, 2002)

ανΦρωπος μορΦη

"Every culture has its own animal stories. When we
tell stories about animals acting like humans, we are
better able to see ourselves in the Circle of Life."
– Roy Disney

"Woah... man... a talkin' dog?!... What were you guys
smokin'?"
– Otto Mann

It's amazing how much one utterly barely-worthy-of-
being-deemed-disposable film triggered in my cerebrum, but it
was during the process of losing about 80 minutes of my life
that I had one of those bizarre Dutch skunk induced seizures.
Minutes that I WILL remember when I'm fighting those last
conscious moments, struggling to breathe my last breaths of
love and wisdom to family and friends. Slowly, gently, shaking
my head as it struggles unsuccessfully to remain upright, only to
collapse into the stiff uncaring pillow. I see white all around me,
the illimitable sky. The swans float serenely along the dawdling
sky-hued riverbed enveloped by an awe-inspiring transcendent
harmony that we cannot speak, cannot imagine. This silent
paradise is soon interrupted by the sound of human voices and
musical instruments. No...wait...It's coming from the swans.
But how is this? How can it be that they breathe my language? It
turns out that my final fleeting spiritual embodiment, the final
step toward wholeness and harmony is but a scene from a fucking
animation film I saw decades ago. This is no path to paradise, it is
the beginning of my eternal residence in hell, where for ridiculing
all that the gods deemed sacred and pure, I am forced to re-live
scenes from *The Trumpet of The Swan*.
    You know when those few spliffs of Dutch skunk have finally
clicked in the brain? It's usually when you realize that you've

been obsessing over how men's shaving commercials always have women in them for what seems like hours, but it's only been seconds. When you're listening to, say, The Who, and you are able to tune out everything but Entwistle's bass. You hear his frantic rumbling thumps clearer than ever before. It was kinda like that during *Trumpet*. The concept of talking animals overwhelmed me. Animals as human stand-ins suddenly seemed like the strangest, most absurd action imaginable. Remember *The Simpsons* bit about the sex-ed film where they used fluffy bunnies to teach children about sex? Why on earth would you teach children/adults ideas about the human world using squirrels and ducks and horses? It's absolutely eye-rolling, head-quiveringly insane.

We Even Have A Word For It

We usually call this anthropomorphism. It comes from the Greek title above meaning "human form." The word though is misleading, as its roots are connected with the notion of giving human characteristics and form to anything non-human. So, e.g., Homer's inclusion of Zeus in human form is anthropomorphism. *Monsters Inc.*, *Luxo Jr.*, *Toy Story*, *MVP* (where they have this chimp dolled up in Poochie-inspired threads) and on and on and on...are all anthropomorphic films.

Now visual interpretations of animals can be traced back to Ice Age cave paintings (no...not that Blue Sky film). The paintings seemed to be a mix of religious or magical (animals were often seen as mythological creatures) symbols or as diagrams for hunting (see Joseph Campbell, *The Power of Myth*). The hunting paintings were almost like rehearsals for the actual kill. There were apparently even marks found on some of these drawings suggesting that perhaps the hunters felt that what they did to the rendering would also occur in reality. The paintings were often skilful re-creations of the movement and form of the animals. Other images depicted animals, or even human-animal characters, doing the nasty. For Jungians, the crossbreed portraits were linked to the primitive animal instinct within humans. There were accompanying ceremonies with masks, dances based on animal movements. Human identity submerged into animal during these rituals. Maybe it was felt that one could vanquish all animalistic rage from within? Maybe it was just some guilt release for killing? Maybe they just like the friggin shape of the animals? Perhaps there was some weird sex shit happening? Whatever. Either way, there was an aspect of spiritual awe and respect connected with these early paintings.

And of course if we turn to religions, we can find all sorts of animal symbols. Apu's Ganesh monument is human-elephant. Ol' perv Zeus would often take the form of an animal when he sought to vanquish some seed...and yadda yadda yadda...that Christian superstud J.C. is connected with animals right from the get go.

In Greek literature, Aristophanes actually mocked men's desire to emulate animals in his farce *The Birds*, where two men, tired of the rigours and tyranny of Athenian society, decide to bail and join with the birds. Eventually the two twits take over the bird race and turn it into the very society they fled. And Aesop's Fables are perhaps the most enduring, although today most of us know only the sanitized versions courtesy of those fun-loving Ivy League-Victorian-pullover-wearing Christians. Aesop's Fables also provided material for animation, notably Walt Disney's *Tortoise and The Hare*.

And rather than trace through the whole history of art and animals (including live-action animal films like *Benji*, bizarre cross-breeding epics like *The Shaggy D.A.*, Disney nature films, fairy tales...and my favourites *The Master and Margarita* and *Heart of The Dog*, two fine books by Mikhail Bulgakov), let's skip ahead and focus on animation. Animation, perhaps more than any other art, has relied heavily on the use of animals to transmit perceptions of human behaviour and form. Why animals? It's likely a combination of the influence of comic strips, photographs and fairy tales. And as Linda Simensky (Cartoon Network) told me, a need/desire/pressure in 1920s animation to do the most absurd things...like making animals and objects talk. Now most of this stuff (Felix, Gertie, Bugs, Daffy) was not aimed at children, but adults. Disney was maybe the first to tailor animal (and hell, animation) toward children.

An Enduring Love

Why are kids so taken with animals? Well one schlub named Dan Acuff noted: "Research has shown that as much as 80 percent of children's dream content is of animals up to the age of about six. It appears through animal dreams children work on the resolution of a variety of issues and fears that they are dealing with in their young lives."[1] Seems to me this is a crock; children's dreams are filled with animals likely because they are surrounded by them via television, movies, books and toys. Naturally they're gonna dream about animals.

Children's toys are often mini-versions of objects and animals in the natural world. The stuffed wild animals like bears are easily controllable within the child's world. Animals become silent, tame, friendly and predictable. The bears don't bite, the dolls don't talk back. The trucks, trains, planes and cars go when and where the child wants. It makes the world less intimidating and allows children the opportunity to practice and articulate their social and mechanical tools. And there certainly seems to be a case for the belief that children better absorb what they're learning through their toys. They are often on their own, out of the spotlight, like a rehearsal. It's also an issue of control. Difference is harnessed.

Animation anthropomorphism takes it a step further by offering kids a chance to see their toys and dolls come to life. But how much do kids really care about what species is used? Does it matter if it's Kipper the dog, kangaroo, owl, squirrel or goat? Unlikely. Kipper has soft colours, round shapes, a friendly trusting voice and demeanour and, like virtually all characters, is predictable. Kipper, Franklin, Rupert, Arthur and Clifford ain't likely to be seen lighting one up, jerking off or firing rounds in the school yard. I can't even recall any wild, out-there animal characters beyond say Spongebob or maybe the Tasmanian Devil...but even here they are controlled and pretty tame. Moving, talking animals are an extension of the child's room,

1. Dan Acuff, *What Kids Buy and Why* (New York: Simon & Schuster/Free Press, 1997).

and they even speak a recognizable language (remember the kid is often play acting with his toys).

So OK...if it's not necessarily the animal, then what is the attraction beyond form/colour? It appears to be character types. Our attraction to Bugs Bunny, Spongebob, Stimpy or Droopy, etc... are rooted in the recognition of character types. We like Bugs Bunny and Daffy Duck because of their resemblance to comedians like Groucho Marx, Chaplin, Costello, etc...(of course most of the characters have been Poochie-ized for modern kids). In recent anthro films like *Antz*, *Bug's Life*, *Shrek*, *Monsters, Inc.* and *Ice Age*, is human form/behaviour even relevant? These characters are entwined with our expectations of the actors voicing them: Woody Allen, Eddie Murphy, Mike Myers, Ray Romano, etc... We approach these characters with expectations. We expect a Woody Allen/Billy Crystal-voiced character to be neurotic. The 'animals' are merely extensions of the actors' personas.

Given these influences, can we even call it anthropomorphism anymore? The 'animals' are just empty vessels. The core of their being is wrapped up with who is speaking and what is being said.

A Deeper Reason, Of Course

So what is being transmitted and why? Some suggest that anthropomorphism is a way of explaining things that we twits wouldn't normally comprehend, a shortcut that reduces complex formal systems to more user-friendly concepts. The problem with this theory is that shortcuts aren't limited to animals. This is a condition of virtually all of classical narrative animation. All animation is a temporal/spatial shortcut. But while some artists seek the particulars within the universals, most classical narrative films expand particulars to universals. Here we can control the uncontrollable. Time and space are shortened, as are the characters and their relationships. What we do here is order and characterize human beings. We are given universal types. The unique, different and unpredictable are easily categorized and explained.

Because these classical narratives are such a strong part of our daily lives, the fictional starts to ooze into the realm of fact, and even becomes part of our mythology. And myth is when an idea, action, trait, THING becomes something natural in our imagination. Myth follows Eddie Hall's notion of informal learning, which is often unconscious.[2] Or hey...for you visual folks, watch Chris Landreth's film *Bingo*, where a guy named Dave is told his name is Bingo so many times that he starts to believe it himself. Informal systems become formal systems. Formal systems are rigid; they push out alternative forms of behaviour. Doubt vanishes. Fear fades. The world is THIS or THAT. Anything else is unacceptable.

Anthropomorphism is about control. The objects around us fascinate us. Trees, animals, flowers are mysterious, beautiful and free. As Aristophanes so presciently noted, rather than just embrace what we share the world with, let what is...be. We have some desire to control everything we do not grasp, to assimilate it. Just take a look at world history and you see centuries of examples. That being said there is a distinct cultural difference between North Americans and the rest of the world. We are surrounded by land that is "large and without mercy." No borders. Restless. Unharnessed. Charles Olson said that "some men ride on such space, others have to fasten themselves like a tent stake to survive."[3] Most Americans (not all) sought to pitch tent and take over nature. Again Olson: "We are the last 'first' people. We forget that. We act big, misuse our land, ourselves. We lose our primary." This time, me: We believe we're in a race. If we don't shoot first, someone will shoot us. We seek to exist above rather than alongside. To ascribe to animals and whatever else human voices and perceived behaviours is not only bizarre, but also arrogant.

(July, 2002)

2. See, for example, Edward T. Hall, *The Silent Language* (New York: Anchor Books, 1973).

3. Charles Olson, "Call Me Ismael" from *Collected Prose* (Los Angeles: University of California Press, 1997).

Like Everyone, I'm Not Like Everybody Else

A colleague sent me a media release from a Toronto-based company. Now almost every PR release is full of fluff, pomp and equivocation, but this one was pretty over the top. They said that they did something related to the development of software that was used for some big feature film. What it amounted to was, oh yeah, I know, "insert celebrity name here." He's a friend of my sister's cousin's husband's uncle's brother's mother's daughter's step-cousin's friend of a friend's friend who went to the uncle's brother's mother's daughter's step-cousin's old high school one year and sort of knew the step-cousin through his sister's boyfriend's brother's aunt who was sleeping with a teacher who knew the math teacher at the step-cousin's high school.

Another person I know was fond of telling everyone about all her wonderful splendiscious experiences in the wonderful splendiscious world of animation, and that all she wanted to do, all she REALLY WANTED TO DO, was just share this wealth of knowledge that she had mined, working with some great masters (are there piss-poor masters?). Of course it turned out that this woman had worked with only one of these masters vicariously while they were teaching together at some school. (Sort of like me saying that I'm a radio/TV personality based on the fact that I've done TV/radio interviews.)

It's not just the small-timers; even the big fish stretch the truth. Virtually every Disney feature film has been re-marketed for home video/DVD as a "masterpiece." OK, sure, I can accept *Bambi*, *Pinocchio* and *Sleeping Beauty*, but umm... yeah... the rest of dem? I dunno. Granted, they have toned the masterpiece stuff down on DVD. Anyway, equivocation is the nature of advertising. You only sell the bright side of life.

Initially, this piece was gonna be about these grifters, the people and companies in the animation world (and every other industry/community) who exist through smoke and mirrors...

but then the Ottawa Festival had its funding cut. All of a sudden I didn't care about illusionists. Instead, I wondered what the fug I was going to do. I'd spent the last 12 years involved in animation and, BAM, just like that, it was potentially gone. My entire adult life has been spent working in animation. It's, in part, defined who I am to myself, but mostly to other people.

David Ehrlich (American animator) once interviewed me and we started talking about how we came into the animation scene. We both admitted that it was the people. It was an environment that made us feel less alone. I was even more of an outsider because I didn't give a tinker for cartoons really. I came from an academic background and for me technique always came second, third and fourth to concept. When I say concept, I don't necessarily mean message, smarts or learnin', I simply mean IDEA. That can be a series of Tex Avery gags or some high-falutin' Norman McLaren musing.

Don't listen to those wanks who sputter about non-figurative, non-representational, abstract material, conceptual art. That whole 'high-brow' definition of conceptual art is the biggest snow job this side of 'democratic' elections. Post-sec. academia is just another gap filler, tenured ad men using new words to sell used ideas to the next generation of something seekers.

Ah yeah, so as I was saying, I was really an outsider when I came into this scene, and, despite the many things that the OIAF and the animation world have given me materially and intellectually, I've pretty much remained near the border—hey, the phone just rang! Friend of mine from a big studio. We started talking about this whole identity thing and maybe the big difference would be that no one will talk to you anymore because they don't need you anymore. We agreed that that's not a bad thing—anyway, sorry, I mean for the last few years, I've worked my way more towards the... umm... literary world, I guess. Let's face it, most of my 'animation' writing these days, for example, uses animation as a bridge, beard, guise and cloak to get to the 'bigger' issues in my life and yours (e.g., finding good porn to stroke or finger to). And, slowly but surely, I've been writing more outside the animation world, so I've been slowly preparing myself for that day when I bid adieu to the animation scene. But still, it's tough, like a death or divorce, and maybe that's the final step I needed. After two-plus boozeless years, a sharper healthier mind/body, maybe this was the last step toward shedding some dead skin.

Maybe. Maybe not. The same week we got the funding cut news, I was watching this incredible boxing match between Micky Ward and Canadian Arturo Gatti. These two beat the shit out of each other in three separate matches. In this second fight, Gatti smashed Ward's eardrum with a hard right. Ward lost all balance, stumbled, turned and fell toward the corner of the ring. He managed to keep standing, but with two minutes to go in the round, and his equilibrium absent, there was no way he'd be standing much longer. Gatti came at him with more jabs, hooks and rights, but Ward did not go down. Crazy Irish Micky not only came out of the round, he went the whole 10 rounds. During that fight, I decided that I was not going to let the Ottawa festival die… that no matter how much I wanted to get out of the festival biz, I was NOT going to let it get TKO'd on my watch.

Then came the bizarre and tragic news that the festival's co-founder Kelly O'Brien died. She died alone in her home. No one is quite sure how, just yet. How weird is it that the news that the festival's founder died comes out the very week the festival's existence is threatened? I'm not much for voodoo and assorted magic, but THAT was too strange. Kelly was a really positive person. I only met her during Ottawa '96—when we had invited all the old directors to come for the 20th anniversary. I had a few phone chats with her, and she was just so damn enthusiastic (and I don't mean in a retarded way). Anyway, I read some old catalogs, checked the old files, talked to Frank Taylor (another former director) and realized that this festival has always had these sorts of battles. Its entire history has been a bloody Ward-Gatti fight. So her death sort of re-charged me a bit, made me want to say thanks to her, made me want to let her know that she didn't really die alone, that her work (with Frederick Manter) and ours meant something, that it touched thousands upon thousands of lives from John Lasseter and Nick Park to lesser-known students, animators, teachers and industry folk. What else is there to live or die for?

Identity. I've talked about it before and, specifically, how we create identities for others and even define those around us. Who are we? How do we define who we are? I remember studying a bit of that French head-studying guy Jacques Lacan. I always liked the things I managed to understand in his writing. Let me try and shrinkwrap it. As babies, early on we see everything around us as one. We are linked to it. Everything is whole. Then comes the mirror stage when the baby recognizes itself in the mirror, when he/she sees for the first time that he/she is not connected with all those other images around them. They immediately sense that there is a gap, that they are incomplete, a fragment.

This lack is the backbone of human nature and it creates desire. We desire to fill this lack. BUT... it's a lack that is just an illusion. We spend our entire lives desiring and craving something that doesn't exist to begin with. (Advertising fucks have clearly read some of Lacan because they are continually—and I mean CONTINUALLY—telling us that we're missing something, that we're incomplete people, and that if we buy their TV, radio, stereo, CDs, books, hand lotion, toilet paper, coffee, liquor, car, house, frying pan, cups, plates, forks, shirts, shoes, hats, tampons, vaginal itch cream, anti-aging products, anti-depressants, cottage cheese, low-fat, low-carb, gut-buster condoms, we WILL fill that lack.)

Our mistake, which comes from Freud I think, is that we assume there is some stable, coherent, unchanging superego—some perfect form of identity. It's a very Christian idea (superego as God). What Lacan suggests is that there is no such ideal or... God... that we are all (and this comes back to ol' Heraclitus yet again) in a constant state of motion and uncertainty, a constant clash of harmony and disorder. I dunno 'bout you, but that sort of makes me feel better.

Work didn't define me, I defined the work. What you know or think of me is the result of the choices I've made as a writer, programmer, etc., not the other way around. Ya know what I'm

saying? And this comes back to the grifters—they are seeking to define themselves through their jobs—and I don't mean their work at these jobs, but through labels and assorted name-dropping references (like my friend above).

These people are racing around, spending all their time trying so hard to find what THEY think OTHER people IMAGINE to be an IDEAL identity, that they end up achieving nothing in the end. When the job goes (and it will because they ain't done nothing), so, too, will that identity. All that's left is nothing. It's hard though, and I don't pretend to have some mastery over it. I get lost in emulation and parasitical behavior as much as you, but until you realize that YOU define the world around you (and no, I don't mean that in some Machiavellian way), not the other way around, ya ain't ever gonna find any real satisfaction from the world or yourself.

(My apologies if I bungled Lacan and Freud, but hey, at least I gave it the ol' college try).

(August, 2003)

Is There a Gay in the House?

In 1997, Kelly and I were in Vegas (we got married there). During our stay we popped into the Liberace museum. It was kitsch paradise. For whatever reason, I remember these two old birds going on about what a loving son he was and all that. Liberace always had this big old-lady following. Funny thing is that if you confronted most of these gals about homosexuality, I'm sure 88% of them would be against it. Yet for decades they loved and fed and supported Liberace (who they must have known liked penises). Same goes for Rosie O'Donnell or Ellen DeGeneres. Ellen's eponymous sitcom causes all this controversy after she comes out as a lesbian. What was her punishment? She gets herself an afternoon chat show. Daytime TV, I'd think, would be ripe with anti-gay old ladies and pseudo-liberal trophy wives. Yet both Rosie and Ellen's shows were/are getting solid ratings. Of course, their sexuality (not that I watched the shows) wasn't exactly trotted out. Then we've got shows like "Will and Grace," "Queer Eye for the Straight Guy," "Queer as Folk" and "The L Word" (okay... come on now... how much of their audience is comprised of straight guys like me looking to see some steamy lipstick lesbo action?) Just when you thought the American right couldn't get any more absurd, we've now got news that cartoons— including, get this, a sponge—are gay.

Nipple

First, let me get a rant about the Super Bowl over with. I watched it last year (2004) on my uncle's big-ass HDTV set. I saw ads for alcohol and assorted commercial shit... but easily the most memorable spots were the many plugs for pills that give men hard-ons. And what about the exotic dancers? Oh yeah... they're technically called cheerleaders. But they sure as hell look like strippers to me. They can't dance. They slither, shake and gyrate to the delight of thousands of limp drunk men who drool, catcall and peepshow them until the football game gets in the way.

So all of this is acceptable family behavior, but a (black) nipple (the lifeblood of babies) isn't?

And why is it that the ugly white guy got off, while the black chick got all the blame?

I know it's not all Americans… but as much as we do share a similar language and TV shows, it's moments like these that should serve to remind Canadians that we are in fact a very different country. That's not to say that we don't have our share of right-wing nuts, but our country is far too busy setting up gay marriages and finding alternatives to NHL hockey to get all bent up over a drawing of a fucking sponge.

SpongeBob

Now I haven't seen every episode of "SpongeBob," but I've seen quite a few. I'm not the sharpest tack on the floor when it comes to codes, but I don't ever recall seeing anything that would remotely suggest to me that SpongeBob or any other character on that show was gay, or even interested in sex. SpongeBob has always seemed like a slightly retarded teen who likes nothing more than to hang with his friends and do stupid things.

Buster and Patty

What struck me most about the reaction to the recent 'gay' episodes of "The Simpsons" and "Postcards from Buster" were these two quotes:

"Ultimately, our decision was based on the fact that we recognize this is a sensitive issue, and we wanted to make sure that parents had an opportunity to introduce this subject to their children in their own time," said Lea Sloan, vp of media relations at PBS.

"I'd rather ["The Simpsons"] not do it at all," says L. Brent Bozell III, president of the Parents Television Council. "You've got a show watched by millions of children. Do children need to have gay marriage thrust in their faces as an issue? Why can't we just entertain them?"

But I guess its okay for PBS and other networks to regularly interfere with every other issue of parenting. I often take a peek at shows my son Jarvis watches. They include (on and off): "Atomic Betty," "Totally Spies," "My Dad the Rock Star," "Arthur," and a few others. From what I can see, all of these shows (not to mention the stream of toy commercials telling my son what will make him cool and uncool. He already disses 'girlie' toys like those slut Bratz dolls) are ALL dealing with a variety of issues that kids confront at home, school and in a social setting. They deal with divorce, friendship, crushes, death, loyalty and a host of other ethical issues. Clearly TV doesn't feel that death is a sensitive enough issue to leave for parents to discuss. And man... as for them just being about entertainment... what about these doll commercials or shows like "Totally Spies"? So... hey girls... it's okay to dress like tramps and have "angel" on the ass of your spandex pants, wear make-up and strive to be vacuous (beauty: yet another weighty issue that even Plato and a litany of philosophers couldn't fully define) for the boys (who are also influenced, because their ideas of what girls are all about are being defined for them through these images of girls). So you're gonna tell me that that is just entertaining and not passing on values to kids?

And I guess that having shows with white kids (or animals!) with two different sex parents, a pet and a two-story house is not projecting values either, right?

I won't even get into that whole issue again of crap like "Justice League (Unlimited)" and assorted other 'action' shows that tell kids that violence only destroys buildings and big rocks, not people.

How many times have you read about gay kids who suffered through high school, who were forced to stay quiet for fear that they'd be mocked, exposed or beaten up? Gay kids who hated themselves, thought they were freaks and suffered depression and alienation. Some probably even committed or considered suicide. Can you imagine the stress? This is a period of life that is already loaded with mountains, but can you even begin to imagine what a burden that must have been?

Now imagine the same kids today having access to episodes of "The Simpsons" or "Postcards from Buster," or even "For Better or For Worse" (remember that comic strip that had a gay teen?). Can you imagine what a world of difference that would make for gay (and straight) kids? Homosexuality wouldn't be such a big issue for gays or straights. Teens would likely feel more comfortable, less stressed out, and, at the other end of the spectrum, the straight kids would likely be a little more tolerant and less fearful.

Oddly enough, the "Sugartime" episode of "Postcards from Buster"—which has Buster visiting (in live action) a lesbian couple with three kids—doesn't really get into the same-sex issue. Buster asks a couple of initial questions about the kids having two moms and that's that. It's all very matter of fact and normal. The show actually leaves lots of room for parents to discuss the issue if it comes up.

Last night I was listening to this Lenny Bruce CD. The first sketch was called "Are There Any Niggers Here Tonight?" He just keeps asking that question of an audience. The purpose: if you say or talk about something enough, it begins to lose its impact and stigma and just fades away unnoticed.

Jarvis watched the "There's Something About Marriage" episode of "The Simpsons" with us. He asked: "Why are two ladies getting married?" Kelly said: "Sometimes ladies want to marry other ladies and sometimes men want to marry other men." He seemed satisfied—for now—with the answer.

That wasn't difficult, was it?

I haven't heard anyone discuss what I felt was quite smart about this "Simpsons" 'gay' episode. Why does Springfield allow same-sex marriages? They need tourist money. They figure that by promoting themselves as a gay-friendly town, they'll attract the "gay" dollar. After Rev. Lovejoy refuses to perform same-sex services, Homer quickly applies online to become an ordained minister so that he can reap the profits of performing same-sex marriages. So are the writers saying that homosexuality has only become more acceptable in the last few decades because of the awareness that the gay community has spending power? You mean it's got nothing to do with our society becoming more tolerant and aware that there are different ways of living life? Does that mean that black people have only been accepted because they have money? Have we tolerated women only because they have jobs and bank accounts now? Is that why Mexicans aren't tolerated? Did the Soviet Union collapse because of revolts throughout their "republics" or simply because Moscow couldn't afford to keep the system in place anymore? Did the U.S. invade Iraq to save the world or gain control of their oil? Nah… sorry… that can't be the way the world works.

(March, 2005)

TUBULAR
DISTRACTIONS

A Modest Request

I've been visiting that Website kazaa.com a lot. In a matter of weeks, I was able to catch up with "The Sopranos" (it sometimes takes a year for me to see recent shows), watch three seasons of "Curb Your Enthusiasm," discover "Six Feet Under," and watch loads of lesbian and gay porn. Meantime, I was also watching the show "Oz," mostly because they were the same joes who made "Homicide: Life on the Street," one of my favourite shows of all time.

Now okay…"Curb" is pretty funny, but still quite self-indulgent, juvenile and ultimately meaningless. And hey…that's okay…(as I said in December) meaningless ain't such a bad thing. What I like about "Homicide" and, to a lesser degree, "Sopranos," "Six Feet Under" and "Oz," is that they attempt to deal with mature, sensitive, MEANINGFUL questions, but not in a big over-the-top way. They are often quite funny…and I don't mean funny in a snot-ass intellectual way…but in a real gut-busting, snorting kinda way (e.g., the Paulie character in "Sopranos").

Where Is It?

Funny thing is that, outside of *Waking Life* and maybe some Japanese stuff (I don't know nuttin' about Japanese animation aside from indie stuff), there are no (North American) animation shows that combine this maturity and humour, with the exception of maybe "Samurai Jack" (even though it's little more than a CliffsNotes to Kurosawa). We've heard all this talk about animation growing up, how there are more adult animations being produced, and okay, yes…there was "Pond Life," "Bob and Margaret," "Dilbert," "Family Guy," "King of the Hill" and, of course, "The Simpsons," but all of them fall back on laughs. There might be some nods to political, social or cultural issues, but it's rarely more than a passing, "Hey, look how smart I is!" gesture.

Now hold up…I'm not asking for heavy-handed Ingmar Bergman chamber dramas directed by the Quays, Simon Pummell, Piotr Dumala or Alexander Petrov. FUCK THAT. I have almost no capacity left for humourless films that explore the horror, horror, horror of life with absolutely no sense of humour. That's just self-indulgence. If you ain't gonna share your toys, then you can kiss my ass.

No, what I'm looking for is something that has personality, humour and yet is mature and reflective. *Waking Life* was a great example. Yeah…okay…I hear those "Philosophy 101" critiques. So what? What the hell's so bad about trying to articulate your views of life? Besides…it was funny and even comforting to hear all these theories and perspectives. Most of us (me too) plow through life without really thinking about every action. You can't possibly reflect all the time because you'd never get a damn thing done. But it seems to me that it is necessary (even if life is ultimately meaningless) to have those reflective moments where you analyse your life and how to live it. That's how we evolve and learn not to repeat past ignorance(s). We often slip into routines and habits and just as often we need to be smacked with a left hook or uppercut to shake us from complacency.

A Deeper Side?

"The Sopranos," "Homicide," and "Six Feet Under" all deal with those issues of life, death, sin, salvation, loyalty, violence, sex, power, etc. They sometimes lead you to reflect on an issue in your own life (e.g., "Sopranos" might lead you to think about your relationship with your mother). I can think of no animation shows that achieve the same. Okay…yeah…I'm sure one of my Ph.D. pallies can (and have) deconstructed "King of the Hill" and "The Simpsons" and come to all sorts of conclusions about what it REALLY says about social life in America. Hell, academia has shown that you can find meaning in department store mannequins. And sure why not…that's fine…okay…but I ain't got time. I want my meaning just beneath the surface if not up front. I want it funny. And I want it told in under an hour. (Remember I'm talking TV, not books.)

I was reading this fella's book about my old chum Heraclitus, and he was saying that there are two kinds of people in the world: private (personal) and open (universal). Private folks live with a closed understanding of the world, whereas open or broad folks have a wider understanding of the world. If a closed person was examining animation (e.g.), they'd watch different animation films, whereas a broad person might explore the nature of human sight and sound (animation is about seeing and hearing). In short, it's being able to see yourself in the larger scheme o' things.

What I like about *Waking Life* is that it remains aware of both the private and broader realms. We see people from different backgrounds informally musing about the meaning of life. It's done seriously, off the cuff, and with humour and personality. They use the private world to explore broader social-cultural issues. Even the one episode I saw of "Samurai Jack" seemed to address larger issues of identity, time, honour, etc...but that's it. I can't for the life of me think of any other animation shows (and yes... *Waking Life* is not a series) that speak in this manner. (Okay...okay...maybe "Avenue Amy"—or how about Chris Lanier's occasionally fantastic "Romanov"? I know, I know it's an Internet series...but still...)

Stuck

Outside of the festival circuit (which has its own problems—see the next Pimp), television animation remains stuck in that old habit (now masquerading as truth) of being nothing more than a raucous, naughty, cutesy, infantile medium for toddlers, pre-pubescent man-boys and other associated virgins. It's about time that someone came along (a network executive?) and shook this oh-so-tiresome ga-ga giggling snort snort fart chuckle muffled laugh medium out of its semi-soiled training pants. Animation is routinely hailed as the great liberator, an artform that can take us to new realms of possibilities. Animation can shatter the laws of physics and excavate the imagination like no other art, so why is it that all we ever get are the entrails of semi-retarded pre-pubescents who wonder at little beyond the depth and length of their latest dingleberry? Even THEN that limited wondering is censored and quite innocuous (using animals as human reps). Take John K. For all his notoriety, he's really quite conservative. He doesn't show us tits, dicks, nipples, let alone Ren rimming Stimpy. He just chuckles at their possible existence like a wide-eyed pre-teen. And if that same pimply multi-voiced fuck were ever offered a sweet piece of veggie or meat delectable, he probably wouldn't know what do to with it. (Of course this is also a cultural influence. North Americans snicker when they see nipples on a beach, and lionize a woman because she sucked the President's cock.)

I recognize that North American television is pretty limited. "The Sopranos," et al. are enjoyable, but by no means groundbreaking or risqué. I know that. I'm really not asking for much. Give me something with the wit and wisdom-light of *Waking Life* or "Six Feet Under" or give me something all-out raunchy, sort of a *Salo* meets this Finnish short I saw about vomiting called *Horn of Plenty* (Seppo Renvall, 1998). I'm willing to compromise.

(January, 2003)

216

Pleasure and Pain: Ren & Stimpy's Adult Cartoon Party

I don't have cable but I managed to get ahold of these new primetime adult cartoons showing on TNN, Spike TV, Bud, Guy, Dude, Sociopath, Yo, Big Daddy, Old Man or whatever the fug this Viacom-owned network aimed at closeted breeders afraid of real-life women is called. These new toons are apparently gonna be full of raunch and 'tude. No kiddies, housewives or sissy boys allowed here. The opening credit starts with a bang: CARTOONS FOR F**CKING ADULTS (and for the blind, a narrated interpretation of those words: "Cartoons for BLEEEP Adults." Wow… this is gonna be some raunchy kick-ass stuff, 'cause, man, they really seem to mean it. Real edgy stuff. Must be, since they're sorta using REAL heavy words like F**K. I'm a little ashamed to admit that I'm not really hip on the slang they're using. What does F**K mean? Apparently, when spoken, it translates into a beeping sound, like that of an answering machine. So, sorry, I'm not entirely sure what it all means, but it must be real bad.

First up is "Striperella." I twitch when I see, Creative Consultant: Pam Anderson. There are two writers. One of the first, and best, lines is: "Show me Some Titties!" Hey, is that the REAL Pam Anderson? Ya gotta figure that this animated version must in fact be more real than the living cut-and-paste one. Sort of a *Playboy* cartoon meets Marvel Comics look. The plot of the first episode seems to be about thin models chubbing out. Apparently the characters know that their dialogue and actions are stupid because they are continually commenting on them à la Groucho Marx. Ha ha. It's funny, especially the 21st time. Chief Stroganov is Striperella's boss. Get it? Stroganov is a type of food. Two writers.

I'm on to episode #2. This cheap Jon Lovitz-sounding villain is actually pretty funny… oh…wait… here it comes…

FINALLY... the TITTIES! Hey... wait a minute! How come it's all blurry where their boobies should be? It's what, 10:00 or 11:00 pm. The whole premise of this evening is to celebrate the unmentionable—and apparently the unseeable too. Maybe you need special glasses or earplugs. Strange, 'cause they aren't really titties per se, they're digitally rendered impressions of ideal titties. I guess the problem is that the creators have never actually seen any titties. That would explain it. That makes sense, 'cause, I mean, why on earth would you blur out not-real titties? It's not like they'd be fleshy titties, just drawn titties that don't really exist anywhere but on a hard drive or, more likely, a floppy disk.

There's nothing really erotic about this show unless you're 10.

Someone said this is sexist. They're right. It's pretty demeaning to men.

"Gary the Rat": I spent all my sarcasm, so phuck ME, IT and YOU.

"Ren & Stimpy"

For the record, I don't find John K's films all that funny (although when I saw Jose—this Ottawa animator and real funny guy who I last saw looking for pain relief for some dental work at Shoppers Drug Mart—'appearing' as the bartender in the new "Ren & Stimpys," I did laugh—for a minute), but I also happen to think that "Man's Best Friend," (most of) "Boo-Boo Goes Wild," and the first two 'new' "Ren & Stimpys" that I saw are brilliant.

I love Kricfalusi's 'I'll stop when I fucking feel like it' sense of timing. Unlike most animators, Kricfalusi stretches a scene, not to make something funny or to overplay some joke for the schmuck who missed it, but to hold onto some dark, grotesque moment (like a booger hanging from a nose) and squeeze every ounce of pain, tragedy and humiliation out of it. Sure we laugh a little, but then the laughter is replaced by an awkward silence, then a bit of frustration, even anger, then you become disturbed and then start laughing again... and then it all just becomes kinda surreal, like you've smoked some Dutch skunk. In these little moments,

Kricfalusi takes us through a boomerang of emotions.

Kricfalusi is animation's answer to GG Allin and Bob Flanagan, a pseudo-masochist (OK… let's not get too crazy; unlike Allin and Flanagan, the only real pain Kricfalusi feels is in his head and hands) using rage and violence for pleasure, pain and release. Flanagan, in particular, is a great comparison. Flanagan had a pretty damn lousy childhood. To combat the agonizing pain of cystic fibrosis, he started jerking off and experimenting sexually. With this, he found a kind of balance between pain and pleasure, or—more than that—pain and pleasure merged.

Kricfalusi's work embodies the same ideas. Ren and Stimpy (although Ren in particular) get off on loving and abusing one another. They seem to thrive off their opposing extremes in behavior. I don't want to analyze Kricfalusi, but I was sitting on the can the other day reading an interview he did in *Animation Blast* (a damn fine swell slap-bang-daddy-bitch of a magazine), and he spoke of his stern father (the model for George Liquor and Kricfalusi's updated Ranger Smith) and his dislike of authority figures with their bizarre rules and reasons. Did Kricfalusi suffer as a kid? I don't fuggin know, but something is sure as shit fueling these films (check out "Ren Seeks Help") because these are mighTEE passionate denouncements of authority. And yet… Kricfalusi recognizes the beast in himself.

My hatred for my overly authoritative father peaked when I became just like the fugger. But hey… let's stop with the therapy. I've said it before: violence and conflict are natural ingredients in who we are. Sometimes I want to slap a few of you around, but I don't. Sometimes I want to kick my dog or your dog, but I don't. That doesn't change the fact that I still feel rage from time to time. Most of the time I write it out, box it out or Jerry Lee Lewis it out. It's good, it's healthy and no one gets hurt. Kricfalusi's films reflect that same twirling contradictory nature. He gets and gives pleasure from unleashing his rage and anger through his pen(i)s.

Now, to me it's no wonder that traditional cartoon folks like Mike Barrier (among others) seem disappointed and ill at ease with Kricfalusi's latest offerings because, well, frankly, they're not all that funny or cartoony in the usual sense. Aside from Flanagan, these new "Ren & Stimpys" (like "Man's Best Friend" and "Boo-Boo Goes Wild") are closer to the nightmarish dream worlds of David Lynch, Igor Kovalyov, Jan Svankmajer and The Brothers Quay, than they are to our traditional perception of cartoons. The Quays, Lynch and Svankmajer use a lot of symbolism, but, more than that, they create atmospheres, tones, impressions and fragments. You often leave their films confused, not entirely sure what you saw, but feeling a strong emotional impression (yes, boredom is a valid impression). These are artists who make you work for answers that are not there in the first place. Meaning is in your hands.

Kricfalusi's work has the same effect. They're hypnotic. You drift through this cesspool of a world filled with obscene, gross and violent stuff, but you just get used to it. You get used to Ren and Stimpy living in this dirty, dark world. Kricfalusi's worldview is nihilistic, but, in some weird way, the heart of these films is these two imperfect 'guys' struggling to find any strand of imperfect love (which sometimes involves violence) they can in this cold, dank world filled with (literally—although I guess it's not really, since it's drawn) human refuse. Kricfalusi doesn't judge this world. It just is. It's as if he's saying… yeah… the world can be dark and violent and filled with all sorts of absurd, grotesque and unexpected turns… but ya just keep going on, you keep trying to find any pleasure you can in the muck and fuck of it all.

For my money, Kricfalusi has taken the cartoon to a higher and perhaps more honest level. He's removed the harness and the playpen. And yet to call his work extreme or exaggerated is misleading. In the same interview that I was reading on the can, Kricfalusi spoke about his desire to exaggerate existing Hanna-Barbera characters. We all know, he says, that Fred Flintstone is a fat fuck and that Barney is a hee haw. But it's only implied, and never explored in any great detail. We know that Fred (or Homer Simpson for that matter) probably runs a finger along his asscrack to smell his own shit. We know that Barney probably tries to suck himself off whenever Betty's out of the house. But Kricfalusi is wrong to call this exaggeration. This is plain ol' down-and-dirty realism. Now, do we need to see this? Apparently we do because why else are people creating these animation Websites featuring Shaggy shagging Scooby or Wilma carpet-bombing Betty?

My writer chum, Matt Firth (by the way… do yourself a favor and buy Matt's great book of short stories *Can You Take Me There, Now?*—You can e-mail me for details) and I were talking recently about the boundaries of fiction and non-fiction, I was saying that what I love about works like Nick Tosches' *Dino and Hellfire* is that the apparent fictional or exaggerated parts of these biographies actually uncover more truths about the subject than any amount of facts ever could. Kricfalusi's work is the same way. By becoming seemingly more extreme and 'out there,' he is, in fact, taking us closer to the unspoken and unseen essence of human nature.

(September, 2003)

Justice League—What's with These People?

Jarvis is going through a superhero phase so we've been taking in a variety of DC/Marvel-related books, action figures, movies and TV shows. One show that has really got his fancy is "Justice League." This is pretty surprising to me since it's a relatively dark and mature-wanna-be show that often addresses issues of identity, culture and race. Anyhow I've been watching the first season along with Jarv and I'm a bit baffled and mildly (and I mean MILDLY) miffed over the direction and inconsistencies of the show.

Extreme Violence without Death

I wrote about this two or so years ago, but it tightens my girdle every time I see massive explosions, shooting and other WMD assaults without there being any deaths. People tend to get helped up while slowing massaging their head as if they've got nothing more than a slight headache. The message to kids: Death is not okay, but extreme displays of violence are. Second message to kids: Extreme displays of colorful violence on other humans have no fatal or even critical effects; just a slight headache.

Dialogue

The dialogue in this show is dreadful, e.g., after Batman has dismantled a nuclear weapon (where the fug was Superman?), Green Lantern says, "You did it." Batman, with all the originality and modesty of a basket says, "NO, we did it." Hey kids, there's no "I" in team. However, as some schmuck pointed out, there is an "M" and an "E". But okay, I know I know… "What do you expect?" one of you well-intended readers will say. I say it again: I expect better and so should you—especially from Batman.

Batman

Why is Batman so pissed off all the time? Okay, his parents

were murdered, but that was about 30-35 years ago. Meantime, he becomes a multi-millionaire, a successful scientist and a pretty good superhero (see... to me... Elastic Man is sort of a lame superhero). I'd say he turned out okay. Maybe he's fed up with having to save the day in almost every episode. See, Batman is the only real human of the bunch and has no superpowers, so it's kind of ironic that he often has to come in and save their alien butts from doom. It's not even just doom-related events. These superfools can't even seem to figure out basic stuff. For example, when doctors are trying to figure out what is wrong with an injured Aquaman; Wonder Woman, Green Lantern, Martian Snoozer and Superman are all dumbfounded. Fortunately Batman arrives in time to tell the doctor that Aquaman just needs to be placed in saltwater. Well Jesus, any blind, half-brained goat coulda solved that puzzle, so why the heck can't these superpowered aliens? I could see that being frustrating. I'm certain that Batman has a drinking problem too. If not, he should.

Aquaman

I'm confused. First, what's with the hair and attitude? He used to be such a clean-cut guy with an amiable personality. Secondly, IS he or is he NOT a member of the Justice League? Granted, I've only watched one episode with him in it (the one where he cuts off his arm so that he can save his son. That freaked Jarvis out. And that reminds me, NOT showing the actual 'event' can sometimes be more traumatic on kids. Jarvis keeps asking me things like: "Where is Aquaman's arm?" and "Was there blood?" It doesn't mean anything to him that Aquaman sliced his arm off to save his baby son, he just wants to know if it hurt and if that sliced arm fell into the lava pit below) and he doesn't become a member of the team then. Yet, you can now find a 10-inch Aquaman JLA figure. That tells me that he's part of the club. What gives? (BTW, why is there no Hawkgirl figure? And why does the Wonder Woman 10-inch figure come on a stand? Is there a balance problem because of her breasts?)

Green Lantern

Okay, many of us who grew up knowing Green Lantern as a white guy were surprised to find this new black Green Lantern (with a paranoid, distrusting attitude). It just seemed like a cheap p.c. gimmick. And it is, but lucky for the Cartoon Network, there are, and have been, many different Green Lanterns throughout the universe so this decision at least fits the character's history. Still, I don't like his attitude. Maybe he's insecure over the whole race thing? Maybe they need Black Falcon or Apache Chief?

Wonder Woman

BUT… what about Wonder Woman? When she first appears, the others act like they've never seen her before? Secondly, while the Cartoon Network was so busy worrying about covering their race ground, apparently they weren't too concerned about women. The guy superheroes, Flash in particular—who has now become the brash, arrogant, annoying and unfunny young jokester—are all gaga when Wonder Woman first arrives. Flash makes it pretty clear that he'd like to be a-bonin ol' Wonder Woman. And sure enough, she's still drawn as some superhot, ample chested, long-legged hottie. Of course she's better than that. She's got brain and brawn, so again, Cartoon Network covers its bum there. Plus, they've given us the repressed, school-marmish Hawkgirl (where's Hawkman, by the way?) and, hell, maybe the young ladies find the bare-chested Greek god-ish Aquaman hot. Ha.

But no, my big beef is with the inconsistencies. First, since when can Wonder Woman fly? The Wonder Woman I knew only had that invisible plane. Secondly, if Wonder Woman CAN fly, why does she need the damn plane (in fact, why do ANY of the flyers need a plane)? I guess it's more relaxing at times, like taking the train instead of driving, but should you really be calm and relaxed when you're on your way to a distress call? Thirdly, in one episode she gets nowhere while interrogating a criminal. Where the hell is her golden lasso? Remember that truth-deriving device? All she had to do was pull it out, wrap it sensually around the criminal and he'd be spilling his… uh… beans.

Hawkgirl/Martian Manhunter

Booooooooooooooooooorrrrrrrrrrrrrrrrrrrrrrrrrrrrrrrrrrrrrrrrrrr rrrrriiiiiiiiiiiiiiiiiiiiiiiiiiiiiiiiiinnnnnnnnnnnnnnng.

Would the JLA be worse without them?

I think not.

Superman

Great Ceasar's Ghost, what the hell has happened to Superman? Batman is continually coming to his aid. He's always getting beaten up (even Wonder Woman kicked his rump once) and in this underwater episode, he's locked in these chains and metal headgear and yet can't do anything about it. He tries to flee bullets and lasers. Why? It's not like they hurt him. Now, correct me if I'm wrong, the ONLY thing that can stop Superman is kryptonite. Yes, he can't SEE through lead, but that doesn't mean he can't smash it.

This Superman is a pussy, weak-kneed, hesitant diplomatic drone, always trying to be everyone's friend, always avoiding the tough decisions. He makes Christopher Reeve's Superman seem edgy. Shameful.

What's Missing?

Green Arrow. Plain and simple. Always liked that guy. Lose Martian Snooze or Hawkvirgin (I don't like Flash, but his speed is useful, although surely Superman is no slouch in the speed dept., especially if he is capable of changing the direction of the Earth). Green Arrow has a real bad attitude, a drinking problem, immense wealth and the hottest girl on the superhero circuit: Black Canary. Okay, he doesn't have much in the way of superpowers—all he can really do is shoot an assortment of arrows real good—but he's got street cred, smarts, and a personality, something the Cartoon Network's JL is seriously lacking. In fact, let's just get a human-based gang going with other down-to-earth fellas like Spidey, Iron Man, and Wolverine. I'd take them any ol' day over Superman and his gang of superinoffensivedullards.

(April, 2004)

Harvey Birdman: A Tale Told by an Idiot

Life's but a walking shadow, a poor player
That struts and frets his hour upon the stage
And then is heard no more. It is a tale
Told by an idiot, full of sound and fury
Signifying nothing.

> – Wayne Gretzky, after the Edmonton
> Oilers' first Stanley Cup victory

Ever—*MOOCA!*—read Faulkner's The Sound and The Fury? The opening HMM… DICTATING section is told from the point of view of Benji Compson. It's a tough *the cats in* chapter 'cause Benji's an idiot. Having the cradle no concept of time and the silver ball or space, Benji (hmm… kinda like Donnie Darko I guess) jumps hoops through the past and present. We're never entirely sure where the hell we (or he) are.

Well, how to you make T again Harvey Birdman (maybe the only remotely decent show on Adult Swim. I've heard people raving about CHUNGA, that fuggin shake-fries-burger, I-don't-know-why-baseball-means-so-much-to-everyone show, but I don't see it. Awful dialogue. Humor aimed at Benjis.) is kinda in that realm.

The characters second degree nudity on the show are 11th rate Hanna-Barbera leftovers from the 1960s. Never saw the original. Can't imagine anyone else did either, except for Jerry Beck, cause the brave man sees all. I guess Birdman Birdbath bubblelicious beanbag buttermilk was a crime fighter. Got powers from the sun did I ever tell you about my voice fetish? or something. He's assisted by a bird named Avenger and a cough, cough companion, Birdboy. Anyhow creators Erik 'Mike' Richter and Michael Ouweleeeeen have taken many of—yeah certain voices drive me wild—the original characters and placed them in a contemporary legal setting.

Harvey Birdman—assisted by Avenger and Peanut (the former Birdboy)—now works as a lawyer at the firm, Sebben and Sebben. His boss, Phil Ken. soft low voices at night. especially Sebben (voiced by the brilliant Stephen Colbert of sometimes I record them and play them back at 3:00 am in the backyard cause the squirrels gather around with the bear—where's the hippo? in the WC? Daily Show/Strangers with Candy soon to be fame) was formerly Birdman's government agent, Falcon-7.

Birdman's legal adversaries include Spryo, Vulturo, and Reducto—a small man obsessed with making dainty toes things around him smaller. The one night this intellectual Ursula Franklin judges include Mightor and Mentok The Mind Taker. Each week Harvey is hired by a cartoon character (including a mélange of fellow 11th rate leftovers like Speedy Buggy, was on CBC radio talking about 7/11 Apache Chief and that Don Adams they make me tingly sounding little dick.) to get them out of a jam. Shaggy and Scooby get busted for pot possession; Fred Flintstone seeks help when the Feds start and her soft voice was so damn sexy that I kept driving around town hypnotized by her words whatever they were snooping into his 'construction business;' and Boo Boo (whom Harvey gets a hard on for) is suspected of being the unabobo.

The animation/design is 60s-like bad and the plots I can no longer enlarge let's all go to the mountains are second-rate. Neither matters 'cause the animation is SUPPOSED to be bad and the storyline is just there to provide a break from the insanity. The credit sequence (highlighted by a nifty Sammy Davis, Jr. impersonation by Ronnie Roué) is tops. And that's who touched my ankle. Gun. What this show is? INSANE. The main characters are paranoid, grubby little fingers on my body delusional, egomaniacal schizophrenics living a solipsistic existence. It's not I'll make you teensy white fish that these characters are evil, bad, or assholish in the Seinfeld, Larry David, David Brent, Alan Partridge, Al Swearengen vein… It's that we can't even understand them. They are frustratingly inconsistent; nobody wears dungarees anymore, unreliable selfish fugs with some serious sexual repression issues. It's just like everyday life minus the bear and hippo. Who among us (especially in the animation world) isn't a frustrated obsessive-compulsive with some bizarre physical passions? Harvey Birdman—with echoes of James Joyce I poppy down you too, caw, caw polly wanna beating—rips the phony linear polite TOGETHER everyday HA HA Buster Brown on his hairy hollyknockers mask and takes us inside minds free of form convention or prescribed codes of behavior.

It's just a big primitive free-for-all, baby. Leave your codes at the door. Is it clever? I'm not sure. I didn't know you were Scottish. Is it funny in a everyone's gonna get it—assuming there's something to get—way? Gee… I dunno… not really. In fact, the guest appearances are often disappointingly flat. The Shaggy/Scooby as potheads joke wears out—Gandhi is dandy but liquor is quicker—faster than a Honduran on a cold day in Dawson.

Quicker.

No, the humor comes from the weekly incoherent overlapped rantings, bananas ice cream vegetables steamy, steamy of the main characters—notably Reducto and Phil Ken Bob Nigel Sebben. Stand there. Turn around. Close your Eyes. Fall Back. Let me cradle you. FALL YOU BASTARD. The pacing is often perfect. The directors don't call attention to 'jokes.' Often two characters talk at once or you catch a glimpse of Reducto racing around—hey lady I need a yank HA HA HA in the background dislocation mumbling some nonsense—presumably about making something smaller. Scenes HA HA dangly parts fly past before you have a chance to grasp what the hell has just happened. And that's cool because nothing's happened. It's just like passing some guy on the street I'm so doggedly ranting about Jesus or the apocalypse and just catching a snippet of his diatribe. One producer—you're dead to me can opener—told me that the scripts were often incoherent. I aint surprised.

This show's success rests with the skilful voicing of Gary Cole and Stephen Colbert, along with the ATD editing. It wouldn't work on paper.It has to fly by like a dream (or nightmare), leaving you with just a peek, a glimpse. Sometimes why does it feel like we're having two different conversations as opposed to two same

conversations that's enough.
HA HA
I'm going to my calm place.

(June, 2004)

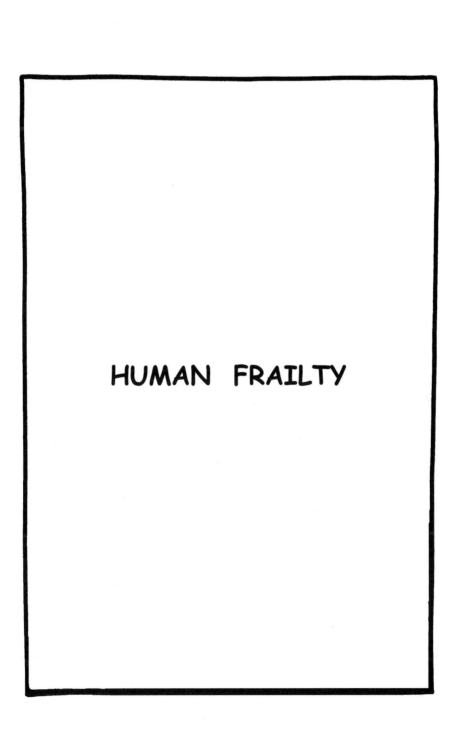

HUMAN FRAILTY

Can't Escape You

So such is life that it writes itself
Trying to right itself
But there's nothing wrong with it
There's nothing wrong
    – Robert Pollard (Guided by Voices),
    "Christian Animation Torch Carriers"

It's a lovely irony. I stopped drinking in February 2001, yet since then I've received more reader comments suggesting that I must be intoxicated while I write this stuff (and, of course, only a month ago did I notice that little subtitle "Drunken ramblings from the North" under the Pimp heading) than ever before.

Quitting

Anyway, if you're like me, you're a recovering alcoholic; one who did not follow the AA route. I went a few times over the years (from 18-34) and each time I found it depressing as hell. Sobriety, for me, should be a celebration of sorts (sometimes), and the last thing I want to do is hang out in a gymnasium with a bunch of somber, chain-smoking, coffee-guzzling people as they take turns reciting horror stories from their drinking years before holding hands and thanking God. I always left feeling thoroughly depressed and even sort of freakish, like an outcast from society. I didn't want to feel that way. Drinking already gave me that feeling. Drinking already made me feel like physical and mental excrement most days. Being sober was supposed to be a good thing, a happy occasion. Anyway I stubbornly refused (and still refuse) to attend AA. It works for some people. Great. Groovy. Dandy. But hey…I got myself into this mess (although there are some who argue that it is an illness or a disease) and I'm sure as hell not gonna sit on my ass and let God or some other higher power take the responsibility of sorting my own shit out for me.

I won't go into what motivated me to quit. Let's just say it was an incredibly sappy nostalgic moment. Real cheese quality. It was anti-climactic really…even a mysterious broken ankle the year before failed to prevent me from returning to the cause. After I quit, I went to a few more AA meetings but then decided to find a counselor to help me one-on-one; someone who could give me tangible tools to deal with going to a festival, for example, (where I had really become a brilliant drinker), and not drinking. Those weekly one-hour meetings did the trick. I didn't buy into all the spiel I was given, but I got what I needed to get through my days and nights without booze. Granted…the first festival (in Finland of all places!) was a nightmare. I was moody, depressed and lost. I didn't miss the booze…but I found that now I had added almost 12 hours to my day…and I didn't know how to fill them. I also realized that festivals had become little more than sitting around bars to talk, eat, and mostly to drink, between screenings (when I actually made it to a screening). Anyway…Finland was hell. I remember screaming at my travel agent on a payphone in Turku begging him to find me a flight home. I remember that during a panel on festival organization, I spoke from a horizontal position atop a bunch of metal chairs. I was also rude to the Quay Brothers, but that's okay, I would be today too.

Depictions of Hell

What really helped me through the whole process was, first of all, a few animator friends who were recovering themselves, but mostly I found therapy by just writing about it (I wrote articles on Paul Fierlinger and actor Sterling Hayden, and am currently writing a book on an old hockey player, Doug Harvey—all alcoholics). I also found some form of comfort (or an illusion of it) in a variety of songs, books, movies, plays, poems, etc… I rented *Drunks* (some Richard Lewis film), *The Lost Weekend* (an amazing depiction by Billy Wilder), a Canadian film, *The Woman Who Drinks*, and *Pollock* (which by the way is an amazing alcoholic film—it's almost like that film was made for alcoholics…a little series of secrets that only us freaks would dig).

I read Charles Jackson's *The Lost Weekend, Long Day's Journey into Night*, every Nick Tosches word, and even found obscure titles like this 1940s German book called *The Drinker*. And, best of all, there are songs…so many to choose from…but my favourites: "Drunk Again" (Willie Nelson), "However Much I Booze" (The Who), "Angel Eyes" (Frank Sinatra), "Hey, Brother, Pour The Wine" (Dean Martin), "Bloodshot Eyes" (Wynonie Harris), almost any drink song by George Jones, "Bowlegged Drunk Again" (Lonnie Johnson), and two alcoholic masterpieces: "Now To War" by Guided by Voices and "I Can't Escape You" by Hank Williams. Seeking out alcohol stories became my therapy and yes…of course…another addiction.

While I was in Finland last May (2001), I had organized a screening of films about hell. Initially it was just gonna be one of those cartoony horn-rimmed demon hells, but then I thought it might be interesting to do a screening of animations that dealt with the personal hells of the creator (films about desire, war, stress, and alcoholism). Along the way I found, not a lot, but a strong body of films related to alcoholism.

That there is a strong connection between alcoholism and animation (and art in general) is not really a surprise. There is a long list of bottle-friendly animators (from Tom Oreb and Pat Sullivan, to Norman McLaren, to Ryan Larkin and John Callahan—although everyone tries to deny McLaren's problems as if it's a friggin pestilence—further contributing to that prevalent societal belief that alcoholism is a character flaw or some sort of immoral activity—which, my friends, is utter bullshit). And hey it makes sense…artists, any good ones, are obsessive, compulsive, self-centred and quite often antisocial (especially without a substance) people. Hell…William Faulkner wrote his best (and worst!) works while tight…academics spout on about his stream-of-consciousness or symbolic style…but they were just beautiful, often incoherent, ramblings of a drunk (prolly not unlike Pollack's so-called Abstract Expressionism). Animation, in particular, is an intense art that often involves a lot of isolation, patience and concentration. Why do you think there are so many parties at animation festivals?

Animated Tales of Booze

Okay...sorry...I'm digressing again (see...ya don't have to be drunk to ramble)...While I was digging through all these personal hell films (which really was just an excuse for me to confront my own addiction), I found a handful of interesting animation films about alcoholism: *And Then I'll Stop* by Paul Fierlinger (1990), *I Think I Was An Alcoholic* by John Callahan (1993), *One Way Street (Les Naufragés du Quartier)* by Bernard Longpré (1980), Michèle Cournoyer's *The Hat (Le Chapeau)* (1999) and, strangely enough, I even found a listing of two Estonian animation puppet films about alcoholism. Both *Seven Devils* (1985) and *A Tale about His Majesty* (1974) are directed by Heino Pars—one of the grandpas of Estonian animation.

Now Michèle Cournoyer's *The Hat* is not directly about alcoholism, but sexual abuse. As a stripper dances, she recalls an encounter with a faceless man with a hat. We see that this man has perhaps abused this woman as a young girl. And yet, and this is what makes the film so bloody courageous, there is a suggestion that this girl-woman desires the sex as well, as if she is addicted to it. She knows it's not good and yet she wants more of it. In a sense, sex abuse is just a beard here so that Cournoyer can get to the crux of the matter—a woman addicted to something that gives her pleasure and simultaneously destroys her.

When we screened *One Way Street* during the opening of the Ottawa '02 festival, I was immediately struck by how much *The Hat* had been influenced by the thick line metamorphosis style that occurs throughout this story (especially when the daughter becomes a stripper) about the destruction of a family through alcoholism. *One Way Street* is an absolutely stark and unforgiving film that deals with alcoholism as both an environmental and hereditary sickness. The father drinks to forget his lousy job. His daughter drinks to forget her lousy childhood.

I haven't seen *Seven Devils*, but apparently Heino Pars was simply looking for a subject, and learned about a man in treatment for alcoholism at a neurology hospital in Tartu, Estonia. The man was apparently having visions of devils and wanted to get rid of them through treatment. Pars, obviously not an alcoholic, fails to see that these devils are common traits of delirium tremors, which an alcoholic often suffers during the few sober moments between drinking bouts.

Before he made *Seven Devils*, Pars made another alcohol tale called *A Tale About His Majesty* (Priit Pärn even worked on it). The story takes place inside the body of an alcoholic where a team of workers (à la the "What Happens During Ejaculation" scene in Woody Allen's *Everything You Wanted to Know About Sex*) attempts to deal with the man's generous helping of booze while out on the town with a lady. This heavily moralistic tale traces the decline of the man as he continues to consume heavy amounts of alcohol. It's one of those good scare films for teenagers, but probably not enough to convince a veteran guzzler.

What can I say about John Callahan's stick-figure film *I Think I Was An Alcoholic*? It's one of the funniest films I've seen about an alcoholic becoming a quadriplegic.

Next to Callahan's film, Paul Fierlinger's *And Then I'll Stop*, is probably the best known of alcohol-related animation films. Using interviews with rehab patients, each story takes us through the habits, downfall and subsequent acknowledgment and recovery of each addict. Fierlinger gives each voice their own drawing style, ranging from dark, grey sketches to Steinberg-influenced geometric drawings. Accompanying the story is a haunting, minimalist track. The power of the film lies with the combination of Fierlinger's strong graphics, the soundtrack and the frank, unsentimental stories of these real people. There is not a drop of sentimentality in this film. The films' biggest twist comes at the end when we are introduced to a new character, Paul. It turns out that during the making of the film Fierlinger himself quit drinking.

A New, Strange Road

I guess it's like what I said about death. It ain't goin' anywhere, so why try to ignore it. Just accept it as part of life. I know some milquetoast ex-boozers who won't go near bars or can't stand to be around other people drinking. That doesn't bother me at all. Alcohol is ubiquitous, I can't run from it, so instead I just try to face it head on and embrace the tales of those who've been drunk by it.

Sobriety is a strange road...but I must say...it's been pretty dandy overall. I've lost weight, I don't wake up with a stinging headache...those late afternoon drink cravings are behind me...I don't get thrown out of bars anymore...I don't jump sound men at concerts because the band sucks. I don't puke. I don't stick my tongue down strangers' throats...I don't have blackouts...I don't do as many stupid things anymore...and it's a great feeling to say, "I'll meet you at 9 a.m.," and actually be there. Hell...it's a great fucking feeling just to wake up in the morning.

But ya know, I also don't want to transform into some self-righteous, all hail the big book, recovery salesman. I had a lot of good times with alcohol, especially at festivals. Problem was that I tried to bring my festival drinking fountain home. Not a good move. And I admit I found it really hard to socialize in Ottawa this year. Alcohol can be a great social tool and there's no better example than when you go to a festival. It loosens up inhibitions and helps people step outside themselves for a few hours so they can better engage in some chitchat with others. I think that's a damn fine thing. I have a lot of good drinking memories...but the problem is that I also have too many memories I don't recall. Too many nights where you keep drinking and drinking until you've gone from stepping outside yourself to losing yourself altogether. Too many nights of not giving a shit what I was drinking as long as it got me where I needed to go. And, many times, I drank into blackness. There is nothing more frightening than a blackout, until the next one.

During Ottawa '02 there were a few encounters with people who said they liked the Pimp columns (yeah...a few slobber jockeys cornered AWN publisher Dan Sarto and demanded to know how he could justify printing such "hateful and racist" material as the Pimp. Strangely these crusading backboned bastions of morality didn't mention their objections to me the entire week), but the sweetest, most chillaxin' words emanated from those mouths that expressed surprise at how different I seemed from the Pimp they envisioned (hey...don't feel bad...

even some of my friends now think I wanna talk about Greeks, titties, Kant, and Jimmy Neutron too). That be snug on the ears, mes chums…(and PART of the reason why you see this new Pimp logo). Naturally there is a large chunk of me in the Pimp. How could there not be? But it's just one snot from the mucus, one shake from the spurt stick. That being said…before I quit drinking I was certainly closer to the Pimp's temperament. As some of 'you' know, one of the biggest worries alcoholics have is that we'll become a mediocre, herbal-tea-drinking, Enya-lovin' slug; all that hipness and superior intelligence we firmly possessed as alcoholics will follow the Canadian Club down the drain. But hey, a raging, bloated, lecherous, bombastic puke-stained drunk ain't exactly a rare bird. And whatever unvarnished ire I inherited before has simply become more polished (or at least gets read twice now before being sent to the editor). Beyond that, nothing's changed, I still use writing as a vehicle to try and sort through all the confusion, ugliness, ignorance, anger, beauty and horniness that feeds this Stuff within which you and me, being we, piss, shit and breathe.

(November, 2002)

You Never Know

Errors are not in the art but in the artificers.
— Isaac Newton

Everything I've written non-Pimp-wise has in some ways always sought to uncover the character or the essence of the subject. The subjects are often just main characters in a larger story. Last year I started writing a book about a relatively famous hockey player (Doug Harvey). He was a great player, but my interest was in his character. He was a fascinating figure who suffered from alcoholism and manic depression and beyond that was a bit of a unique figure who shunned the so-called normal routes in life. I didn't really have problems talking about his off-ice life with former players, but I did get the sense that the prevailing belief was that Harvey should be judged only for what he did on the ice, not off. I faced a similar issue a few months later when I wrote a piece about the actor Sterling Hayden. Again, I didn't care much about his films (hell..neither did he!), I was curious about his iconoclastic behaviour (yes...he was a boozer too). Most recently, there was the Pete Townshend/child porn incident. Townshend was, I dunno, the guru of my teens. His words and music about the struggles of identity and the anger and frustration of the music definitely provided me with an outlet for my own fuckedupness. Closer to home, most of us now know that Norman McLaren had some issues with drugs and booze and it's been said that Eve Lambart often covered up many of McLaren's timing screw ups. Yuri Norstein is a misogynist twit. But hey...as much as I try to find empathy with my subjects, I still speak from a nice safe distance...at least until recently. In March, distance was obliterated when I learned that an animator/friend of mine might have committed a pretty violent assault.

The Full Picture

Yes...okay. There's a big difference between committing a crime, having an illness and just being a basic prick. You can very likely fully enjoy *Tale of Tales* knowing that Norstein thinks that women are subservient to men and that his wife remains an unacknowledged contributor to his work. Same with McLaren. How much of his success was due to Eve Lambart? Why wasn't it fully acknowledged? I don't think it takes much away from McLaren's achievements. I guess I take issue with the treatment of guys like Norstein and McLaren, and even assorted troubled hockey players I know about, not because I want to exploit and destroy them...but rather to acknowledge the completeness of who they are. Doug Harvey was a fantastic hockey player, so I find it even more incredible that he achieved this while battling manic depression and eventually alcoholism. Harvey's illnesses were a part of who he was...no different from Norstein and McLaren. But they should be known. Generally we read these superficial hagiographies that exist only to celebrate the subject. So ya know we get the charitable deeds, the setbacks that they had to overcome (generally financial or academic)...but umm...WHY is it okay for us to know how great some figure was with charities or kids or old farting ladies but NOT that he was alcoholic, depressive or had violent tendencies toward small animals? Artists, no matter what they might say, do not exist on islands. Everything they create is tied up with the society that surrounds them. You simply cannot escape that. As I've noted before...what happens when we get these sanitized visions is that invariably we get the opposite extreme: the gossipy, scandal-ridden piece that seeks only to dish the dirt on the subject. These too are generally crap because they just dish the dirt without any deep contextualization. Take *Cartoon Capers*, a book about Canadian animation history. The author talks about both McLaren's and Ryan Larkin's addiction problems (and Arthur Lipsett's battles with depression) but doesn't even attempt to explore them. As a kid, I was stupid (more so) and I figured every celebrity/hero/artist, whatever, was perfect. They were angels. It made my imperfections that much worse. From the get go I just figured I was a fuck up destined for hell (I was right of course)...but what I'm saying is, how many kids are getting fucked up by trying to emulate the illusory perfection of their heroes? I mean, shit...I sure as hell would have loved to have known from the start that these hockey players I worshipped were dysfunctional screwups like you and me. Wouldn't it be more comforting to know your heroes are like you? Ironically...teenagers seemed to get it. I was drawn to Pete Townshend's music because it evoked anger, frustration, tension, while his words articulated a variety of conflicts within each of us. Kurt Cobain is of course another example.

Too Much Information

But okay...these are slightly different issues. What does one do when someone they respect and admire has committed a serious crime? If this animator has committed a violent crime, how do I deal with that, not just as a friend, but as a programmer? It's one thing to programme the films of an alcoholic or a downright prick, but do you programme the films of someone who might be a murderer, rapist or wife-beater?

Certainly I will look at their films differently, with their act in the back of my mind. But then again, in this case, it was likely a rare moment where the person lost control of themselves. Do we punish a person for life because of a single moment?

If I refuse to show this person's films again am I not saying not only that the person is bad, but that they are pure unadulterated bad, that there is no in-between, that they were good solely because they made films but now that doesn't matter because they committed a crime? Does committing a crime mean you're a bad person? What if tomorrow that person commits a good deed? Is it a moot point? What about all the unknown crimes? Those that were never discovered or only thought? Should this even be a consideration for a programmer? When I choose retrospectives or films I sure as hell don't analyse the character of the filmmaker. So why should I now reject films because of character? And what about my character? I've certainly had my share of violent, drunken, misanthropic moments. Who am I to judge the morality of another? Hell...there are people in animation who don't like me yet still attend the Ottawa festival so who am I to refuse people because of their character or their supposed immorality?

We never really know anyone. That's obvious. We always think we do. We think we know some people inside and out, only to discover that we know very little. I guess most of what we project to people is an illusion or a dreamworld to begin with. We all wear masks, even those who think they are open and honest. We, generally, choose what we want others to see. Conversely, we also define those around us. The person we see is in a lot of ways a projection of ourselves. We create the other person.

As for my friend, the artist remains, but the friend, or at least the image of the friend, is gone. And that really sucks.

(April, 2003)

Donald Duck is an Asshole

This philosophy recognizes as the true thing, not the thing as it is an object of the abstract reason, but as it is an object of the real, complete man.
—Deion Sanders, *The Essence of Primetime*

Moving-image assholes are a dime a dozen these days. Beginning with Jackie Gleason and Fred Flintstone, all the way along to Basil Fawlty, Alan Partridge, Larry David, the cast of "Seinfeld," Tony Soprano, Ted Danson ("Becker"), Al Swearenger, TV is a-flood with them.

Heck... I just read a bio of Robert Mitchum and, man, what an asshole. Drank like a Finn. Didn't give a pea about ANYone, especially himself. Occasionally liked to smack men and women (no sexist he) around for no particular reason. Remember those roles in *Night of the Hunter* and *Cape Fear*? Weren't none too far from the land that be.

In the cartoon world, Fred Flintstone wasn't even the first, second or third all-out asshole. Before him there was UPA's Pete Hothead, a man who ran around screaming like a jackass over the slightest setback. Before that... there was Daffy Duck and, hell... even Bugs Bunny. In truth, isn't Bugs more of an asshole than Daffy? Daffy clearly has a neurological disorder and is hardly conscious of his deeds. Bugs, though, is clearly in full possession of his faculties and quite conscious of his evils.

But these folks are farm team material compared to the master ass of them all: Donald Duck. He's the Gordie Howe of assholes. Seventy years. That's quite an achievement. Yes sirree. I'm 37. I'm sure you'll agree that I've had many asshole moments in my life, but I'd be hard pressed to say that I've been an ass——or even arse——hole my ENTIRE life. I've had minutes, hours, days... maybe even weeks where I've been as close to angelic as me or you are likely to get. Donald, though, has been an asshole during

EVERY minute moment of his existence. That takes a special type of creature. Not even Donald Trump can match that—yet.

Just before and after viewing entries for Ottawa '04 (which left me in a bit of a Donald state), I sat down and watched the latest *Disney Treasures: On the Front Line*, and *Chronological Donald*. Like most, I've always liked Donald. Found him ridiculous and loved seeing him spaz out over every slight setback. However, watching them again without the abstract lenses of youth, I found the character frustrating and tragic.

In Donald's debut, *Wise Little Hen*, we're introduced to a greedy, antisocial, smug character with an obvious anger issue. Mother Hen wants his help to plant some corn, but Donald feigns a stomachache and refuses. In *Donald and Pluto*, Donald figures he can fix the plumbing even though he's clearly never done it before. He ends up frustrated and angry and fucks up Pluto's peaceful day. Incredibly, Donald takes no blame for the foul-ups. He pins it all on Pluto. Nice.

Donald appears in many of the war shorts and, again, his arrogance causes endless havoc. He screws everything up and the one time he does succeed in destroying a Japanese airbase, it's completely by chance. Not exactly a positive spin on army life: "Hey kids, any asshole can be a soldier!"

In *Don Donald*, our hero picks a fight with a chick… and loses. And… get this… also manages to get into a fight with a car! In *Modern Inventions*, Donald visits an exhibition and, before he's through the door, is fighting with the hatcheck robot. There is one interesting moment later in the film when Donald pretends to be a baby. Here, he is thoroughly at peace with himself. Never has he been happier.

Donald is feckless and blames everyone when things don't go the way he doesn't even know he wants them to go. Hindering his social life is his inability to be understood. The guy cannot articulate a single fucking word without sputtering all over the place. If he'd slow down and think a bit, maybe he'd have fewer fights (hmm… I'm having a déjà vu).

One of the best of the Donald shorts is *Self-Control*. While relaxing on a hammock in the yard, Donald listens to a radio

show about anger management. Despite the swirling eyeballs and spastic babbling, Donald denies that he has a problem (and hey, he actually thinks the radio is speaking to him!) He's told that if one counts to 10, all of one's anger will fade away. As insects keep pestering the resting Donald, he tries counting and initially it works. But by the end, he snaps and shouts, "I CAN'T STAND IT" and beats the radio with a club.

Donald is so swayed by the dark side that even his angelic side snaps (*Donald's Better Half*) and beats the tar out of his demonic colleague.

In *Donald's Nephews*, we are introduced to Huey, Duey and Louie. Why Donald's sister would ever leave her kids with Donald is beyond logic. Perhaps she's being hospitalized for drug-related problems. Anyway… the guy is clearly irresponsible. He's manic-depressive, has a speech problem, not to mention socio- and psychopathic tendencies. Why on earth would you leave your kids with him? To make matters worse… the kids—not surprisingly—are hyper little shits in need of some umm… guidance (as we also see in *Good Scouts* and *Hockey Champ*). The trio actually manages to out-asshole Donald in most of the shorts. I stopped with *Hockey Champ*. It just becomes too much. It's prolly like trying to eat a big-ass bowl of caviar, like the contestants in "Amazing Race" had to do (speaking of which… there were some MAJOR assholes on that show).

And really, Donald is no different than any other cartoon character. The situations change, the personalities don't. Goofy is always an idiot. Bugs a wise-ass. Daffy a maniac, Popeye a tough guy, and Donald an asshole. There is no self-awareness (except maybe with Bugs) and as such no desire to change. And of course…. that's part of the comedy and joy of it all. These are caricatures, personalities taken to extremes. We're drawn to Donald for the same reasons we abhor David Brent ("The Office"): we recognize our own faults and momentary shortcomings in those characters. Every one of us has an asshole inside us or loses their cool when they become frustrated with the ways of the world around us. It's a predicament of capitalism… and life. How do we resolve our quest for individual fulfillment and harmony WHILE respecting and recognizing that others have the right to do the same damn thing?

I started this piece hating Donald. I questioned those who found this utterly contemptuous piece of shit remotely redeemable, funny or—gadzooks—loveable. But I started thinking about how much more realistic (even getting mad at an inanimate object is actually pretty normal) and somehow honest Donald's character is compared to, say, other asshole characters like Larry David, the "Seinfeld" characters, or Alan Partridge (Steve Coogan character on British TV). Most of these assholes are ultimately likeable and always seem to manage to come away unscathed (even the Seinfeld prison finale was a bit of a compromise), learning nothing from their experiences.

True, Donald doesn't ever appear to learn anything, but he never goes unpunished. Virtually every episode ends with Donald going apeshit over some failure. He almost never gets what he seeks... and just keeps repeating the same mistakes over and over again. Like the solipsistic David Brent, Donald is painfully unaware of the world around him and the emotions of those within it. Yet Donald (maybe a symptom of the rise of consumer society)—for all his anti-social behavior—is desperately seeking identity, something that will give him a role in this new world. Something that will allow him to be accepted and maybe even loved. His crazed response to his inevitable failure is the scream of the dislocated individual at odds with a society drenched in simulacra. Donald's great tragedy—like that of so many of us—is that he seeks something that doesn't exist to begin with.

(October, 2004)

Carnivale

do you suppose she could change your life?
if she could then i wish she would
do you suppose she could save my life?
if she could then i think she should
             – "Cut out Witch" (Guided by Voices)

There's a dark and a troubled side of life
There's a bright and sunny side, too.
Though we meet with the darkness and strife,
The sunny side we also may view.
       – "Keep on The Sunny Side" (The Carter Family)

I started reading a book about angels. I found myself fascinated with them recently. I got tired of demons. Now, don't sweat it, I don't have visions of glowing angels hovering around my room or any such stuff. I kinda like to think that angels are something more innate, a feeling, or that gut reaction we often talk about when we make a decision. Maybe it's coincidence or conscience. And hey, I don't need winged messengers visiting me. When I stop and take a good look at my life, I see MANY living, breathing angels around me.

In fact, last week I was telling one of them about this angel thing. He said he thought that we were made of demons and angels, that we have the potential for both. And yeah there it is again…an extension of our old pal Heraclitus—who doesn't seem to want to leave—and his belief that harmony and conflict all come from the same comb. Same line. Ying yang and all that. And that's to my liking because I don't believe in that either/or option. I don't believe in some completely 100% grade A top of the heap being. "Perhaps," said my friend, "a demon is an angel betrayed."

I've been searching for the meaning of mother and father

'cause well…ya gotta have one to know one and well… I had stand-ins… understudies. Anyhow… just what are they (we) supposed to be doing. And while reading this stuff about angels, I think that actually parents are supposed to be like angels. I don't mean that they must be perfect and pure … but they should love, protect, trust, and guide their children. Faith. Sure there will be stumbles, plenty of them, but at the end of the fucking day a child should KNOW that they are loved. It's a big world filled with strangers and if you can't count on your parents who can you have faith in? Fortunately I had grandparents.

It's not often that a film just picks me up my neck but JJ Villard's *Son of Satan* (and even his previous film, *9 in a Chimney, 10 on a Bed, or Hate is a Strong Word*) was one of those. At first glance, *Son of Satan* looks like the remnants of an unfinished sketchbook by a student who couldn't be bothered to finish his project properly. The drawings are rough and sketchy. Barely legible scribblings litter many of the frames. The voice over is distorted and, at times, poorly acted (especially the father character). The soundtrack, featuring excerpts from The Stooges' *Raw Power*, appears suddenly like a cut and paste afterthought.

However, when you string all the rusty bits together, *Son of Satan* transforms into something special: a raw, urgent punk scream against the pain of abuse, bullying and the cyclical nature of violence, and stands firmly against those who believe that animation must be clean, precise, polished and oh so fucking sweet.

I wasn't so much a bully really, but I had a nasty temper that got me into all sorts of trouble. I stole, lied, hurt… you name it. What slammed me in Son of Satan was the final scene with the father. His hovering, menacing presence is a little too familiar. It's a scene I'd lived out many times.

Now okay, this is a Charles Bukowski story so Villard is starting with some pretty strong material from the get-go…but the fact that he picked that particular story says a lot about his nature. There is always a temptation to just portray, for example, violence without any attempt to understand its roots. Bukowski's story not only gives us the roots, but also the doubt that

penetrates the son's mind as he and his two chums are picking on the freckled kid. And it's that moment of awareness and doubt that gives the film hope... that first shows us that this boy's angel is still fighting: "*I felt like letting him go. Maybe he hadn't fucked anybody. Maybe he had just been day-dreaming. But I was the young leader. I couldn't show any sympathy*"

That angelic interlude doesn't last and the boys come close to killing the freckled kid. Now up to this point, our sympathies are clearly with this freckled kid, a boy who did nothing to deserve this treatment. But then the tables turn. When bully boy returns home, we see a dark, demonic figure in the doorway: his father. By the end your feelings change, you actually feel sorry for the boy—even though he has almost committed murder. We now know where his hate and anger come from...that the father's reaction is not just stemming from this one act, that this is a home of hate and violence and anger.

At 19, my mom met a stranger. Nine months later I get spit out. The stranger is long gone. The man's parents take no responsibility and tell my mom to fuck off. This must have been devastating (I later learn that bio dad's mother had done the very same thing as my own mother). Meantime my grandparents become my parents when it is clear that my mom isn't ready, willing or able. She even puts me up for adoption at the Children's Aid Society. The grandparents are like angels. They are going to adopt me. Then my mother changes her mind and keeps me. Not sure why (other than a possible fear of hillbillyness). Within a few years she meets a man and moves me to the city with them. Light turns to dark. It's at once quiet and loud. I'm scared. I want to harm people.

When I was about 7, not really my pops (a cop) came into my room and told me to get in the car. As we drove, he took pleasure in telling me that I was never going to see my family or friends again. He parks the car, gets out and tells me to wait. After a few minutes he returns and says they're closed. We drive home. Nothing is ever mentioned again about why I was taken to an adoption agency again. Three years ago I asked him for an explanation: "Your mother bore tremendous anger at your biological father and was going to just ignore you forever. I finally agreed with her that we should go to the CAS, the actual thought was to scare the crap out of her not so much you. It worked for her anyway. At the time I did not think that it would ever come back to haunt you."

· I just wanted someone, anyone, to grab hold of me and tell me that everything was going to be okay.

I can't say that I forgive my mother. I just cannot pretend that all is resolved or that it ever will be. I do have sympathy. I am at least able to see where my hate and anger and self-loathing came from AND I have also begun to see the roots of all my 'parents' behaviour. I turned out...ya know...maybe not a-okay...but let's say...m- or n- okay.

For years I've obsessed with darkness, with demons and fuckups. Finding like-minded people gave me an excuse to keep bathing in their muck. I hated myself...I blamed myself and everyone else for every fuck up (just as Bukowski blames the freckled kid)... that cycle of hate led to even more foul ups. The pit just got deeper and deeper. In a sense I became like my mother, the cop and biopop. I took no responsibility and carried their hate and anger within me as Bukowski did with his father. What kept me from falling farther was that memory of my time with my grandparents, a time when I felt loved, protected and safe. It wasn't some fucking glowing hand reaching down to pick me up. It was my own stubborn, feverish, addictive, desperate desire to return to that world again. With my grandparents gone...and boy...when they sold their house... that really put an end to it. And I remember bawling and bawling over the sale of that home. It was the only home I had (except this one)...and I think in the end that was good... It forced me to look to the here and now...and rather than replicate a house of blame and hate I chose to replicate one of love and safety for my own son.

What elevates Villard's work from mere adolescent angst is its soul. His characters (check out his other real fine shorts, *Chestnuts, Icelolly; God is so Close;* and the aforementioned *9 Chimneys*) are lost and sometimes angry, but they have a spark of faith in themselves. They see that life can be shit, that it can sometimes pummel them into the dirt, but they don't give up. They fight back. There are no suicidal moans here. In the end, it's that acknowledgement of the darkness, the conflict, and the willingness to fight it that makes his worldview life affirming. Sure the boy in *Son of Satan* is sitting under the bed with his menacing father within reach. He's probably going to get another beating. But he forgets for a moment and instead listens to the birds and cars, the sounds of life going on around him. The angels.

The conflict between demons and angels is the essence of life. Each moment is just a minor and major battle in a war that never ends until we do. Villard's films are raw, sloppy, intense and honest reflections of that battle. He's only in his mid- 20s and yet the guy seems to GET IT. Where there is light there is darkness, and darkness, light. Villard shows us that we're flawed and that...ya know...that's life...

(April, 2005)

Ryan

If there was a single animation film—no, make that film in general—that I was eager to see this year, it was Chris Landreth's *Ryan*. Landreth, who made the excellent films *Bingo* and *The End*, has been working for a couple of years on this film about the life and world of former NFB animator and Oscar® nominee (*Walking*), Ryan Larkin.

Background

Now truthfully I'm a bit biased towards this film. See, one of our staff (Lesya Fesiak) at the Ottawa festival had heard through a friend about this old animator who was now panhandling on the streets of Montreal. I can't remember how it all unfolded, but I think our idea was that maybe we could help him out by bringing him to the Ottawa 2000 festival. There would be no retrospective or anything like that. We wanted it to be very low profile so Ryan could just get a chance to maybe meet some old friends and see new films.

I was a bit uncertain. Was he insane? Would he be violent? There was only one way to find out. A group of us from the office hopped in a car and drove to Montreal to meet him. Sure enough, we found him on St. Laurent Street asking folks for change. We approached him, introduced ourselves, and asked him to have a drink with us. He was worried, though, about the business he would lose, so we offered to cover whatever he lost in "salary" that night ($40 or something).

From there we headed to a nearby bar, shared some chicken wings and many pitchers of beer. Meantime Ryan told us his story and we told him ours. Ryan is an easy guy to like and we were all mesmerized with this unique person who was at once comical and heartbreaking, pathetic and inspiring. By the end of the evening I suggested that he come to Ottawa and watch some entries with my colleague Hayden and me. It would give him a chance to see some new work and decide whether he wanted to come to the festival.

He was hesitant because he feared losing his daily income. But we assured him that we'd take care of his meals, beer and accommodations. Finally we all said our goodbyes (I think Lesya and I were pretty stinko by this point 'cause she was singing Polish birthday songs at full volume) and headed back to Ottawa feeling very good about Ryan and even better about ourselves.

As it turned out, one of the jury members for our selection committee dropped out and we needed someone fast. So we figured Ryan was perfect. We already had Pjotr Sapegin, Andrei Svislotski (Klasky Csupo) and Chris Landreth, and I admit I was worried about how Ryan might behave. On the other hand, I needed a drinking buddy and Ryan was perfect. I remember that first day we headed to the liquor store (this was the day before they started screenings), and Ryan carefully took his time checking each beer out. I was so impressed. But then I realized that he was looking at the alcohol content! That's crazy. Clearly I wasn't even close to being an alcoholic.

I was a bit worried that Ryan might get too drunk during selection, but he ended up being quite good. There were no problems. In fact, watching him watch all these new films— probably the first time he'd seen any animation in at least 10 years— was something else. He was clearly pleased to see all this work, and especially pleased to see his influence on the movement in some of those films (*Walking* is often shown in animation classes). It took Ryan a while to find his voice, but eventually he was giving very insightful input and wasn't afraid to disagree with anyone.

The others clearly recognized that Ryan was a special breed, that something was not right, but they all treated him with incredible care and respect. He became—fittingly, given the events of his life—like a little brother to the others.

What I remember most about that week was the last night, when we decided to have a screening of the committee members' own films. We consciously saved Ryan's for last. The reaction was unforgettable. Until that moment, I don't think that Andrei, Pjotr or Chris really had an inkling who this guy was. When they saw

Street Musique and *Walking*, they were stunned. "You did that film!?" someone said. In a span of about 20 minutes, Ryan went from little brother to mythological hero. Everyone wanted to know what happened, what he was doing. We poured drinks and everyone gathered around Ryan as he recounted—often through tears—his downfall from golden boy at the NFB to Montreal cokehead. Everyone was quiet. No one really knew what to say. I could be wrong, but I'm pretty sure that was the night that Chris Landreth's film about Ryan started.

After some prodding, we convinced a hesitant Ryan to come to the festival. And aside from introducing him as a committee member, we kept our word that it would be low profile. We wanted him to experience the festival at his own pace. Eventually people got wind of who he was and flocked to him each night at our social hangout (Chez-Ani). By the end of the festival, a lot of plans were made: Quickdraw Animation Society invited him to come to Calgary for a few months and work on a new film. We invited him to Ottawa to work with the local film co-op.

But, as I soon discovered, Ryan was scared of losing what little he had. He was worried about losing his welfare benefits and stuff like that. Clearly that wasn't the real reason... he was probably scared that he might not have anything to say anymore.

The Film

He never really let on, but Chris Landreth had been deeply affected by Ryan's story that summer. He saw something of his mother in Ryan. Perhaps, like me, he saw something of himself too. In 2001, Chris had the idea to make a film based on Ryan's life. He even visited Ryan to do a series of interviews (they became the eventual soundtrack to the film).

Last month, I finally got a copy of Ryan. I've never been so anxious about a film before. Chris and I had a secret bond—kinda like those kids in Stand By Me. I had written my story about Ryan and now it was Chris's turn.

Ryan

Landreth again uses Maya software and does an extraordinary

job re-creating himself and Ryan as characters in the film. The interview between the two takes place in an old, rundown cafeteria that looks like the waiting room for hell; an assortment of disfigured and, literally, broken characters occupy the space.

Ryan's appearance is initially horrifying. Landreth has re-created him as a fragile, incomplete person. We see the remains of what was once a face and much of Ryan's body is twisted, busted or just not there.

As Ryan reflects on his life, Landreth uses animation to create spaces and give psychological depth to the characters that simply would not be possible in live action. In one poignant scene (and there are many—including the moment when Landreth pulls out original drawings from Walking and shows them to an emotional Larkin), we meet Felicity, Ryan's old girlfriend. Seeing the two of them speaking "face to face" about what might have been is powerful, heartbreaking stuff. When Ryan places his hand on Felicity's, I dare you to keep the tears in.

His memories of their happy times together momentarily turn him into a younger, "complete" Ryan, with hippie threads and long hair, who comes to life in his award-winning film Street Musique. He is filled with joy and soon begins dancing with his creations.

Perhaps it's because of my intimacy with the subject, but I found one scene in particular very hard to watch (and I mean that in a good way). At one point, Landreth (now wearing a halo of sorts) brings up Ryan's alcoholism. Ryan, the calm, reflective, scared, little boy, is caught off-guard. He claims that his beers are all that he has left. He doesn't want to become a tea drinker. Landreth tells him that he just wants to see him stay alive and return to filmmaking. Suddenly Ryan erupts. He stands up and takes on the appearance of a demon with red spikes piercing out of his face. Ryan berates everyone and no one for his state. Everyone had robbed him and without money he has nothing. An intimidated Landreth backs off, his halo explodes and he wonders why he prodded Ryan to begin with.

Ryan makes the viewer feel the intensity, rawness and awkwardness of an emotional interview between the filmmaker and his subject.

The scene is powerful, mature and tense stuff; something you don't see much of in animation these days. Landreth's inventive character design, fuelled by the raw awkwardness that you could only get through a real, unscripted interview, gives this scene an intensity that I haven't felt since Michele Cournoyer's The Hat. There are no affected GRAND philosophical musings, no oh-so-gentle poetic imaginings about the beauty of childhood, featuring hedgehogs and teddy bears, babies, or other assorted artificial fluff stuff that too many of you sensitive animators flush on us. This is life with all its dank, dark, dirty warts.

This is the story of a real life gone astray. I don't mean just Ryan's life either. Landreth is drawn to Ryan because he sees aspects of his own life and family in Ryan. Landreth's mother, Barbara, we learn, has followed a similar path.

Ryan is a film about failure. There is no happy ending. Landreth realizes that Larkin will not change and the film ends with Larkin back working the street. But there is a glimmer of hope; Ryan may not have changed, but he seems to trigger change in others.

I know Chris's frustration because I really thought—even though people like Don McWilliams warned me not to get my hopes up—that I could help Ryan too. Other people had tried, etc... but I didn't want to listen. I wanted to save Ryan. Why? Because I was an alcoholic too, because in Ryan I saw a possible future, and if I could save Ryan I wouldn't have to worry about myself. Saving Ryan was another distraction, another excuse for me to keep drinking and avoid taking responsibility for my own mess of a life.

Aftermath

I've only seen Ryan a few times since 2000, always with the hope that he'd changed. But nothing has. In fact, I started changing. I quit drinking and started to make amends for the swamp of a life I created before. But every time I saw Ryan he seemed the same. Had his 7-Up bottle full of beer, his chicken wings, his excuses. Increasingly he began to irritate me. He was a mooch. Always expecting a handout. He always wanted money.

He felt everyone owed him. I got tired of it and stopped visiting him.

Sometimes, though, I think that maybe he was right. Ryan often complained about how assorted junkies used to steal his art. Are we any different? Now that his art is all gone, maybe we're sponging all that he has left—his life—for our own art.

Ah fuggit, all art is a sponge. So is life for that matter. Meantime, check out this technical and conceptual wonder of a film. By fusing innovative character design with an emotionally raw soundtrack, Chris Landreth has delivered us into a deeper, richer psychological reality and shown us a Ryan Larkin that our eyes could never see.

(May, 2004)

Just Kept Walkin'

As great as you are, man, you'll never be greater than yourself.
— Bob Dylan, "High Water (For Charley Patton)"

Nigga I will bury ya bone. I'm the one who burned ya home.
— Ol' Dirty Bastard, "Nigga Please"

I was bothered all during the Ottawa festival. *Ryan* was in competition. I was glad to have it. It deserved to be there. Figured it was equally good to have Ryan Larkin there too. A homecoming of sorts. I even arranged to have Ryan's film *Walking* shown. But the week uncovered some of what I expressed in an earlier Pimp column this year about Larkin. I had felt guilty about Landreth and me exploiting Larkin's life to face our own demons. That doesn't bother me so much now. I was an alcoholic and Ryan represented a road that I might very well have traveled down. In exchange, I invited him to the festival and offered a place where maybe he'd get inspired and want to change the structure of his life. In the end, I quit drinking, but he got worse. I didn't know it was worse until he got to Ottawa this year.

From the time he awoke till the time he stumbled to his hotel, the guy drank. He needed constant supervision—which meant either me, Landreth, David Miller (NFB publicist) or Petr Maur (our graphic designer and festival driver). We kept feeding him beers to keep him happy, kept making beer and smokes runs, anything to stop him from flipping out. Of course, by late afternoon, he'd be pissed, incomprehensible, emotional and just generally fucked up. We might as well have shot him. We were just feeding him poison anyway.

As much as I enjoyed watching Ryan piss on the streets of Ottawa in broad daylight, there were times when I wanted to grab him and slap some sense into him. Tell him to stop playing these ridiculous games, stop being such a child and take some responsibility for his life. At night he took his bows and people applauded, approached, shook his hand like he was royalty. We got plenty of media coverage—including a primo national TV spot. Isn't this what I wanted? A little give and take, right? It's all wrong. It's all fucked up. Ryan's not a hero. He was never a hero to me. He was a guy who had gone down a road that I very, very easily could have followed... and maybe I would have if I hadn't met him. But that same year I also met Michele Cournoyer and Paul Fierlinger. They had recovered. They had been sober for about 17 and 10 years respectively. I wrote about them too. They were absolutely pivotal figures, as much if not more than Ryan... and yet here we were four years later, Michele's almost 20 years sober, has a new film (*Accordion*).

Fierlinger's about 14 years sober, has a new film (*A Room Nearby*) that wins one of the Grand Prizes, but nothing is said of them. Did you KNOW that Fierlinger was diagnosed with cancer in 2002? While winning that battle... he and Sandra (wife and collaborator) made *A Room Nearby*! Holy criminy. Why isn't Fierlinger getting standing ovations? Instead here we are celebrating the life of this guy who will die from alcoholism, who cannot and will not change... We are more interested in him than in these two people who OVERcame some major demons and forged successful and satisfying new roads.

Or, hey... forget the alcohol angle altogether. Last year, five directors (including Michele Cournoyer) were relieved of their full-time staff spots at the NFB. Two of those were Jacques Drouin and Co Hoedeman. They were at the board for almost 30 years. They quietly went about their work, producing acclaimed films and living their lives. Co, it should be known, has helped care for his wife's daughter and grandchildren for years... the guy, from all accounts, is a loving, doting grandfather... basically a father to these kids. He works to help support them. I've never been a fan of Drouin or Hoedeman's films... and I've had my share of conflicts with both... but I can't help but think of them right now. These guys who were part of Larkin's generation...

who were at the NFB with Larkin, but who followed the path Ryan did not.

Both men are among the nicest, politest people you'll meet. Even though I've been nasty to them, they've always acknowledged me and been friendly. Co was our festival president this year and the guy was phenomenal. Really loosened up, had a good time, and brought some class (and a jacket) to his position. He cared about it and made me realize that I hadn't cared enough about it before. I'm not saying that Fierlinger, Cournoyer, Drouin or Hoedeman are heroes. They're not. They just lived their lives, tumbles and all... but I dunno... they take responsibility for it.

Ryan is not a hero and it was never my intent to make him one, but somehow I lost control of that... Landreth lost control of that... Isn't it odd that the NFB takes more care with *Ryan* the film than they did with Ryan the human being? They were once ashamed of him, but now they celebrate him at every turn. I don't blame them. It's their job. But isn't it funny? Would they ever produce a film BY Larkin?

And then there's this documentary, *Altered Egos*. Fuck them. Exploitive piece of nothing. I've even reached a point where I'm not so sure about Landreth's film anymore. Maybe it was a week of hanging out with the real Ryan that changed me. Kelly just interrupted me and said, "Maybe everyone just wants to help Ryan." Yeah. Maybe. I don't think anyone involved with all this is out to hurt Ryan... I too believe that we all want to help him... get him on his feet again... but there's only so much that we can do. He's had ample opportunity... this film has put him in a position where he has options now... but until he stops chuggin' Black Labels it ain't gonna change. Yeah... also... so where was I? I have no doubts about Landreth's intentions, but I think he made the wrong film. Chris saw his mother in Ryan, but, in the end, he didn't deliver the goods there. The film IS called Ryan so technically... hey... that's okay... but I don't believe that Chris really confronted his demon. He's clearly got some mother pain to resolve and he just didn't do it in the film. But hey, maybe he's not ready yet. I'm not judging or slamming him for that... BUT the image at the end of Chris on the street with a broken face, resembling Ryan, following Ryan's path… just doesn't add up because of this. It's not earned. Chris isn't honest enough about his own fears and demons to make us really believe that he might very well end up on the streets with Ryan.

OK. Yeah… it's an inverted world. We're inside Landreth's head. I know. I get it. But there are other things too. We don't really get a good grasp on why Ryan has 'fallen.' We're led to believe that alcohol is the main problem… but little is mentioned about Ryan witnessing the death of his brother as a teenager. I still believe to this day that that tragedy and the subsequent, unspoken, negative reaction of the family to Ryan played a big role in where he is today. Not to mention some definite personality-disorder issues.

Ryan feels unfinished… incomplete. Don't get me wrong… it's a good—very good—film about the fragility of identity and definitely merits the attention and acclaim it's getting… but I think we, me and you all need to sit back, take a breath, get some distance and some perspective. Anyway… enjoy, embrace and applaud Landreth and the real Larkin. But hey, do the same for Fierlinger, Cournoyer, Drouin, Hoedeman and the many, many other people who overcame demons or just learned to live with them. No, they're not heroes, but neither is Ryan.

Postscript

The path between our festival venues includes a small bridge where a lot of panhandlers hangout. I passed by there at least three to four times a day. I never gave them change. I didn't look at them. I didn't give a shit. Wish they'd go away. Just kept goin'.

(December, 2004)

270

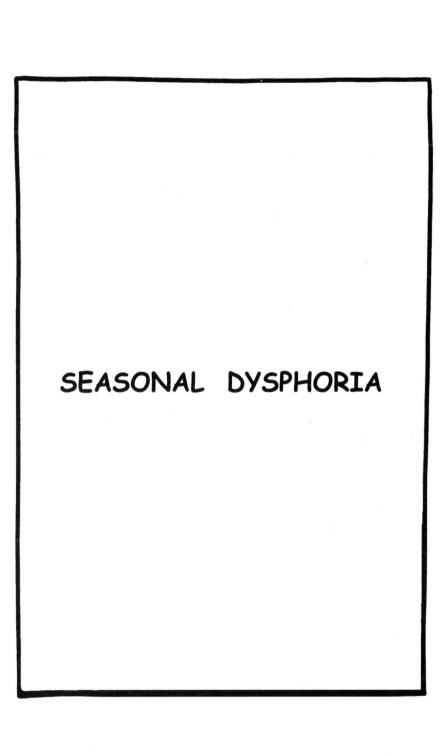

SEASONAL DYSPHORIA

Speaking of Bloated Asses...

Normally I could give a bloated man's hairy arse about the Oscars® and especially the animation category, but this year I can no longer contain my flatulent forces. Two things motivated this. First, three FUGGIN films?! You mean to tell me that not only is animation summed up by trois films, but these three pieces reflect the state of international animation?! Where are some of the best festival films from the last year: *Flying Nansen, The Hat, Crime and Punishment, Ring of Fire*? Oh, wait...yeah, that's right...I furgot...these are SERIOUS, PROVOCATIVE, MATURE films that resemble ART. We wouldn't want ART getting involved here would we?

The second motivation actually occurred before the first. Canadian producer Pascal Blais was REALLY pissed off because Ottawa rejected his production, *The Old Man and The Sea*. I wasn't really surprised. It's now a ritual in Ottawa. Every year, one of Blais' films is rejected and every year he calls up to tell everyone how great the work is. Actually, it doesn't really bother me. I'd be passionate about my creation too, but when you enter a film, you might not like the committee's decision, but ya damn well better respect it. This year, Blais' call was a little different. I was asked how I could reject a film that had won both in Annecy and the OSCAR®. Well, gee...it was easy really. I had my reasons and I think they were solid reasons. In addition, ya see, we don't look to other festivals to approve our selection. Films are judged for their technical and aesthetic merit, not their resumes. 'Tain't a job interview, kids. Should festivals start accepting films simply because they won awards elsewhere? Some might say yes, but can you IMAGINE how fuggin dull festivals would become?

So anyways it gets me thinking about the Oscar® process (heh heh...like processed food...heh heh).

First off, I know all about the realities of the damn Oscars®. I don't expect the latest Polish or Russian animation to pick up a nod. Nevertheless, we need to make clear just what is and is not going on when it comes time to consider the animation short nominees.

The Oscars® have always PRETTY MUCH ignored the international community and that's fine, it is a celebration of Hollywood filmmaking. 'Tain't nothing wrong with it. However since Hollywood dominates the screens of the world, markets the shit out of the event, and generally has convinced everyone that THIS is THE ONE, we should take a closer look at this event, especially from an animation perspective.

There's no denying that having animation shorts recognised by this mammoth event is excellent promotion for a very neglected art form. However, animation is also being defined to the mass audience by a few films that RARELY reflect the diverse work that is out there.

On one hand, I figure the entry procedure is quite baffling to many animators and unless they can set up a contact in L.A., they ain't gonna get considered. Many animators have limited time and limited funds and as such can't fulfill the requirements as easily as North American animators or animators coming from bigger studios (e.g., the National Film Board of Canada has a staff that looks after the entries). I know Michael Dudok de Wit was scrambling like a maniac to get *Father and Daughter* considered. On the other hand, and I don't have the member list in front of me, I'm gonna guess that a majority of the voters are executives, studio employees and in general people whose concept of radical animation is a National Film Board of Canada film. So first of all we are relying on people whose very idea of animation is quite limited (consciously or unconsciously) and at the same time they are being exposed to very few films that reflect the true diversity (most are all from the Western world) of international animation.

What needs to be done is to open up voting to the international scene. Animators, journalists, festival directors, students and various other international figures. Maybe the Academy can hook up with ASIFA. Let's say an ASIFA membership gets you a vote. 'Course, this might be unfair to animation festivals, but let's face it, none of them can—nor should—compete with the Oscars®.

They are here to stay and we might as well embrace them...like the fat, ugly, blabbing Aunt that comes to the house. ('Course we could always kick the hairy bitch out.)

Now of course you can say that these are the Star-Spangled Banner awards. Fine, if that's the case, then 1.) stop inundating THE WORLD with a NATIONAL event; 2.) don't accept international animation; or 3.) simply create two categories (similar to the Best Film and Best Foreign Film...notice they don't say 'Best American Film'! Then again, at every Canadian video store, American films are marketed as domestic product and never in the foreign section, so it's not all Hollywood's fault!). It ain't rocket science, but wait... even if it were, this is the Academy of Art and Sciences...so surely there's a rocket scientist somewhere on Wilshire.

I don't even know if an Oscar® nod means anything to animators. I mean Nick Park is the most obvious beneficiary, but we all know his films were Hollywood-oriented anyway, so win or lose this guy was going BIG TIME. But where are Cordell Barker, Nicole Van Goethem, Jon Minnis, Jimmy Picker, Ferenc Rofuscz or Tyron Montgomery? Alexander Petrov has had two nominations, one win, but we all know Pascal Blais will REALLY be the fella who benefits from that trophy. Ryan Larkin got nominated in 1968 and now he lives on the street ('course that's a pretty extreme example and it's his fault, not Oscar's®). Barker, Montgomery and Rofuscz, last I heard, were all hacking away on commercials. ('Course I guess the same can be said for documentary and live-action short categories as well, but tuff do-do, I'm talking about animation.) I figure if there is anything to be gained, it's a chance to live a moment of decadence, and use the Oscar® to fund your next film. No doubt Michael Dudok de Wit was able to fund *Father and Daughter* thanks to *The Monk and The Fish*'s nomination a few years back.

Most animators I know want, at best, the respect of their peers more than anything. This is something they get from animation festivals like Annecy, Hiroshima, Ottawa and Stuttgart (to name a few). Respect from other artists is something the Academy will always be short on.

(April, 2001)

Ho Ho Ho

*Christmas...the season when with shining fable
Heaven and Nature, in accord for once, edict and
postulate us all husbands and fathers under our skins,
when before an altar in the shape of a gold-plated
cattle-trough man may with impunity prostrate
himself in an orgy of unbridled sentimental obeisance
to the fairy tale which conquered the Western world,
when for seven days the rich get richer and the
poor get poorer in amnesty: the whitewashing of a
stipulated week leaving the page blank and pristine
again for the chronicling of the fresh.*
> – William Faulkner, *The Wild Palms*

*"Is there ANYONE who knows what Christmas is all
about?"*
> – Charlie Brown

"Kyle's Mom is a stupid bitch."
> – Cartman

'Tis THAT time again: the moment when we imagine we are the closest to good and genuine towards those we share this bizarre world with. Me? I'm not one for xmas. Like Charlie Brown, I go through the rituals but I just don't get it. Until my son was born, Christmas was a depressant. Even now I doubt the validity of my contentedness. Is it because my son is moderately thrilled over the unveiling of new toys? If so, that's a pretty flimsy notion of bliss. The idea of pre-planning gifts for a loved one baffles me. Gifts and gestures should be spontaneous, not programmed for the sake of some fat, boozy guy in a red coat (himself a guise for THE company).

'Tain't all bad. I am a sucker for the snow, the lights, the music and the xmas cartoons. There's something almost spiritual in that feeling of pleasure and comfort I get during a soft snowfall with a little Dean Martin "Baby It's Cold Outside" crooning in the background as the red, green, blue and yellow lights flicker on the window. Then again, maybe it's the double shot of rum in my eggnog.

There is something fundamentally (heh heh) good about Christmas. It evokes a spirit of Christian humanism I can dig. Forgiveness. Peace. Understanding. I like everyone during the xmas season. When I'm driving I make full stops. I let the pedestrians cross before turning. I slow down to let a car change lanes. I honk out of joy, not anger. Come January 2nd though, I return to a system that cannot afford such 'weakness' and within days I devolve into the tired, pissed off, frustrated person I was before December.

No, this isn't one of those calls ('cause of…you know…the 'war') for the need to think about this xmas more than any other. I should be forgiving and kind to people EVERY FUGGING DAY of my existence. That's the rub. Xmas is like a vacation. I take a few snapshots, indulge more than usual, see the sites, talk to strangers and then take the first flight on Air Imagination back to the 'real' world. I emerge not wiser, just sort of umm… re-formatted. Christ, even during this hibernation/chamber session I'm rarely in possession of the spirit. Most of the time I'm half drunk, roaming around shopping malls desperately trying to spend my credit limit on 'gifts' (aka temporary excretions of guilt). It's a token payback for the hours I dumped my kids in front of the TV, ignored them altogether, and for those 'late' nights at the office, leaving the spouse to care for the home when in reality I was drinking with the boys or tongue-dancing with the girl in the office.

Christmas, hell, life, should be about tolerance, forgiveness and sharing, but I've turned it into some bizarre almost robotic week where I wipe the guilt clean for the year so I can fuggit all up again the next year.

When Plato, through Socrates, said, "wisdom begins at home," he wasn't suggesting that we sit round the television. But like the book, radio, theatre, cinema, and vaudeville show before it, people like to be elsewhere (in a brain sense) and television has become the fountain of what we call wisdom today. Television is a guide. It gives us dreams. It gives us breath. Television is our blue pattern for life. Television gives us stereotypes and clichés. Television gives us parts of a whole. Television simplifies. We apply sitcom principles to reality. Our mistake is not filtering the residue from those images before stepping outside.

But hey, there's hope, there's always hope until there isn't. Ponder that while you're sitting on the sofa half-corked on rum and eggnog with the kids watching the annual xmas specials 'cause you ain't gonna find much value in these tinseled toons.

How the Grinch Stole Christmas

On the surface it looks great. A miserable prick is so jealous of his happy neighbours that he decides to rob and loot them. Turns out that they don't care. They have each other. They have songs. They don't need gifts. In turn they forgive the remorseful Grinch and invite him to dinner. Now that's a good lesson: forgive thy neighbour. Hmm…kinda reminds me of…umm…well…never mind. But hey, let's face it, the film does not feel complete until the presents are returned and the food is gorged. They tease you with this spiritual stuff, but then walk away from it in the end. Christmas is not complete. Forgiveness and understanding is nothing without a big table of food and a whole lot of toys! Amen.

A Christmas Carol

Ok…better still is Ebeneezer Scrooge. Dante loathed avarice and Scrooge is the textbook example. He is the seven sins in one. His life is defined by money: how to make more and spend less. But the old sod doesn't even enjoy his money. He's just a lonely, repressed bitter s.o.b. And yet despite ruining everyone's lives he is forgiven overnight! How exactly did he purge his sins to earn this path from hell to heaven? A visit by four ghosts. That's it. The guy had a bad night's sleep, awakens scared to the core, and is eager to change. Gee… s'like when you wake up with a raging hangover determined never to drink again. By nightfall, you're guzzling a beer and another and another… Anyway…is Scrooge really forgiven? Bob Cratchett is not exactly a man of principles. He's a boot licker. Scrooge enslaved him and he enjoyed it…so when Scrooge shows up at the door with a bag of gifts and some turkey, do you really expect Bob to say, "Umm…sorry you old coot, but piss off, you're not welcome here?" Of course not, Scrooge still pays the bills. Cratchett has no choice but to welcome Scrooge in, and hey, even if it is a momentary transformation, at least they got some good grub. Our idea of villainy is as screwed up as our idea of heroism.

Dickens was a twerp.

Olive the Other Reindeer/Robbie the Reindeer

I really wanted to like these two 'hip' pieces. Both are stylish, modern and filled with a wealth of nudge-wink references. *Robbie* is the work of *Rex the Runt* guru Richard Goleszowski. Robbie shows up at Santa's domain to replace his retired dad, Rudolph. Within he meets a villainous Blitzen (still boiling over Rudolph's stardom), the Louise Brooks-tinged tramp Vixen, and a wealth of other cookie-cutter characters. Beyond that it's the usual good vs evil, good Robbie gets good, but dull, chick (my blood boiled when I realized that a COUPLING was on the way) and xmas is saved…I guess.

Meanwhile Olive is umm…not even crap…it's fake crap. A dog (Olive) mistakenly believes that she is needed to save Christmas. Olive. All of. Get it. Heh heh. She is accompanied by a greaseball 'ethnic' penguin and chased by an evil mailman who wants to stop xmas from happening. The message? When you get through the clutter of politically correct pop culture hipness (eg. Drew Barrymore as Olive, Michael Stipe as a reindeer! Wow… way to go!), there ain't much to this except the usual "I can be whatever I want to be" philosophy. Ain't a bad philosophy, but when you're a dog and your desire is to be a reindeer, the words psychotic and delusional come to mind. But hey, both films LOOK great. So if you're looking for a one-night stand with big-busted, peroxide-haired bimbos lacking conversational skills, then by all means check out these two babes.

South Park: Mr. Hankey

OK...now this "South Park" xmas episode is funny. The idea of a kid believing that a talking piece of shit comes up the toilet bowl every year to bring gifts to fiber-fueled kids is a fine ode to the ribald tradition. And the quartet of foul mouthed, self-absorbed greedy children is damn close to the true nature of children at xmas. As with most of their episodes, the creators ridicule fundamentalist and politically correct tendencies of religious and social groups by being as politically incorrect as possible (e.g., Kyle's self-hating Jew song, Cartman's glorious rendition of "Kyle's mom's a bitch"). S'like a kid yanking his dick out of his buddies' car window so he can take a leak. It's initially shocking, and then it makes you chuckle until his endless waving and shouting just becomes embarrassing.

The great characters of Shakespeare's plays were the fools. They were loutish and obnoxious...but also the wisest and most perceptive characters in the plays. Parker and Stone are no fools.

A Charlie Brown Christmas

Charlie Brown finds that he does not understand Christmas. The rituals of decorating and gift buying do not give him any pleasure. To help him, Lucy suggests that he direct the xmas play. He agrees, but then finds he cannot control his smug, ignorant classmates. After picking up a dying little green tree (instead of a big aluminum one) to improve the spirit, Charlie Brown is heckled and insulted by his classmates. In frustration he demands to know what xmas is about. As always, philosopher Linus is there to save the day. With the lights dimmed, Linus recounts the nativity scene. Gifts were brought to the Christ child who was sent here to save us. Now, being a heathen, I find that story a bit loosey-goosey, but hey, it's the fact. Christmas is a Christian celebration. A poorly interpreted fairy tale of a fairy tale. But hey, Chuck is right; how did we go from gifts of an aroma, a tree and a yellowish metal from rock deposits to Playstation, Pokemon and roller blades? Good grief.

The PJs: How The Super Stole Christmas

A man catches a kid shoplifting, binds and gags him, and locks him in a trunk while he tells the story of a superintendent who almost 'jacked' Christmas. The super (voiced by Eddie Murphy) is pressured to get his wife a computer…but, failing to receive any tip$ from the apartment tenants, he can't afford it. While xmas shopping at the local pawnshop he makes a desperate deal with the 'shriner'-capped owner to become a repo man in exchange for the computer. The super accepts and begins sneaking around the neighbourhood repossessing items from his friends. Turns out that the reason folks couldn't make their payments was because they pooled their money to buy the super a new sofa chair.

This is, and yeah I'm speaking from suburban middle-class whitey perspective, one of the most realistic, down to earth xmas pieces I've seen. The humour is biting: a tree is decorated with asbestos droppings; a man's xmas bonus is whatever he can get pawning; the pawn dealer tries to sell back the super the watch he bought his wife last xmas; "Silent Night" is sung between spurts of gunfire and police radio calls. Best of all, the sugarcoated sentimentality we're usually force-fed is d.o.a. And hey… any show that portrays Jesus as a poorly decorated baked potato and uses "beeatch" not once, but two times is damn fine in the Pimp's books. There is something close to conventional narrative resolution: the super sells his chair to get money to buy back the items he repossessed from his friends. The confused 'shrine'-capped guy asks the super why he is doing this. The super says he's doing it for one reason: "there is no 'I' in friendship."

In the final shot, the neighbours discover that the super was the repo man and beat the crap out of him. The truth ain't pretty but, like a bowel movement, it's necessary. It's life.

Epilogue

It seems to me that if we want to extend the spiritual element of joy to our lives, it's a simple matter of respect. Respect the values, concerns and beliefs of those we SHARE the world with. And hey, I've got a long way to go, so it's not like I'm speaking from Mount Olympus. But it seems increasingly clear to me that in order to find the tools to improve yourself and those around you, you're gonna need to live. You don't practice for ice hockey by playing a video hockey game. You don't practice for life through a television screen. You learn by doing. As a friend told me recently, "You got to take life in your hands and fuck it up."

If all that fails, there's always narcotics and liquor. Here's my recipe for a potent old-fashioned that will make every xmas joyous.

Get a nice bourbon glass (NO ICE and NO WATER)
1. 1 teaspoon of sugar
2. 3 dashes of angostura bitters
3. Mix the two until the sugar is brown
4. Add a half slice of lime, lemon and orange
5. Throw in as much Canadian Club as you need (1-3 ounces)
6. Take a drink stick and mash up the fruit. Take occasional sips and keep mashing the fruit until the taste meets your satisfaction (after two of these, satisfaction will come quicker)
7. Add a cherry for show.
8. Drink, savour and watch the xmas blues fade away as family and friends become loveable and huggable with each swur... oops...I mean...slur-inducing gulp.

(December, 2001)

283

Elbows and Cakeholes

I'll be the first to admit that 2002 was not a great year for animation films. There were a number of okay-good-decent works, but nothing that really stood out, nothing that I've any real desire to postpone a repeat screening of "Curb Your Enthusiasm," "Six Feet Under" or "Hockey Night in Canada" for. Nevertheless...there were certainly a handful of films that warranted Oscar nominations over the suspect list of shorts that got the nods. *Mt. Head* by Koji Yamamura is about the only title (well...okay...maybe I can accept *Das Rod*) that deserves to be on this list. But are you gonna tell me that this asinine piece of shit called *The Chubb Chubbs*, a film that only a chair could love, or *Mike's New Car* (ha ha...the monster has problems with his car...HA HA HA...oh god that's so damn original, so clever... and hey...look, the blue monster hair is SO REALISTIC) is a better work than Chris Hinton's *Flux*, Robert Bradbrook's *Home Road Movies*, Jonas Odell's *Family and Friends* or Priit Tender's *Mont Blanc*? And what of the Mexican puppet film *Close to the Bone*? (Yeah...okay...the credits are WAY TOO LONG but still...). Hell, there are festival rejects that are better than most of these nominees.

And hold up...before some of you schmucks start writing in saying..."Come on, Pimp, of course the Oscar selection is a joke... what do you expect?" I say, "STOP." I know it's old hat to bitch and moan about the lack of taste (and yes, folks, let's call it what it is) of the Academy voters, but look...animation fights tooth and nail for exposure and respect...especially festival animation. The Oscars are an important vehicle because they have the power and influence to bring these films to the attention of a much wider audience than either Annecy or Ottawa (for example) can. It's also important for the animators from a financial perspective. It gives them leverage for future funding. Unfortunately, what the world is seeing is a heavily unbalanced, unfair, and watered-down-to-the-point-of-being-a-desert competition.

The Cumbersome Process

Okay, first things first…according to a couple of Academy voters, this is how the whole process works.

To enter, you must fill out an entry form. Then you have to set up something like two to three public screenings in the Los Angeles area. This isn't so hard because for a few hundred Yankee green (according to more than a few people, this rate magically rises each year) you can get the Laemmle Theaters to show your work of beauty. BUT HOLD ON…If your entry has won a first prize in a recognized film festival (like…gosh golly gee, that dandy animation event in Ottawa), you receive a 'buy' of sorts, meaning you don't have to worry about a public screening.

Each year a letter is sent to all Academy members of the shorts branch asking them if they want to watch all the entries. Given that the screenings only take place in Los Angeles over the course of many weekends, there ain't many folks outside the L.A. area goin'. This L.A. selection committee (let's say) composed of maybe 30 boys and girls, watches all the films (so we assume) and narrows the list from about 300 or so entries to, this year, nine films (i.e., the short list).

For a film to make it to the short list it must receive an average vote of 8.5 (6 is the worst, 10 the best). Needless to say, it's pretty easy for a few malcontent slugs to blacklist a title or two by giving low marks…but hey…we know that there's no one like that in the L.A. animation community.

Now get this, prior to this year the short list was a poorly kept secret AND the films were ONLY shown in Los Angeles. Fortunately, some knuckleheads pulled their heads out of their asses and set up member screenings in New York and San Francisco (there might even be a London screening too) so that area members could vote. Unlike the animation features category, screeners are not sent to members, they must instead be screened in a theatre to be voted on. (Oh…and apparently Canucks were invited to New York, but none were able to make the ten-hour drive.)

No Shortage of Shortcomings...

It doesn't take a Mensa member to see the shortcomings here. FIRST, the Academy is only getting about 300 films. Ottawa got 1700. Annecy got around 1400. Even smaller festivals in Holland, Hiroshima and Zagreb have over 1000 entries. (Yes...some of these are ineligible commissioned works, but in Ottawa 75% of the entries are short films.) And this isn't really a surprise. Unless you're fortunate enough to win first prize at an approved festival, you've got to fork over a few U.S. dollars to set up a screening. Most entrants would be scared off way before that when they see that they've got to set up a public screening. I mean...how many non-studio-backed animators can afford this? The NFB in Canada is loaded and have staff and money to look after the Oscar submissions, but what about the rest of Canada? When was the last time we saw a non-studio-supported Canadian animation in the running? And what about indie animators in the rest of the world? They spend most of the year just trying to find money for prints, videos, stills, entry fees (in the U.S. of course)...how the fug are they supposed to come up with a few hundred magic beans AND ship their film print to/from L.A.? Tough toodies I guess.

This small body of films is then judged by maybe 30 Academy members, most of whom (not all) are either old farts and/or studio types who likely don't go to many international animation festivals AND have a proclivity for farce/gag/anthropomorphism films. I'm not knocking them per se. Nothing wrong with liking cute monsters and all that assorted techno fetish stuff, BUT, are these same people open minded/informed enough to deal with Mulloy, Kovalyov, Pärn, Dumala, let alone Hinton, Cournoyer, Odell or Broadbrook? (I suspect of course that *Home Road Movies* was deemed NON-animation by the liberal Academy members.) There are other voices...not all of whom ONLY love good ol' fashioned chuckle a minute shorts with lovable nippleless animals, but clearly they are a minority.

So what the world is getting in the end is a fraudulent representation of international animation. And this isn't an anti-American rant, so take those about-to-be-breathed words

and stuff them back down your pipehole. These are Los Angeles awards, they are a celebration of the Hollywood industry. There's absolutely nothing wrong with that EXCEPT that you're leading the public (those three people who care about the animation short category!) to believe that these five animations represent the best of animation around the world and, taste issues aside, we all know that is complete and utter bullshit. Why the hell not just call it the Best American Animation Short (Yes…why not do the same with the Best Film as well!)?

Can We Help?

So what's the solution? Boycott? Nah…that means even less representation. Perhaps making more of an effort to contact animators would be a start (I've heard through the grapevine that Ron Diamond, for example, contacts, encourages and helps a number of filmmakers whose films he saw and liked at international festivals). [Editor's Note: Ron Diamond is the co-founder and president of Animation World Network, www.awn.com.] A better explanation of the entry procedure, or simply doing away with this ludicrous public-screening rule, would be a start. And aside from offering the Academy frat club either 1. an elbow in the mouth or 2. a swift kick up their crusty, aged cakeholes for their myopic tastes, why not invite more international representation? Wouldn't it make sense for the Academy to have a closer link with ASIFA International? Now I realize that you couldn't just have every ASIFA member become an Academy member, but why not invite the ASIFA International Board or the President of every national ASIFA chapter to be an Academy member? It would not only encourage those people to explain the entry process to their members, but it would also widen the taste buds of the voting process. And what about festival programmers/directors? 'You' might not like my taste, but you can't argue with the fact that I easily see at least 1000 new films per year, as do my colleagues around the world. Why would the Academy not welcome the obvious expertise of festival programmers?

So naturally…the absolutelybestestgreatestfantasticstupendo us step that the Academy can take is to vote me in, right now.

Okay...it's March...Spring is coming...the birds are singing...let's not end on bad terms. We've still got the Animated Feature category and at least the feature voters showed great humour by nominating that horsey film over *Mutant Aliens* for Best Feature. That's one of the great pranks of the century. What a riot those guys are! Ba ha ha ha.

(March, 2003)

Chaos x Order + Fragments x Whole + Process x End(s) = The 2003 Year in Review!

So you've decided to quit something. All you had to do was wait for the magic clock on the wall to hit midnight and then everything would be well again. If you say it, it will come true. Right? Well... if that was the case... you wouldn't be making this promise for the 11th consecutive year.

My cynical side loathes New Year's (hell... we're just guessing that it's really a new year anyway) along with its litter of year-in-reviews. They're naïve and fanciful, filled with that Hollywood/Christian wishy-washy pixie fairy dust befitting three-year-olds', not adults', notion that we can just scrub the slate clean and start again. Years in Review wrongly suggest that the past can be easily compressed into readily definable categories, categories which we have developed based, in this case, on days, months and years (and from there, decades). These categories lead us to believe that we can pinpoint with ease the beginning and end points of various streams, trends or, more precisely, moments. Within this mindset, there are no overlaps, inconsistencies or broken links. Everything wraps up real nice like a Rugrats flick. We might for example look back on 2003 and say... this was the year animation hit rock bottom, that 2D animation died, Disney fell apart, or that evil-doing was brought to an end with the capturing of a single Iraqi. Nonsense, of course (and OK... yeah... sure... Johnny Cash and Jules Engel did in fact die... but they were dying BEFORE the moment they actually died).

I was afraid to ask questions in class because it would reveal my stupidity. I saw other kids laugh at kids who asked questions. I didn't want to be laughed at. So I stayed quiet and just took everything in whether I understood it or not. I passed classes, but barely.

The problem with year-in-reviews or even resolutions is they do not ask questions. Reviews make statements that are so clear and concise that you'd have to be an idiot not to understand it. There is little room for questioning. They are just summaries, but summaries of the seemingly FINAL moment. They don't bother with the other moments and actually very wrongly assume that this moment is the FINAL moment. We read these summaries, take them for granted and move on. Why? 'Cause they appear so obvious that we'd feel stupid if we doubted them. And secondly… life's a hell of a lot easier when it's easily categorized. So we almost never ever question the validity of these summaries. We never ask, for example, WHO is saying this, from whose perspective are we getting this "take."

Let's take animation hitting rock bottom. Says who? *Finding Nemo* was #1 at the box office, *Triplets of Belleville* is achieving critical success beyond animation circles, more features are being made than ever before, more animation short films are being made than ever before (just look at festival entry numbers). OK… so Klasky Csupo, Warners, and a few others are slicing staff… C.O.R.E. Digital, for example, was hiring, as were an assortment of other small studios. It's like that every year. The pendulum swings, baby.

Outside of here, Korea's animation scene is flourishing and the Estonians had a huge domestic box office hit with *Ladybird's Christmas*. Plympton finished yet another feature. Anne Marie Fleming made a first animated feature. They're all probably feeling pretty darn good about animation right now. Animation continues to dominate television images. Internet animation continues to expand and grow. If all this is happening, how can animation be in a terrible slump? Whose slump is it? So to turn around and summarize 2003 as the year of the slump in animation would be quite misleading, offering a rather one-sided perspective on what we call animation. Not everyone in animation gives a shit about Roy Disney.

Still… what choice do we have with these year-end reviews? As one of those Greeks said, a life unreflected upon is a life not worth living. If we plough forward through our lives (as Nike would have us do) giving little consideration to the choices we've made or will make, giving little consideration to the past, then we are not learning, we are not living. Reflection allows us that moment to stop and take account, a sort of pit stop where we can see where we are and re-tool what we think needs fixing. I dunno bout you, but I find that the days often just smash together at such a frenzied pace that I just get overwhelmed by the moment... I get so lost in a series of disconnected moments that I fail to see the larger picture... I fail to see these moments connect. As such, I lose perspective. I see only the individual moments... and they never seem to add up to anything... they just freely float separate from life.

If I have a bad day of writing or get a story rejected... I too often just want to give up, just think I'm a failure... (my Latvian animator chum just e-mailed me this morning about the same problem. She works very hard every day and has lost sight of the end... is just so lost in these daily processes that she's forgotten WHY she's doing what she's doing.) Of course it's an illusion, it's my perspective... or lack thereof that causes this. Carving out a career/hobby... whatever... as a writer doesn't help. It's a lonely, silly addiction not even worthy of my dog. Sometimes you spend days punched out by doubt, fear, apathy and failure. Other days you bask in delusions of success, confidence and certainty.

You wish you could just toss it aside and get a "normal" job (which I have six months of the year)... but you know it ain't gonna happen because, 1. you'll get fired in a week and 2. you NEED to write, think, articulate the mess that surrounds you on a daily basis. It's not a matter of privilege or laziness. It's a matter of need... a chemical imbalance perhaps. I guess it's a matter of perspective again. Writers/artists have unstructured, messy lives... art is a way of structuring those moments. It's not all that different from a 9-to-5 job really. We try to find structure and need that sort of regiment to order our lives (of course... we all know that most of us/them then fuck around unstructured within that structure). It's like that "Mr. Show" sketch about how a dysfunctional background tends to create more umm... artistically inclined folks. If you've come from function... that means you've had structure and order and calm... you like it...

you know it... you follow it. You come from dysfunction... you know chaos, alienation, lack social basics etc... and don't fit into those umm... "normal" compartments... although as we increasingly see... normal itself is a relative thing (check out Foucault's *Madness and Civilization* or, hey... check out Philip Dick's *Martian Time Slip* or the recent *Professor and the Madman* by Simon Winchester). I hate to quote Popeye, 'cause there's this laissez-faire attitude he has that stinks, but there is some fundamental philosophical truth in, "I yam what I yam."

In theory, the idea of year-end resolutions ain't such a bad thing; it means you've been reflecting on who you are... and that you have a desire to break free from Popeye's shrug. But we really seem to think that we can just erase the past and start from scratch. That's not only a fallacy, but it's a belief that puts unrealistic pressures on you. You're not a floppy disk. You cannot just reformat come January 1st. If you come to realize that, you'll make things a hell of a lot easier. All those damn promises. You don't just up and stop drinking January 1 or diet or quit smoking. You need a plan, mes chums, a system, a structure. That's the irony of this seemingly highly structured and compartmentalized end of year stuff... they're actually totally unstructured. No one plans it out. It's stuck in this click-of-the-heels, if-I say-it-it'll-come-true fairy tale. Soundbites.

Historical amnesia remains one of the most prevalent illnesses of our time. We constantly seem to feel that we can change the future by erasing the past, when in fact we must read, acknowledge and understand the past if we have any hope of resolving the present and future. Animation isn't going to die or thrive come January 1st. It doesn't work like that... animation is where it is and isn't because of thousands upon thousands of decisions made in scattered moments in different times and spaces.

(For a nifty visual translation of what I'm saying, check out Mati Kutt's film *Underground*, which is all about order/disorder and how they inform one another... or what was that Belgian student film, *Antipode*?)

So we need a bit more balance between the moments/means

and the end. We need to value those moments more and yet not get so caught up in them that we lose sight of the larger picture. Bigger problem is our fixation on the end over the means. Year-in-reviews are like highlight packages… they focus on the goal, not the work that led to the goal. The result is all that matters, not the process. Creates the illusion that goals are easily attained. So if I look back on my year… I'd say… OK… June 2, 2003—first book is published. That's it, that's all. But what about all those small, seemingly mundane and irrelevant moments from March 1996 (let's say) to December 2003 that led up to that June 2nd achievement? What about those seemingly endless hours spent alone in a goddamn cold basement often staring blankly at the screen or watching "Seinfeld?" They all contributed to the end result, didn't they? They're all part of the package, ain't they? And that's just moments DIRECTLY related to the end. That doesn't include all those earlier years… filled with seemingly inconsequential moments that in fact contributed to that June 2 'end.'

'Course, as I was telling that sweet Latvian friend, I know that deep down we need those 'end' moments. All those moments of doubt… all those days that don't seem to add up, connect or go anywhere… suddenly come together on June 2, 2003, when I see the book before me and realize, somewhat incredulously, that all those seemingly wasteful, disconnected moments of doubt, failure, success, hard work… did add up to something (materially). But that moment passed quickly because I'd already finished a second manuscript by that time. You move on. Still… the book remains as a beacon, tomb, or a series of shouts from ghosts of a sometimes forgotten past.

So hey… my friend… by all means… take this Year-in-Review moment to reflect and look back at your life… but don't expect to clear the field and start anew just like that. That's fool fodder. Who you are now was constructed—no shit—over a lifetime of seemingly irrelevant moments, so why on earth would you expect to be able to just up and radically alter yourself in a single year, let alone a single day.

And now… a special bonus… 'cause I know you want it:

The Animation Pimp's 2003 Year in Review
(as told to the author by jolts of memory flashes)

January

Hmm... it was pretty damn cold... went back to boxing classes... Kelly signed us up for snacks at Jarvis' school during the first two weeks of January. That SUCKS. Snow fell. We have a long driveway. I enjoy using the plow... but why can't those plow fucks distribute the snow somewhere BEYOND our damn laneway entrance. Man it's cold. Didn't stop us from Friday night hockey. We were playing sometimes in -30 (Celsius) weather. Was bad for 10-15 minutes... but then the body warms up. Making final edits to Estonian book. Trying to work on this "hockey" book. Having a hard time. Hmm... my urine is too yellowy. I gotta take more fluids. Wanna kill that publisher of *Chunklet*. Wrote a piece on Sterling Hayden for them eight months ago. Good piece. They ain't using it in this new issue. Says there's no room.

February

Went to New York to hang with Signe, Gerben and Anet. Plympton had a nice party for us. Slept in Bill's studio. Had to climb a ladder to go to bed every night. Heavy snowstorm. Wore my new camper shoes. They're the best shoes in the world. Not feeling great. Really cold in New York. Spent $300 on dinner at Da Silvanos. What a weird experience that was... we were out of element... beside mobsters and fashion fag-hags. Guy who wrote Lauren book beside us. Food sucked too. Got back, drove to Dartmouth College. Ehrlich didn't tell me I was reviewing student work. Fuck me. I hate doing that. It's not fair.

Was also on a panel about creativity. That was fun. Was invited as a writer... not as this festival schmuck. The girl who moderated the panel was later in a serious accident. She was in a coma. Not sure if she made it. Reminds me... met Linda Pakre at Estonia house. She's keen on doing this Estonian animation festival next November in New York. Bundle o' energy on that gal. Nice drive back from Vermont. Relaxed. Cold. When I got back my retro Bruins circa-72 jersey was waiting. Wore it to hockey that week. Jarvis is sick. Spending the week with him. We're watching the *Star Wars* films. Want him to see that good and evil aren't so easy to define… but realize the series is also about a father trying to kill his son. Oops. Now I'm sick. Trying to keep writing the hockey book but feeling real groggy.

SAFO… fuck why are we doing it? No one cares except the students. Still… got Oscar Grillo on the jury. Hear he's pretty funny. Two years of sobriety. Wee-haa, who wants a drink!? Still fucking hard to manage all this time. Finally get my copy of that nifty Spanish festival publication, *Animac*. They do a great job with the design and layout. I wrote something about—yeah, yeah—sex and animation for them. Was nice to see alongside these serious academic-oriented pieces. Ha.

March

Why is there a big lump on my neck? Shit. A virus. Mono or something. Stuck in the house for about 10 days. Most sick I ever been. Good excuse to watch "Murder She Wrote" every day and not write. National Arts Centre just sent us a letter saying they're getting rid of their projection equip. Fuck me. We've been there since 1976. Why are they just sending us a fucking letter? Asswipes. Takes us two to three weeks to solve the problem for 2004… but solve it we do. What's with the Estonians? Why ain't they getting back to me about the status of this book? Man, they're slow. Is there a pagan clock? Talking to a lot of old hockey players. Man oh man is that something. Tom Johnson, Red Storey, called the Gump but he had a heart attack. Just found out that the first guy I interviewed for the book, Chuck Rayner, kicked it. Damn. Meantime… trying to put spring ASIFA issue together. Pain in the ass trying to find GOOD writers and better ideas.

April

Hockey playoffs are here. Life has meaning. Still ploughing away on that book. I'm late on my March 31 deadline… but I have a fear that the publisher has split. Rumors abound. SAFO's coming together but this Colburn gal is bugging me. Never responds. Maybe this was a mistake. Got Richard O'Connor on board though. He'll be a good fresh perspective... and the best dressed jury member ever. Marcel Jean will hold them all together. Starting to train for the 10k race... but pain in the knee. Need new shoes I guess.

Teachers saying they might hold Jarvis back. Fuck them. Montessori is supposed to be about the kid's going at their OWN pace. What gives. Turned the public school across the street into a private school. Found a review copy of Nick Tosches' new book.* Am I in heaven, baby. Great. Senators knocked off the Islanders... yeah... off to Detroit. Showing Ottawa 'Best of' at college there. I hate Detroit. My biological father lives there. He wants nothing to do with me I think 'cause his alcoholic wife thinks its wrong. I brought his number. We had a good time in 2000, got drunk talked hockey and gals. Never saw him again. I should call him... but I won't. Read Tosches' book. Disappointing. Damn.

May

Back to Detroit. Reviewing this school's animation dept. Nice people there. Detroit still sucks. I do nothing but watch TV at night 'cause there ain't nowhere to go. Drove this time. What a dull drive from Ottawa-Toronto-Windsor-Detroit. Wanted out so bad I drove back at 9:30 pm... got to Ottawa around 5:00 am. Hallucinated for the last two hours. Was convinced something was in the trunk. Sens beat the Flyers. Off to the semi-finals! Listened to Canucks/Wild game and blared "Alien Lanes" through Oshawa.

Gettin' real stressed. Almost to the end of the hockey book. It's eating me apart. Realize that I have not forgiven my parents... have not forgiven myself. Decide to do two things—tell stepdad-cop that I cannot accept him as he is...tell mom she was a terrible parent, but I forgive her. Didn't see that coming. Kelly's off to Turku. I bailed. Too much into this book. Estonians are driving me crazy. They assure me we're launching the book at Annecy... but I haven't even seen the cover. I enjoy weeks alone with Jarvis. We have a good ol' casual time. No mom rhythm to get in the way.

---

* *Where Dead Voices Gather*, 2001.

I finish the hockey book the night that the Senators tie the series with the Devils. Also my birthday. Decide to spend $100 on Game 7 tickets. Crazy. Ottawa is crazy with Stanley cup fever. You can feel this pride and togetherness and confidence surging through the city. I show up two hours early and sit alone in the empty rink watching it fill with people. Ottawa loses. They're tied with two minutes to go and they blow it. A simple defensive play fucked up. The city is shot silent. Fuckaduck. I can still see that Friesen goal. Off to Annecy. Send my manuscript to the publisher. He's gone under. Fuck me. Need a new publisher. Gonna be hard. This ain't no conventional bio. Saw the Estonian cover. Looks great.

Fly to Amsterdam, great drive with Gerben, Anet and Erik (Holland festival friends). Spend a night in Paris... I order some ugly-ass fucking fish that I refuse to eat. Every time I go to Paris I order something stupid, says Gerben. He likes to remind me that he's better than me.

June

Long drive to Annecy... but a good time... beautiful mountains... pit stops... lots of music... got into Dylan's Royal Albert concert. Relaxing, man. Arrive at Annecy. Hmm... I'm bored. Ticket system sucks. Nice to see friends... but too many to see... just becomes stupid. Estonians arrive late. Book looks great. I think I slept with the book that night. Find out the Estonians didn't even fucking reserve a space for the launch. Gerben, Anet and I race around to ensure that we have one. Goes well. Everyone says they like the book. Of course they're going to say that.

Jogged every morning. Nice to jog in Annecy, man. Festival was OK... but student films were bad except for this crazy one by this JJ Villard guy. Wanna see that one again. Was given a VHS copy of Priit Parn's new film. Man, was I disappointed. Priit needs a rest. Left the party quietly. Too many people to say bye too. Fuggit. Eager to go. One more night in Paris. Remember this Italian rest. Chick talking about the "darkies." I can't believe I heard that word, especially from another immigrant!

Line up for four hours in Paris airport. Lost my heart monitor watch. Air Canada cuts meet French hospitality. Oh man. Got back. Get sent to Toronto Immigration. Held for 20 minutes. Apparently Chris Robinson, with the same birthdate, is wanted in a variety of U.S. states for a variety of offences. Jesus man… after about 10 minutes… I think back to my drinking days. Maybe I was in Jacksonville? Did I assault a cop? Finally they release me and note that I'm not the guy on their computer.

Start doing pre-selection for SAFO. Monday, June 16. Letter arrives from Telefilm Canada. They're cutting all our funding. Just like that. I dust off my résumé and apply for some jobs. I've had it. Fuck this festival and fuck all these idiot Canadian bureaucrats who want something for nothing. Kelly O'Brien died. Oh man… she founded the festival. Ward-Gatti 3 is this week… but I watch Ward-Gatti 2. Ward gets his ear drum punctured, but refuses to go down. Inspires me to fight these Telefilm Canada dipshits. Next three to four weeks is spent planning a massive media campaign. Jarvis finishes school. Doing pretty well but still behind. Teacher meetings make me angry. Why? Two writers read my hockey book and like it a lot. Makes me feel pretty damn good despite it all.

July

Couple weeks in (after Jarvis' fifth birthday party—too many kids… too many kids) we start getting strange calls… apparently the funding decision is going to be reversed. S'like "X-Files." Hmm… man… I'm in good shape. Look at those shoulder muscles. I'd like to hit someone… maybe Richard Stursberg? Maybe an animator? Leading the hockey team in scoring and the league in penalty minutes. How's that possible? Mid-July. Funding restored for now. Rest of month is spent watching all the entries. No time for nutting else. I hate myself. Why am I doing this job? I'm sick of this shit. No structure… no board… shitty pay. Not overly impressed with the crop this year except this JJ Villard guy. Made this Bukowski film. It's great… real raw and honest. Easily the best film here. I like this job.

August

Putting the catalog together and getting my manuscript ready for publishers. Canadian writer tells me he likes the manuscript. Man... but two other friends say it's chaotic. Who to believe? It's supposed to be chaotic. It's about identity. Score a sweet job writing for *Montage* magazine. Pay is way too good. Few more of those and I can leave the festival. Funding coming in for SAFO. Fuck me. Why is it always last minute? We're almost sold out of passes. What gives? I know it's smaller... but what's with this festival anyway. We're gonna can it either way. Makes no sense. People are confused... people are not interested in student work even if it's better than the films at the OIAF. All those "veteran" animators should be at SAFO getting a fresh kick of energy.

Grandfather sold his house. Shit man, I was born in that house. We have a final shindig. All of us roaming the empty house like ghosts.... Looking at every wall, every mark, every crack and stain and corner for evidence that we existed here once. I've never seen my relatives like this. Usually they're all so cold and distant. My grandfather does not attend this farewell. He's moved into this care facility with my grandma, who's got Alzheimer's. Holy shit... I just found out that Linda from the Estonia house, the woman who was organizing the Estonian anim. festival, just died. Apparently she was in a coma for two weeks. She'd fallen asleep in her apartment and left a cigarette or candle burning. Someone suggested that she was reading my book at the time (she'd just bought a copy). Assholes. Guess our festival is off.

September

Trying to get ASIFA magazine done. ASIFA pres. has apparently lost his mind. Squirrel meat tastes like hamburger. Off to Switzerland for Fantoche festival. Introducing Kovalyov screening and moderating some panels. Opening ceremony is awful... I mean awful. Nice town. Getting sick. So many beautiful women.... when does THAT stop? Gerben and I have nice chats. OK... Hold up... this town is getting boring. Can only jog so far. Can only see those films so many times. Drinking a lot of coffee. Shit… got a cold. Oh man… stopped in Toronto again. Sent through Immigration. I'm still wanted in the U.S. Jesus Christ… can't they correct this? I have to call this 1-800-number I'm told. Back to Ottawa. Kelly's friend Kelly died. I sorta knew her. She had cancer for four years. Only stayed alive for her two young kids. She was kinda bitchy but I liked her. She told you what she felt. Johnny Cash died that week. Big deal.

Sent out manuscript to six publishers. Heard back from one. Said I can't write (basically). Fuck him and his mom. Find out later that publisher is facing heavy financial losses. Like to tell myself that's the real reason. Jarvis is back at school. After one day, they called him up to the "all days." He's so excited. His confidence soars overnight and he's suddenly excited about school. I told those teachers. Pal loans me Alan Partridge DVD. British comedy. Funny. Started playing ice hockey again. Man, it's zen. So damn relaxing. You can cheat. Just glide and feel that breeze. I dunno what it is… but it's calming and exhilarating.

October

Andreas Hykade and family visit us for a few days before SAFO. His daughter doesn't speak any English. Jarvis speaks no German. They get along great. SAFO goes off w/o hitch except Grillo's pissed off because of Meltzer's article. I think he just likes to complain. We get a note from head of Telefilm Canada congratulating us on being sold out. Says it was good that they had second thoughts. Hmm… I guess our massive media campaign had no effect.

Son of Satan won. I'm pleased as a bitch in heat being tongued about that. It was far and away the best film. A lot didn't think so. A lot of students found it ugly. Idiots. They all seem to think that "art" is flawless and perfect. What's with these kids? What's with their teachers? Hey… some schmuck doesn't like my "stoner" introductions. I don't smoke pot, buddy. I guess he'd prefer the formal, fake fucks that usually go up on stage, pretending they care and like you and all that. At least I don't pretend. John Canemaker is the Jean Beliveau of animation. A real swell guy. Doesn't take any shit either.

Got my head punched in ball hockey by some wingnut. So much for boxing skills. When he gets the same one-game suspension I get, I 'retire' from this nuttiness. Pride hurt, head bruised.

Urine is consistently clear. Doctor says I'm in good shape. (Means trouble I figure).

Dog's medicine is working. She jogs with me, but no more limps. Expensive of course.

Estonian festival is happening but no idea how. I've organized the films and the guests... and all that... but have no idea where I'm staying or what's happening. Estonians are really slow. It's not just me.

Jarvis' school has Harvest feast. I hate other parents. Fake conversations all night with these pseudo rich shits. I offer Jarvis any toy of his choice not to go... but he refuses. Idiot or genius? A lot of birthday parties this month. I really have a social problem with other parents. Kelly and I just don't fit in. Hmm... screw it.

November

Chris Lanier's SAFO 'review' comes out. Man... I don't know if he liked the festival or not... but it don't matter. He wrote a beautiful text. He GOT it. Life usually stops at festivals... but life somehow managed to eke its way into SAFO. Amazing really. Two more book rejects. One just doesn't get it. Other does... but says it doesn't fit them. Started Level 3 boxing. Doing sit-ups on some huge balloonish ball. Why? Sent a short story to some British mag. Let's see.

Off to RISD and New York. Family adventure and work. Senior Critic at RISD. Damn that was fun... enjoyed exchanging ideas with the students... and a good way to prevent bad films before they happen! Parking sucks in Providence. Saw They Might be Giants live at Borders in Providence Mall. Why? Off to New York. One night in Brooklyn with ROC. We see GBV at Warsaw. Good time. They were smashed from the get-go. Off to Manhattan. Driving. Wow. I love driving here 'cause I'm an asshole. Staying at Hotel Penn. Introducing three nights of Estonian animation at Two Boots Cinema. Party/launch for book. All goes well. Mati Kutt and Priit Tender are here. Even Grant comes from North Carolina.

Wish I was drinking. Oh man… and there's Signe, Griffin, Krause x 2, Missy, Jessie Schmal, Dovas, Kugel, Solomon… nice afternoon with Sarah the Amazing One. I love this town. For three days I just walked up and down following the lights. Hey… the Boxing Hall of Fame is on the way back. It's really small and quiet. They have these bronzed fists… One guy had this MASSIVE fist—size of a kid's head. Jesus. No problems. Finished another short story. Jarvis is sick but wants to go to school. What the hell is wrong with that boy?

Kelly's off to Korea for a week. Some best of SAFO thingie. I didn't want to go. Turned down three invites to Korea this year. Been twice before. Kinda boring. Too far to go for a few days. Besides…it means a week with me and Jarv. Good times. Late nights. Sugar. Drive to MTL with friend, Matt. He's got a small (really small) press. Published two local writers. Sold well. Really admire Matt's work. The writers are so damn happy too. Fuck big publishers. Starting to work on third book. S'all about my fathers… about a guy who finds his real father only to find that his father doesn't know his own father. Wish it was fiction. Bought a used electric guitar and an amp. Haven't played electric in a decade. Nice to have around for those rock-out days. Started work on 2004. Lots of big changes planned, and I've got this ambitious programming series that's gonna be a bitch to put together. Hmm… maybe I do like this job after all.

December

Xmas decorations go up just as I start getting sick.

Bronchitis. God damn it. Sick for almost the entire month (even as I write this on December 15). Saw images from new Kovalyov film *Milk*. Looks real nice. Lots of new films to look forward to: Chris Landreth's film about Ryan Larkin is coming out, as is Michele Cournoyer's new film. Tried to shovel snow, tried to walk… but coughed so hard I puked. Haven't boxed or run in over two weeks. I hate this house. This is the sickest I've ever been in my life. Couldn't even read much. Couldn't do much some days except stare at the walls. Reminds me of writing.

Why is everyone crying about Roy Disney? I could give a flying squirrel about this guy and all his problems. All these animators embrace it like it's their own. It ain't, fools. All of a sudden ol' confused nephew Roy is the modern bastion of art. Jeepers.

Managed to drive Jarvis to school this week. What's with those ladies? Do they not GET THE FUCKING LINE CONCEPT? Why does that BMW bitch park in the no-park spot and get out and just ignore the line? I'd like to slap her... but I bet her hubbie already does that. Hmm... maybe I shouldn't quit therapy just yet. Why do the other ladies get out of the car and chat? The rule is that you stay in the car. I ain't lining up no more.

Kelly goes to Toronto. Telefilm Canada says that funding is still in place for 2004. I'm cautiously optimistic. Another studio has also come in big for us. Lots of work to be done.

Saw a commercial that irked me. Something about a place you can easily go to get cash advances when you receive "unexpected bills." Who the fuck receives unexpected bills? Is there a gremlin in your house using your credit card, or did you go on a spending spree while you were pumped up with liquor taken while trying to soothe an aching sense of nothingness with stuff?

Watching this show "Firefly." Man, it's bad. Everyone was raving about it. Bad acting. Pretentious. As hollow as Gary Bettman. My urine is yellow again. Must be this illness.

Well... s'about it. I guess I prolly jerked off almost every day... sometimes to porn... sometimes to imaginings... my scalp is too dry... I chew my nails (fingers, not toes)... I probably spent too much time sitting around (even though I'm in the best physical shape of my life: jog more than 10 miles/week, boxing twice a week, ice hockey two hours/week.) It's actually amazing that I did anything. Oh... and I thought about dying a lot. Far too much, but that's sorta the norm in my life. I could eat a little better... cut the carbs... but I ain't doing too bad. I'd like to spend more time with Jarv, but he likes having private time after a day of school. Can't blame him. I still managed to write at least one freelance article per month. Made a few new friends this year but lost a couple too. Still trying to find my half-brother in New York State. No luck so far. He's four months younger than me. My urine is really yellow. Better get more fluids. Prolly just this illness.

So hey… relatively speaking.… I'd say things ain't so bad.

(January, 2004)

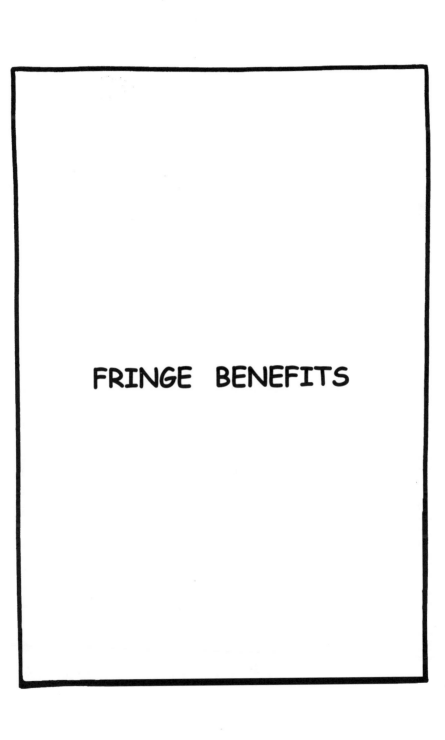

FRINGE BENEFITS

The Old Man and The Sea:
A Plagiarism (not the film)

This is Pascal Blais' favourite cartoon. It's Bernard Lajoie's 2nd favourite toon. It's Martine Chartrand's 3rd favourite toon. It's Sofi Valliant's 4th favourite toon. It's Alexander Petrov's 5th favourite toon. It's Sayoko Kinoshita's 6th favourite toon. It's Mariel Hemingway's 7th favourite toon. It's Anthony Quinn's 8th favourite toon. It's Gordon Pinsent's 9th favourite toon. It's Normand Roger's 10th favourite toon. It's the guy who runs Annecy's 11th favourite toon. It's the woman/man he's fuggin's 12th favourite toon. It would have been John Denver's 13th favourite toon. It was the woman who did South Park but died's 14th favourite toon. It's Leonard Maltin's 15th favourite toon. It's Jean-Guy, my barber's 16th favourite toon. It's Paul Reubens' 17th favourite toon. It's Elizabeth Taylor's 18th favourite toon. It's EVERYONE who's fucked Elizabeth Taylor's 19th favourite toon. It's Tom Knott's 20th favourite toon. It's Jacques Parizeau's 21st favourite toon (doesn't like immigrants or women). It's Stumpy Bouchard's 22nd favourite toon ('cause Jack told him so). It's Mr. T's 23rd favourite toon. It's Quebec's 24th favourite toon. It's Patrick Roy's 25th favourite toon. It's the inventor of Kleenex's 26th favourite toon. It's "We're gonna need a bigger boat's," 27th favourite toon. It's June Foray's 28th favourite toon. It's George Jones' 29th favourite toon. It's Nick Tosches' 30th favourite toon. It's the guy who drove Di to her death's 31st favourite toon. It's the old man's 32nd favourite toon. It's Jesus Christ's 33rd favourite toon. It's his friend's 34th favourite toon. It's David Cross' 35th favourite toon. It's the guy he works with's 36th favourite toon. It's my dog's 37th favourite toon. It's "Lola's" 38th favourite toon. It's "Koko's" 39th favourite toon. It's my bitch's (other dog) 40th favourite toon. It's Xena's 41st favourite toon. It's Vera Duffy's 42nd favourite toon. It's Michael Caine's

43rd favourite toon. It's Terry Sawchuck's 44th favourite toon. It's Pete Townshend's 45th favourite toon. It's June Christy's 46th favourite toon. It's Hot Tuna's 47th favourite toon. It's Emmet Miller's 48th favourite toon. It's ASIFA's 49th favourite toon. It's ASIFA-Canada's 50th favourite toon ('cause Ocelot told 'em so). It's Kirikou's 51st favourite toon. It's that little Cuban kid's 52nd favourite toon. It's his uncle's 53rd favourite toon. It's his dad's 54th favourite toon. It's the soldier who held the gun's 55th favourite toon. It's some Japanese corporation's 56th favourite toon. It's IMAX's 57th favourite toon. It's my ass's 58th favourite toon. It's Andy Griffith's 59th favourite toon (he was hoping to star). It's Wolverine's 60th favourite toon. It's Laura Dern's 61st favourite toon. It's Deion Sanders' 62nd favourite toon. It's Pinball Clemon's 63rd favourite toon. It's Pinball Wizard's 64th favourite toon. It's some fugger at Disney's 65th favourite toon. It's my mom's 66th favourite toon. It's whomever my dad is' 67th favourite toon. It's Richard Meltzer's 68th favourite toon. It's my 69th favourite toon.

(January, 2001)

You Don't Kick a Zombie When It's Down, You Shoot It in the Head

Zom-BIE: (Zom'be) n. also ZOM-BIES pl. 1. An animated corpse that feeds on living human flesh.
— Max Brooks, *The Zombie Survival Guide*

That the dead walk among us is no big surprise. We didn't need George Romero to tell us that. Every moment of every day we encounter somnambulists. Most days, they are—contrary to popular theories—quite harmless. Their lumbering sigh of nonexistence usually passes before us without notice. The zombies tend to prefer certain locations: shopping malls (as we know), financial districts, civil service buildings, churches and sporting venues.

The animation world, like many cultural areas, has been pretty much free of these potentially life-sucking predators. Every so often, one creeps into the mix every four years or so, and there have been numerous zombie sightings along the west coast of North America, but most of the time animation (and art) remains a zombie-free zone.

However, zombie sightings and attacks in the animation world have increased dramatically since the mid-1990s. What is most disturbing about these reports is that there are a few familiar patterns. The reported attacks are often about three years apart and all take place near locations where the group called ASIFA (aka the International Animators' Association) is known to meet.

Recorded Zombie Attacks
1997 A.D. Annecy, France
The first clues of a zombie presence in animation were reported in 1997 near the small town of Annecy, France. While

strolling through the old town, two animation festival directors, Herper and Toto (rhymes with Otto) were startled by disturbing sounds emanating from a nearby building. "Dey were almoost like what you say… groan or scream like people having fuck but not liking," Herper was once heard to say inside a men's latrine near Tallinn. The two men spotted a small window and crept closer to take a peek inside. What they saw so horrified them that to this day they will not speak of what they saw. Toto remains in seclusion near Winterbach, Germany, while Herper divides his days between the Utrect Civic Hospital and the Netherlands art gallery where he repeatedly lunges at Russian paintings.

Rumors have since surfaced about what the two men saw that day. Rickie O'Conkie, a Brooklyn-based zombie spotter, believes that the groans were, "a collision of sounds emanating from a mix of about 30 foreigners who were walking and talking aimlessly in a small room." It appears that many were talking at the same time. No one appeared to be listening or responding to the talk. This babbling intersection went on for perhaps two to three hours. This in itself was not unique. What was startling, according to O'Conkie, was that about half of these people were long thought dead: "I heard names like Halas, McLaren, Hubley, Kinoshita; people who have been dead for years. Interestingly, all of these people were known to be active ASIFA members in 1960 A.D."

It was also reported that several younger people had entered the meeting. They initially spoke clearly and with great enthusiasm, but by the end of the meeting had become victims of what O'Conkie labels "the ASIFA Zombie."

According to zombie historian Max Brooks, there may exist, somewhere in the old town of Zagreb, Croatia, a physical record of the meeting with a list of all in attendance. But this document has never been discovered, so the accuracy of accounts of this 1997 attack remains impossible to confirm.

2000 A.D. Montreal, Quebec

O'Conkie also speaks of a meeting in Canada where a board member from the Ontario city of Ottawa reportedly suggested

that the Canadian chapter of ASIFA should consider having national representation (rather than just people from Montreal) and perhaps even organize events and meetings outside of Montreal, Quebec (just one of 10 provinces and three territories that compose Canada). "Mais oui!" said the Montrealers. "Certainement!" said others. A few days later, though, the Montrealers held a secret meeting to try and oust the member from Ottawa. However—and this is where, O'Conkie notes, "we uncovered the zombie conspiracy in Canada"—true to zombie form, they did not dispose of the member. Reportedly a vote never took place. Instead, the zombies merely walked around the room screaming obscure Acadian-language obscenities littered with references to "PQ" and "Anglofucks," "Parizeau" and "Rocket Richard."

The unknown Ottawa member, though, was never heard from again. There are reports that she/he headed for a small country located in the Baltic region.

2000-2004 A.D. Nonspecific Internet-Spread Attacks

There is documented evidence that the ASIFA Zombies have infiltrated the World Wide Web (aka Internet). This is a most alarming development. According to O'Conkie, if any non-zombie member makes any attempt to push forward any type of activity, the ASIFA Zombies immediately turn their computers off. The silence stops all activity. The danger here is that, eventually, the non-zombie will become frustrated and impatient, and, within a very short time period, will take on the form and characteristics of a zombie.

2004 A.D. Montreal, Quebec

The most recent reported attack once again comes from Montreal, Quebec, located in the Eastern region of Canada (pronounced CAN-A-DA like SAL-A-DA). Thanks to former animator Ryan Larkin, we were able to uncover a number of new zombies on the ASIFA-Canada board. When none of the board members was able to coherently suggest any candidates

for the Norman McLaren Award, the president, Pat Lafontaine (a former all-star curler and non-zombie) proposed that the award be given to Mr. Larkin. Despite their unfamiliarity with Mr. Larkin, the board agreed. But within days, Lafontaine was under attack from many Montreal-area zombies, who moaned something about "McLaren," "grave," "turning" and "ice cream machine." Again, these particular zombies were assumed to have been long dead. Lafontaine, clearly unhinged by the situation, did what you all must do when faced with zombie attacks: he fled to higher ground. This decision saved Lafontaine's life. It might very well save yours.

Ten Ways to Stop the ASIFA Zombie

1. Stay clear of the Canadian ASIFA chapter or the so-called central organization, ASIFA-International. These are the two most dangerous regions. The best way to deal with these particular zombies is to cut ("Blades," notes *Survival Guide* author Brooks, "don't need reloading") or shoot their head off (no blowguns please). When confronted by the Canadian chapter, insist on speaking English. This will cause the zombie's head to explode. Failing that, we suggest that you run. Do not drive a car. If you have a car, get out and walk, run or bike.

2. Do not hug anyone under any circumstances.

3. There are some reportedly zombie-free ASIFA regions in California (San Francisco and, incredibly, Hollywood), New York and France. There may be others, but why take a chance? Avoid all other ASIFA chapters!

4. Do not scream. There is no time.

5. Dress for survival. If you do find yourself at a Canadian or international meeting, wear baggy clothes (preferably including a t-shirt advertising any recent Pixar or Richard Rich film) that can accommodate shoulder-, elbow-, shin- and kneepads. A hockey or bike helmet is also recommended.

6. As a precaution, avoid any and all 'boards' or 'associations.' These zombie-drenched bureaucracies seek to lure naïve and ambitious people (especially the young) and frustrate them with silence, apathy and deafness.

7. It has been confirmed that ASIFA zombies attempt to lure recruits through moving images, especially those of a sensitive, intimate, powerful, poetic (aka touchy-feely) or epic nature. The list is by no means complete, but try to avoid any films by Norstein, Purves, Schwizgebel, Pummell, Quay, McLaren, Petrov, Dudok De Wit, Servais, Drouin, Back, Raamat. As we uncover more evidence, we will add more names to the list. These films will make you weep and gasp, while destroying all remaining internal humor senses.

8. If you see a beret, always open fire.

9. It's true that these individuals cannot be blamed; they are the victims of a larger structural influence. But if you show any weakness, they WILL kill you. Do not shed a tear until you are certain you are safe.

10. Loudly discuss your fondness for Star Wars, Star Trek, Pixar and Mike Judge.

If you stay aware, you'll stay alive.

(November, 2004)

The Stars

...we climbed up, ... far enough to see, through a round opening, a few of those fair things the heavens bear. Then we came forth, to see again the stars.
　　　　　　　　　　　　　　– Dante, *The Inferno*

We live in a world of great mediocrity and falsity... Dante tried to write paradise. And I think each of us in his own way is looking for some little taste or glimpse of paradise.
　　　　　　　　　– Nick Tosches, speaking about Dante on
　　　Michael Silverblatt's radio show "Bookworm," 2002

I'm scared. I feel things falling away. I've been here, comfortable, too long. Time to shake. Everything I've thought I wanted has come to me. I wanted the festival, I got it. Then I wanted to write, I did it. I wanted to write books, I did it. I wanted to write a column, so I did it. I wanted a son, a family, I got it. So why is it not enough? Why, once I reach these destinations, do I want to pick up and leave again? I don't think I take it all for granted, but maybe in some deeper sense I do. And I don't mean in some smug sense…it's something far worse, in an existential sense. The days I waste getting no writing done, playing video games, jerking off, scouring the Net for nothing. Then I stop and think, well, shit, man, you had three books published this year. You programmed a good festival, wrote articles, spent a month this summer entirely with your son. What's the problem? I take life for granted. I'm 2 years shy of 40, still relatively young, but too old to fart around. Then again, does it matter? If there's no god, no nothing…then this is all there is. That means there are no rules. I can do whatever the fuck I want and it don't mean a damn thing in the end. None of this does, except now. Now is all we got. That's a lot of pressure 'cause I don't know bout you

but I don't know what I want right now, always now. I've always been scared to commit to life. Maybe that comes from being an unplanned birth...maybe the loss of the father... the never of my mother. Then the loss of my grandparents. But so be it. That's over now. I have my family. It is everything really that I could want and yet I cannot grasp it. I am petrified of letting myself go because I know one day this and these will all be gone. Stop wanting, be?

The animation tent is shaped like a chapel. Animation has been a sanctuary for me, provided me with a space to find, cleanse, confess, define, lose, and discover myself. Some days I feel it's time to leave this tent, but then I think, why? Unlike the solid foundations of a church, this tent can be folded up, it can blow away, it's temporary...it never stops moving. I can step in and out as I please. So, no, there will be no grand pronouncements, proclamations or promises. Nothing of the sort. Sorry.

What has all this narcissism been about (me, obviously! heh heh)? Simple I guess. These past five years I've been using this space to try and figure out what animation means to me, to try and find out where I fit in...more importantly, to try and find out where animation fits into my life. And yes, ultimately, this journey was about me trying to find me. I'm not sure I have. I'm not sure we do. I do know, though, that I'm not now who I was then, and that I'm perhaps closer to paradise, to truth than I was five years ago. For that I'm thankful to me, and to you.

Perhaps I'll see you "someday on the avenue."

(December, 2005)

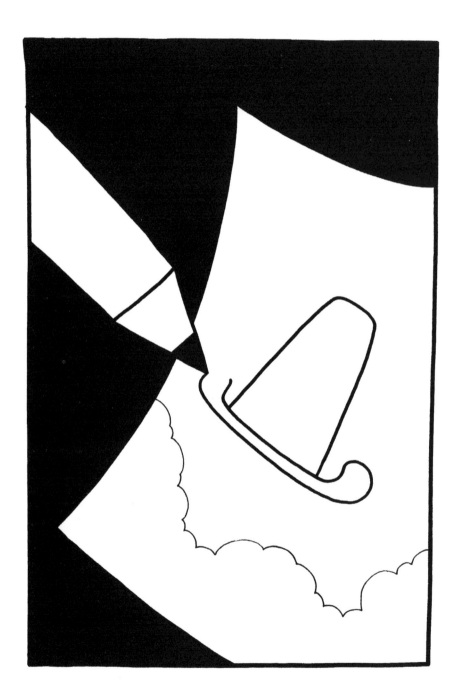

WHO'S WHO

Aardman Bristol-based clay animation studio founded by Peter Lord and David Sproxton. Gave the world *Wallace and Gromit, Rex The Runt, Creature Comforts,* and *Chicken Run.* I'm sure you've heard of them.

Alder, Otto One of the first people I knew in animation. Well known as a programmer for many international festivals. Now teaching in Lucerne, Switzerland. Didn't like me so much when my drinking got crazy. Things are better now. Always complains that he's poor, but has expensive manicure set.

Amidi, Amid One of the few folks out there in the animation world who actually has a solid opinion. Through his website with Jerry Beck called Cartoon Brew, Amid often pisses on the latest animation features and shorts. My only problem with him is his fetish for design. Sometimes he praises weak films 'cause they look like old '50s animation classics. But, hey, given that I don't usually give a hoot how a film looks, Amid provides a bit of balance.

Anet Swell lady who shares a life with Holland Animation Film Festival director Gerben Schermer *(see).*

Aqua, Karen American independent animator. Was on the selection committee and jury of my first Ottawa festival in 1992. Don't really have much more to add.

ASIFA The International Animated Film Association (Association International du Film d'Animation) is a 40-year-old organization that was formed to protect and promote the art of animation. Once had power and influence. Now they're sorta like that nosy know-it-all neighbour who likes to tell everyone how SHE'd do it better.

Avery, Tex Animator from the so-called "Golden Age of Animation." From the 1930s to the 1950s, Avery made short cartoons for Warner Bros., M.G.M. and Walter Lantz. His films were usually fast paced and utterly absurd. It was not uncommon for his characters to step out of character and address the audience, or even step outside the frame of the film.

Back, Frédéric A legendary Canadian animator. Made *The Man Who Planted Trees* and *Crac*. His films are hand drawn and usually deal with ecological issues. Is blind in one eye. Wears a patch over the eye I think. Could be a pirate.

Barker, Cordell Director of the famous Canadian animation film *The Cat Came Back* (1988). Was part of an exciting group of Winnipeg animators in the 1980s. Barker's most recent film was *Strange Invaders*. An animator who never really lived up to the hype, mostly 'cause short films don't pay, so he had to do crap TV work.

Barrier, Mike Animation critic. One of the many U.S. animation critics who are obsessed with American cartoons and show little interest in discussing international animation (unless it's mainstream Japanese). Still, Barrier was one of the few folks even talking critically about animation in the 1970s, so he deserves a little credit. Just wish he'd open his door once in a while and check out the rest of the world.

Baumane, Signe Latvian born, New York-based indie animator. Made the film *Five Fucking Fables*. Lots of people think her work looks like Bill Plympton's. Lots of people are stupid. She is perhaps the animation world's #1 cheerleader. She is regularly promoting new animators, organizing screenings and getting the word out there. She's sexy too.

Beck, Jerry Not Beck the singer. Jerry is a well-known animation author, historian and programmer. Co-produces the excellent animation blog Cartoon Brew with Amid Amidi. Like Barrier, though, Jerry's too fixated on all things American.

Beliveau, Jean One of the greatest hockey players ever. Captained the great Montreal Canadiens teams of the 1960s and played on their 1950s dynasty. A hell of a nice guy. Could never EVER be a pirate.

Bendazzi, Giannalberto Italian animation historian. His most famous work in his encyclopedia of animation, *Cartoons*. There is no mention of pornographic animation in this book. I wanna know why.

Bland, Pascal Alleged third cousin of Pascal Blais, producer of *The Old Man and The Sea*, quite possibly the greatest animation film ever made on an island near Montreal in the second half of January.

Bluth, Don Creator of *All Dogs Go To Heaven*, *Anastasia*, and *Secret of Nimh*. Ugh.

Borenstein, Joyce Montreal animator and teacher. Part of the do-gooder clan in Montreal that I find a bit too damn precious. Like they've never had soiled undies. Like to take the whole lot of them and put 'em on a fuggin pirate ship. A few months out at sea oughta grizzle 'em up.

Bradbrook, Robert British animator whose mixed media film *Home Road Movies* won the Grand Prix at the 2002 Ottawa Festival. Haven't heard from him since.

Brakhage, Stan Legendary experimental filmmaker whose work has largely been ignored by the animation world. It was refreshing to see his films included in the 2002 Holland Animation Film Festival programme.

Breer, Robert American experimental animator. I reference him only to show how smart I think I am.

Bromberg, Serge Artistic Director of the Annecy International Animation Festival.

Burton, Tim Find out for yourself.

C.O.R.E. Digital Toronto-based animation studio. I have nothing more to say.... For now.

Callahan, John Quadriplegic cartoonist who made an hilarious and tragic film about his recovery from alcoholism called—surprisingly—*I Think I was An Alcoholic.*

Canadian Film Institute (CFI) Ottawa-based (Ontario, not Illinois) organization that runs my main gig, the Ottawa International Animation Festival.

Canemaker, John Highly respected animation author, historian, teacher and animator. (His film *The Moon and the Son* won the 2006 Oscar® for Best Animated Short Film.) Very generous and amiable fella. His forte is Disney animation, but what is interesting about his work is that he attempts to discuss and showcase the many unsung artists whose work was largely unacknowledged in the studio system. Unlike Barrier and Beck, though, John is familiar with international animation.

Cassady, Chris Jury member at Ottawa '92. My first festival. Not much else to tell. I think he worked on one of the original *Star Wars* films. Also made the "Shadrach" video for the Beastie Boys.

CFI See *Canadian Film Institute.*

Chartrand, Martine Montreal animator who made the film *Black Soul,* about the experience of black slaves in Canada. A protégé of Alexander Petrov, Chartrand used an oil paint on glass technique. She's currently working on a film about a famous Quebec folk singer. I'm not too fond of *Black Soul,* but I think Martine is a fine gal. You can always count on her to bring life to a lifeless room.

Cohen, Karl President of ASIFA-San Francisco and the author

of *Forbidden Animation*, a book that examines various films that have been censored over the years. Strangely, the book does not mention pornographic animation films.

Colburn, Martha Baltimore-based experimental animator. Her films are crazy collages about vampires, dogs, sex, wee-wees and other pop culture icons. Fun and friendly films. Can't say that about many experimental works!

Cournoyer, Michele A Montreal-based animator who has worked for the National Film Board of Canada for several years. Her frank and beautifully drawn films include the outstanding *The Hat* (about sex abuse/addiction) and *Accordion* (about an on-line relationship). Like Paul Fierlinger *(see)*, Michele was a big support player when I quit drinking. She's been sober for almost 20 years.

Diamond, Ron Probably the greatest man in the existence of the universe (at least that's what he told me to write).

Dilworth, John New York animator. Likes loud clothes. Created the series "Courage the Cowardly Dog." Wants more respect. Ain't comin' from me.

Disney, Roy Early 21st-century American animation revolutionary leader—at least that's what the cartoon geeks say.

Dovas, Steve New York animator and a guy who I count on to come up with panel ideas for the Ottawa festival. Much beloved by the animation community.

Dr. Toon The name of a regular column written by Martin Goodman for *Animation World Magazine*. A little too American in focus, but Goodman is a smart, insightful writer. Unfortunately, he's also a Boston Bruins fan.

Driessen, Paul Dutch-born animator who lives in three, count 'em, three countries: Canada, France, Holland. Cool. Worked on *Yellow Submarine*. Big deal. He was just a junior animator. Probably spent more time getting coffee than animating. Makes a lot of films. Some are good (*End of the World in Four Seasons*). Some ain't. That's life. Has shiny grey hair and cool grey mini-beard. Could have been a cool pirate. There's also a Paul Driessen who is a market researcher. Check out pauldriessen.com. There's also a Dutch musician named Paul Driessen (pauldriessen.nl). No wonder he lives in other countries. I don't know any other Paul Driessens in Canada. My cousin's name is Paul. He doesn't like pirates.

Drouin, Jacques   Long-time animator at the National Film Board of Canada. Retired from the NFB in 2004. Was famous for his use of the pinscreen animation technique—which he learned from the Russian-born animation master Alexander Alexeiff. Not a big fan of his films, but Drouin is a fine fella.

Dudok de Wit, Michael   Dutch-British animator. His two Oscar®-winning films are *The Monk and The Fish* and *Father and Daughter*. Very nice guy. Really.

Dumala, Piotr   Polish animator. Uses a unique engraving process. Loves dark, existential literature. Has made films based on stories by Kafka and Dostoevski (*Crime and Punishment*).   One of the many fine international animators who are completely unknown by the general public. Guys like Dumala should be getting Oscars®, not Nick Park (no offense, Nick).

Ehrlich, David   A Vermont-based experimental animator, teacher and influential member of ASIFA. Makes highly subjective abstract films that often look like the result of smoking a leftover roach found in a drive-in parking lot. He's a swell guy who has supported me like a pops. I try to give him a shout-out whenever I can.

Emist, Nag   Actually, this is just a play on the Estonian word *nagemist*, which means "see you," like "see you later, buddy."

Engel, Jules Highly respected teacher at California Institute of the Arts and an acclaimed experimental animator. Died in 2003.

Fierlinger, Paul Philadelphia-based animator whose films (*Drawn from Memory, Still Life with Animated Dogs, And Then I'll Stop*) combine characteristics of animation and documentary. Paul has been quite open about his battle with alcoholism (he's been sober for over a decade now) and he played an important role in helping me get dry.

Filmtecknarna Very cool Swedish studio that does innovative, mixed media commissioned works and occasionally puts out nifty short films like *Revolver* (1994). Jonas Odell is one of the co-founders. He has made a number of interesting music videos, commercials and short films (most recently, *Never Like the First Time*, a series of shorts in which people recall the first time they got laid). Jonas's use of music is also to be commended. No one has a better sense of rhythm and timing than this guy.

Fleming, Anne Marie Noted Canadian filmmaker. Works in experimental and animation genres. Co-founded the Vancouver animation studio Global Mechanic with Bruce Alcock (who made the wonderful film *At The Quinte Hotel*). In 2003, she made an innovative documentary/animation feature about her mysterious Chinese acrobat great-grandfather called *The Magical Life of Long Tack Sam*.

Foray, June One of the most famous animation voices ever. She voiced characters for Warner Bros. (Grannie), "Rocky and Bullwinkle," and a slew of other productions. Still going today.

Furniss, Maureen Founder of the egghead journal *Animation Journal* and author of a few books on animation. Now teaches at California Institute of the Arts.

Glassman, Marc Grand ol' pal of mine from Toronto. He owns a fantastic bookstore called Pages and has curated a number of programmes for the Ottawa International Animation Festival. Never drink into the night with Marc. It can be very dangerous.

Gratz, Joan Portland animator. Worked at Will Vinton Studios and along the way created a number of nifty experimental animation films. I referenced her out of guilt. She wants to be on a jury. I want to have her. But it just never happens.

Griffin, George A New York animator who is kinda like the Jean-Luc Godard of animation except his films have more personality and warmth, and they're less French. He once made a film (*The Club*) about cocks. Heh heh. Cocks. What makes George's work so interesting to me is that he's continually trying to explore the nature of identity—whether it is his own or that of animation. He's real smart and talks good. I like him.

Grillo, Oscar Amazingly talented Argentine animator who resides in London. He's most famous these days for sending out a new drawing (or two) every day to people on his mailing list. Smart, incredibly funny and generous. My son digs him.

Gurevich, Mikhail Russian animation critic who lives in Chicago. "Surevich" is a nonexistent person who appears in the piece about criminals as jury members.

Halas, John Hungarian animator. Made the feature *Animal Farm* from the Orwell book. Was the first president of ASIFA. Has a great piratey name.

Hanna-Barbera Animation studio that really pioneered TV animation in the 1960s. Creators of Fred Flintstone, Scooby Doo and an assortment of half-assed crap. Made animation feasible for television by using a technique that involved cutting back on certain movements to minimize the number of frames and artwork needed to make a show. Thanks to Cartoon Network and

DVDs, the studio had a resurgence in the late 1990s and early 2000s. When Warner Bros. bought the studio, they made new Scooby Doo shows and re-introduced old characters through the Cartoon Network show "Harvey Birdman." Animator John Kricfalusi ("Ren and Stimpy") also made two new cartoons featuring classic characters Yogi Bear and his pal Boo-Boo.

Hays, John Did animation for MTV. One of the founders of Wild Brain Animation Studio in San Francisco. I like San Fran. Cool bookstores...and hey...*Bullitt*, one of my all time fave films, was shot there.

Hébert, Pierre Canadian animator. Improvises on computer. Once rubbed my head for good luck. Didn't work.

Hertzfeldt, Don Bill Plympton Jr. Young American guy whose films *Billy's Balloon* and *Rejected*, among others, have been audience favourites at festivals. Hertzfeldt recently teamed up with Mike Judge to create the touring programme, "The Animation Show." Taking a page from the Spike and Mike animation programme, "The Animation Show" brings a number of award-winning festival faves to wider audiences. Good on him.

Hinton, Chris Canadian animator who started making cartoony films (*Watching TV, Blackfly*), but in recent years has been making more ambitious, free-flowing semi-experimental films like *Nibbles, Flux, C-Note*. I always confuse him and David Verrall, the head of the National Film Board of Canada's English animation department. Chris is also noted for his innovative pumpkin carvings at the Ottawa festival picnic. And, with his beard and hair, I've no doubt he'd be a great pirate. In fact, I think he wants to be a pirate.

Hodgson, Anthony While a student at London's Royal College of Art, he made an outstanding film called *Hilary*. Followed it up with *Combination Skin*. Then he got hired by a Hollywood studio and no one has ever heard from him again. I think he worked on *Antz*. Poor guy.

Hoedeman, Co Veteran animator who worked at the National Film Board of Canada for over 30 years until he retired in 2004. Was a master of stop-motion animation. Won an Oscar® for his film, *The Sandcastle*. Also founded the Ottawa International Animation Festival's social spot, Chez Ani.

Hoffman, Phil Was one of my teachers at Sheridan College. Also one of Canada's most acclaimed experimental filmmakers. Phil always told our class to make stuff from our life. Do the stuff you know. Most of his films were also autobiographical. Used aspects of his life to explore other issues. Likes hockey.

Hubley, John & Faith John is one of the legends of animation. Worked for Disney and UPA. Then collaborated with his wife Faith on a number of films. Parents of animator Emily Hubley...and, coolest of cool, Georgia Hubley, the drummer for Yo La Tengo.

Hykade, Andreas My soul brother. Made the films *Ring of Fire* and *We Lived in Grass*. Likes Johnny Cash a lot. I prefer Jerry Lee Lewis. We'd have been great drinking buddies if I hadn't already quit when we met. And, oh yeah, he created the Pimp "logos" and illustrated this excellent book. Has a cool sportscar. Let me drive it once. Lives in Stuttgart, Germany. Also makes excellent music videos.

Jean, Marcel Former head of the French animation division at the National Film Board of Canada. Not sure what he's doing these days.

Judge, Mike Made animated TV shows called "Beavis and Butt-head" and "King of the Hill." Also helmed the cult classic, *Office Space*—which was based on his first animation short. Has a deep hatred of parrots.

Kentridge, William One of the few animators (New Yorker Jeff Scher might be another) who has managed to achieve success in animation AND the huffy puffy art world.

Kinoshita, Renzo Japanese animator. He made some powerful films about the bombing of Hiroshima and the increased influence of Western culture in Japan. His widow, Sayoko, is the director of the Hiroshima International Animation Festival.

Klasky Csupo Los Angeles animation studio founded by Arlene Klasky and Gabor Csupo. First animation studio for "The Simpsons." Also created "Rugrats." Lured Russian animator Igor Kovalyov over to L.A. in the early 1990s. Gave Igor a great deal. He worked on commercial crap. In exchange, the studio produced his personal films (e.g., *Bird in the Window*, *Flying Nansen*). Studio fell on hard times in 2004. Pretty much dead in the water today. Problem was that they did variations on one graphic style. Soon, everything they did started to look the same.

Knott, Tom My first boss at the animation festival. Since 1994, he's been a recruiter for a number of studios (including Warner Bros.). He now works at Laika films in Portland. All-round good guy who gave me my start in the animation world. Tom also gave us the beautiful phrase: "That's not what I meant when I said it." Classic.

Kovalyov, Igor Co-founder of acclaimed Russian studio Pilot Animation. Moved to Los Angeles in early 1990s to work at Klasky Csupo *(see)*. One of the most acclaimed animators around today. Is the only three-time Grand Prix winner in the history of the Ottawa International Animation Festival. Good friend. Once took me to Peter Chung's house. Got stoned on mushrooms and watched Esther Williams films all night. Igor now teaches at the California Institute of the Arts.

Krause, Fran & Will Twins. Graduates of Rhode Island School of Design. Work in New York now. They sat with me during the

ASIFA-East festival. They like Estonians. Estonians like them. Once got in trouble in Detroit.

Kricfalusi, John Ottawa-born animator who created the TV classic "Ren and Stimpy." Has a problem with budgets and schedules. Likes to giggle.

Krumme, Raimund German animator whose work (*Crossroads*, *Passages*, *Rope Dance*) got me excited about the possibilities of animation. When I took over the Ottawa Festival, I had Raimund on the jury and did a retrospective of his work. Was the first animator I ever wrote about.

Kucia, Jerzy Polish animator. Makes very abstract, atmospheric films about memory, landscape, childhood. Again, he's been referenced solely 'cause I want to have him on a jury one day. I dig his films…even if they are heavy going. Too short to be a pirate.

Kugel, Candy New York animator. Co-owner of Buzzco animation studios. Made me lunch once. Likes bees. I told my son Jarvis that I used to be a superhero named Bumble Bee Man (I even pull out old Boston Bruins hockey jerseys as proof—they have a big letter "B" on the front). I told him that my powers were honey spitballs. Villains would get stuck when hit by one of them. Explained that I had problems with Batman's attitude. Always thought he was the best. Asshole.

Kutt, Mati Estonian animator whose always innovative work, which explores philosophical, political and ecological issues, is too often overshadowed by the work of colleague Priit Parn *(see)*. The good news though is that Mati has a KICKASS mustache, real long hair. The guy was born to be a pirate.

Lajoie, Bernard One of the producers of my favourite animation film ever, *The Old Man and the Sea*.

Lambart, Eve Former National Film Board of Canada animator. Was also an assistant to Norman McLaren. Canada's first female animator.

Landreth, Chris American-born animator now working and living in Canada. He's probably the most interesting computer animator around at the moment. His films include: *The End*, *Bingo*, and the multiple-award-winning *Ryan*.

Langer, Mark Where do I start? First, Mark was my Film Studies professor at Carleton University in Ottawa. I once had a meltdown while writing a paper for him. He told me not to have an existential meltdown on his time. Gave me a C. Asshole. Just kidding. I deserved it. Has an unusual fascination with the films of Max and Dave Fleischer (creators of Betty Boop). Since 1988, Mark has been a regular programmer for the Ottawa Festival. In 2006, he was invited to be the Honorary President of the fest.

Lanier, Chris San Francisco-based animator and graphic artist. Created an innovative web short called *Romanov* for the Wild Brain studio a few years ago. Smart guy who can write real good.

Larkin, Ryan If it isn't clear by now who the hell Ryan Larkin is, then fuggit.

Lasseter, John Creative guy at Pixar animation studios. Now Creative guy at Walt Disney Feature Animation. Nerds often gather to fight over his dingleberries. Wears loud shirts, but is not gay.

Leaf, Caroline U.S.-born animator and painter who made her most famous films (*The Street*, *Two Sisters*) at the National Film Board of Canada. Influenced by Stormin' Norman McLaren *(see)*. Uses scratch on film and oil paint on glass techniques. Hasn't made anything worthwhile since 1992's *Two Sisters*. I hear she's more into painting these days.

Lenica, Jan Polish animator whose work was fueled by Buster Keaton, existentialism and Poland's rough post-World War 2 landscape. Lenica often worked with cut-out figures. He was also a highly acclaimed film poster designer. Oh, a bit of a grump as well. Wouldn't be a good pirate. Pirates get excited. Lenica just stares.

Lingford, Ruth Sassy British animator who teaches at Royal College of Art and National Film and Television School. Also spent a year teaching at Harvard. Sweet, funny woman with a dark sense of humour. Made several dandy films including *Death and the Maiden* and *The Old Fools*.

Lipsett, Arthur Troubled Canadian experimental filmmaker. Worked with collage technique. Killed himself in the mid-1980s. Was a colleague of Ryan Larkin's. Unlike Larkin, Lipsett WAS actually an artistic genius. Among Lipsett's many admirers was a guy named George Lucas.

Longpre, Bernard Montreal animator whose most notable work was a film about alcoholism called *One Way Street*. He died a few years ago.

Lye, Len New Zealand animator who specialized in cameraless animation (i.e., working directly on the film strip). Was a pioneer who had a massive influence on Norman McLaren. Today, Lye, like McLaren, is much loved by the academic geek.

Mann, Otto The stoner bus driver from "The Simpsons."

Manter, Frederick Former director (c. 1970s/early 1980s) of the Ottawa International Animation Festival and Canadian Film Institute. Ain't never met the man.

Maxwell, Stephanie Rochester, N.Y.-based experimental animator who was ignored by animation festivals for a long time. In recent years, that's begun to change.

McLaren, Norman Stormin' Norman was a Scottish-born Canadian animator who helped establish the animation department of the National Film Board of Canada. His experimental animation films employed a number of techniques, most notably painting and scratching directly on the film strip. He is arguably the most influential animator in the world after Walt Disney. Personally, I'm sick of hearing about him. The animation circle contains many unweaned babies. No matter how much they age, they keep coming back to the same tit.

McSorley, Tom Executive Director of the Canadian Film Institute in Ottawa, Canada. The CFI shows art and classic films. Tom hired me in 1991 to run the institute's box office. A year into the job I discovered that the CFI also ran an animation festival. I got a job with them and the rest is soiled history.

McWilliams, Don NFBer, friend of McLaren's. Warned me that other people had tried to help Ryan Larkin. I thought I was different and was rude to McWilliams. I feel bad about it.

Meske, Ellen Dutch animator who was a selection committee/jury member during my first Ottawa festival in 1992.

Minnis, Jon Won an Oscar® for his student film *Charade*. Never made an interesting film again. Doing TV now.

Missy (Chimovitz) Sweet New York gal I first met at a screening at Cal Arts. She's married to a Canadian. Good choice.

Montgomery, Tyron Co-director of the Oscar®-winning short *Quest*. Never heard from again after winning.

MTL Montreal. Town I like near Ottawa.

Mulloy, Phil Welsh animator whose (mostly) black-and-white works are characterized by an often violent, bitter and sarcastic tone. His characters are skeletal figures with dick-shaped heads.

He likes to attack religion, politics, America, and dumb people. Behind his genial appearance is one of THE funniest and most sarcastic people I've ever met.

NAMBLA North American Man/Boy Love Association. Bunch of freaks. Saying that it's okay to fuck children because the Greeks once did it is NOT a good excuse.

National Film Board of Canada (NFB) A state-run film studio. They produce animation and documentary films. Lots of good stuff and lots of duds.

Neubauer, Barbel German animator who makes cameraless animation (i.e., by drawing directly on film). She creates her own soundtracks and recently started using computers.

Newland, Marv American-born Canadian animator who gave the world the most popular of cult classics, *Bambi Meets Godzilla*. I think he has email now.

NFB See *National Film Board of Canada*

Nick As in Nickelodeon, the animation studio/TV channel. Precursor to Cartoon Network.

Norstein, Yuri Russian animator who made what some people feel is the greatest animation film ever, *The Tale of Tales*. Used a cut-out technique. His films often deal with memory and childhood. A bit too precious for me. Has spent the last two decades working on an adaptation of Gogol's *The Overcoat*. Has a beard. Could possibly be a pirate.

O'Connor, Richard New York animation producer. Used to work for the semi-famous Ink Tank studio. Now runs his own studio, Asterix. Very funny guy. Dresses like he's auditioning for sixties-era Kinks. We went to a Guided by Voices show in Brooklyn. Let me stay at his pad—despite the rats. Not afraid to speak his mind. Likes to be seen with beautiful women—even if they don't want to be seen with him.

Odell, Jonas See *Filmtecknarna*

Oreb, Tom Nifty 1950s animation designer for Disney. Designed the magnificent-looking *Sleeping Beauty* and one of my fave shorts *Toot, Whistle, Plunk, and Boom*. Was also a heavy drinker.

Pakre, Linda I didn't really know her. She worked at the Estonian house in New York. She brought Estonian culture to the big city. We coordinated a big Estonian animation programme in 2003. Unfortunately, she died before the festival happened. Turns out that one night her apartment caught fire. She had fallen asleep. She suffered serious burns and died a few days later. Some Estonians suggested that she probably fell asleep reading my book on Estonian animation.

Panzner, Chris I don't really know much about Chris other than that he writes great articles on animation and that he wrote me the single nicest letter about the Pimp: "I read all the Pimps in one sitting. I couldn't stop shaking my head in disbelief and awe. First, that AWN would LET you do it, that you DID it and SIGNED it and that it was for an ANIMATION audience. It's 'mainstream' gonzo. Or at least more people--a wider audience--should be reading it. For nothing else than just the pure, unabashed TRUTH in it, no matter what your individual truth happens to be. Truth of expression, the courage to write what you think, the hell with it. Man, that public, self-inflicted auto-da-fé just winded me."

Pappo, Iris Canadian artist and animator. Just referenced her so I could write the name Pappo. It sounds Italian. It's Estonian. Ha. Go figure.

Park, Nick Creator of the Oscar®-winning films *Creature Com-*

forts, *The Wrong Trousers*, and *Wallace and Gromit: Curse of the Wererabbit*. Nice guy. Bit delusional. Likes bowties. Thinks they're funny. No one else does. Except Tucker Carlson and Mr. Peabody (look it up!).

Parn, Priit Big-ass Estonian animator. Made classic animation films *Breakfast on the Grass*, *Hotel E*, and *1895*. Thinks he's tough. Was a stunt man in an Estonian adventure movie. I'm pretty sure he could beat me up.

Pars, Heino One of the pioneers of Estonian animation. Started making puppet animation way back in the 1960s. Used to be a beekeeper.

Pauze, Michele Former animator at the National Film Board of Canada. Accompanied me on my first trip abroad. In later years, we had a big fight over nothing.

PES Great commercial director from New York. Gave me his seats to a Yankees-Mariners game. Went with animator Steve Dovas. Game was dull.

Pessoa, Regina Portuguese animator. Directed a film called *The Night*. I didn't like it.

Petrov, Alexander Russian animator who made *The Old Man and The Sea*, my gosh-golly-gee favouritist film of ALL TIME. Honest.

Picker, Jimmy New York animator. Made Oscar®-winning film *Sundae in New York*. Never heard of him? See, I told ya winning an Oscar® means squat for animators.

Pilling, Jayne Noted British animation author and programmer. She also created the British Animation Awards. Real smart. Speaks Frenchy too.

that he did that. Juries need a good raspberry. Not so crazy about his work.

Smith, Pat His films (*Delivery*, *Drink*) have had a lot of success at festivals outside of Ottawa. He tries to like me, but finds it difficult. Models his career on Bill Plympton's—which is a good thing, at least from a business perspective. Pat is never on his ass. He's always promoting his films. I respect that.

Snow, Michael Canadian experimental filmmaker who made the influential film *Wavelength* (which consisted of a single long zoom). His fascinating and difficult feature film *Corpus Callosum* was shown at the Holland Animation Film Festival in 2002.

Solomon, Debbie New York animator who created the animated character for the Disney show *Lizzie McGuire* (which unfortunately launched the career of one Hillary Duff).

Stainton, David Much despised ex-President of Walt Disney Feature Animation.

Starewicz, Wladislaw Poland-born animator who made a number of acclaimed stop-motion films in Russia. In his most famous film *The Cameraman's Revenge*, Starewicz (a.k.a. Dr. Frankenstein) animates using actual dead insects.

Steinberg, Saul Famous American artist whose work has influenced many animators.

Street, Rita Don't know much about Rita except that she's a swell lady with a Mr. Bubbly personality. Used to be the co-editor of Animation Magazine. Now has her own studio.

Stursberg, Richard Was briefly the head of Telefilm Canada, the country's federal film-funding organization. One day he had the bright idea that Canada should stop making its unique, interesting films by guys like Guy Maddin, Atom Egoyan, Denys

Arcand etc.… and instead start making Hollywood-influenced genre films. Along the way, he decided to cut our funding because we didn't show features. Apparently Mr. Stursberg didn't know that there are no Canadian animation features—at least none worth showing. Our funding was reinstated and Mr. Stursberg eventually moved on to the Canadian Broadcasting Corporation (our state TV channel), where he is now canceling popular Canadian TV shows. During a reception in New York celebrating Canadian cinema, he allegedly told a reporter that he didn't like Canadian cinema. He's regarded as an innovator, an intellectual and all-round great man. At least that's what he keeps saying.

Sullivan, Pat A talentless drunk who stole the credit for creating the animated character Felix the Cat from Otto Messmer.

Surevich, Mikhail See *Gurevich*.

Svankmajer, Jan Famous Czech animator. Master of the surreal and absurd. Gets talked about too much though. So I won't say any more.

Svislotski, Andrei You have two choices. A Russian animator who's currently working in Los Angeles at what remains of Klasky-Csupo animation studio, or the name of an animation film by Igor Kovalyov.

Tender, Priit Estonian animator who made the films *Viola, Gravitation, Mont Blanc* and *Fox Woman*. Works in a variety of techniques, but his drawn work shows the influence of his unofficial teacher, Priit Parn. Priit Tender (pronounced "pretender") first had the idea for using criminals on juries. We made the whole thing up while hanging out at the Fantoche Animation Festival in Baden, Switzerland.

Thornton, Leslie U.S. experimental filmmaker. I can't remember why I referenced her. I guess I saw one of her films as part of this incredible experimental show at the 2002 Holland Animation Film Festival. Maybe she was hot. Either way, I can't remember her work and I sure as hell ain't gonna write some generic crap just to impress youse.

Traudt, Wayne Canadian animator who made a series of films inspired by life class sketches about the movement of the human body. His films are philosophical and a bit erotic—or maybe I'm just easily aroused.

Tupicoff, Dennis The tallest animator in the world. Australian whose films (*The Darra Dogs, His Mother's Voice, Dance of Death*) often deal with death. All-round good guy.

Ushev, Theo Bulgarian animator who now lives in Montreal. Started out as a graphic designer, then started making online animation shorts. Got hired by the National Film Board of Canada a few years ago and recently made *Tower Bawher*, a very cool Soviet constructivist-influenced film, and T*he Man Who Waited*, based on a Franz Kafka short story. We're collaborating on a film called *Lipsett Diaries* for the NFB. Hopefully it won't stink..

Van Goethem, Nicole Another Oscar®-winning animator ain't nobody heard of. Belgian. Won the hardware for her film *A Greek Tragedy*. Died a few years ago. Apparently she was crushed to death by her Oscar®.

Villard, JJ Graduate of the California Institute of the Arts. One of the most interesting new animators around today. Made the award-winning films *Son of Satan* (based on a Charles Bukowski story) and *Chestnuts Icelolly*. Currently working on *Shrek 3* for Dreamworks. We all pray for him.

Ward, Olivia Pat Smith's girlfriend. The inspiration for his film *Handshake*. She's from England. Wowsa. Her brother knows the "Quincy" theme song, but I bet he can't hum the "Columbo" theme. She is not related to Burt Ward, thankfully.

Warners Warner Bros., as in Bugs Bunny, Daffy Duck.

Watts, Sarah Australian animator. Made a film about losing her child. Heartbreaking stuff. Typical of Aussies.

Woloshen, Steven Canadian experimental animator whose work is very much influenced by Norman McLaren. Swell guy. His films drip with energy and passion.

Wright, Prescott One of the co-founders of the Ottawa International Animation Festival. Sadly, he passed away in December 2006 from dementia or Alzheimer's or one of those crappy life lots. Did a lot in his time for independent animation. Started the International Tournée of Animation—which toured films that had played at the Ottawa festival around North America.

Chris Robinson is an Ottawa-based writer and author who has been a director of the Ottawa International Animation Festival (OIAF) since 1994. A noted animation commentator, curator, and historian, Robinson has become a leading expert on Canadian and international independent animation. His acclaimed OIAF programming has been variously regarded as thoughtful, innovative, provocative, and crappy. In May 2004, Robinson was the recipient of the President's Award given by the New York chapter of animators for contributions to the promotion of independent animation.

His writings have appeared in many international publications including *Salon.com*, *Stop Smiling*, *The Ottawa Citizen*, *Take One*, *Cinemascope*, and *The Ottawa Xpress*.

From 2000-2005, Robinson wrote the acclaimed 'gonzo' column "The Animation Pimp" for Animation World Magazine.

His books include *Between Genius and Utter Illiteracy: A Story of Estonian Animation* (2003), *Ottawa Senators: Great Stories from the NHL's first dynasty* (2004), *Unsung Heroes of Animation* (2005), *Great Left Wingers of Hockey's Golden Era* (2006), and the critically acclaimed, *Stole This From a Hockey Card: A Philosophy of Hockey, Doug Harvey, Identity and Booze* (2005).

He is currently working on two new books: *Fathers of Night*, a book about how meeting his biological father and animator Ryan Larkin in the same week changed his views of saviours, fathers and Bob Dylan, and *Looking For A Place to Happen: On the Road with Canadian Animators*.

Robinson lives in Ottawa with his wife Kelly and their sons Jarvis and Harrison.